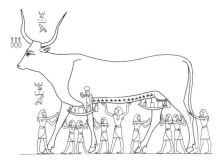

So were gathered together…
All the gods and their kas as well,
Content and complete…

From the Memphite Theology

The Complete Gods an

Goddesses of Ancient Egypt

Richard H. Wilkinson

With 338 illustrations

Front cover: *The goddesses Maat and Serket, depicted in the tomb of Nefertari (Araldo De Luca/Archivio White Star).*

Back cover: *The triad of Hathor, Mycerinus and the goddess of the Jackal Nome, Egyptian Museum, Cairo (Photo Heidi Grassley, © Thames & Hudson Ltd, London).*

Half-title: *The divine cow of the heavens and her supporting deities. Outermost shrine of Tutankhamun, Egyptian Museum, Cairo.*

Title page: *Ramesses I before the enthroned Khepri and Osiris – personifications of the solar and chthonic aspects of the Egyptian view of the cosmos. From the tomb of Ramesses I, Valley of the Kings, western Thebes.*

Contents pages: *Caryatid pillars in the mortuary temple of Ramesses II at Abu Simbel associate the great monarch with the god Osiris through the king's stance and insignia.*

First published in the United Kingdom in 2003 by
Thames & Hudson Ltd, 181A High Holborn, London WC1V 7QX

First published in the United States of America in 2003 by
Thames & Hudson Inc., 500 Fifth Avenue, New York, New York 10110

First paperback edition 2017
Reprinted 2022

The Complete Gods and Goddesses of Ancient Egypt
Text © 2003 Richard H. Wilkinson
Layout © 2003 Thames & Hudson Ltd, London

British Library Cataloguing-in-Publication Data
A catalogue record for this book is available from the British Library

Library of Congress Control Number 2002110321

ISBN 978-0-500-28424-7

Printed and bound in Hong Kong by Asia One Printing Ltd.

MIX
Paper from
responsible sources
FSC™ C006398
www.fsc.org

Be the first to know about our new releases,
exclusive content and author events by visiting
thamesandhudson.com
thamesandhudsonusa.com
thamesandhudson.com.au

Contents

Introduction: Egyptian Religion and the Gods

Three amulets representing (left to right) the goddess Taweret, the god Bes, and the god Thoth in baboon form. Late Period. University of Leipzig Museum.

The spiritual world created by the ancient Egyptians was a richly fascinating one which remains unique in the history of human religion. The character of that spiritual world was both mysterious and manifest, at once accessible and hidden, for although Egyptian religion was often shrouded in layers of myth and ritual it nevertheless permeated the ancient civilization of the Nile and ultimately shaped, sustained and

directed Egyptian culture in almost every imaginable way. The deities of Egypt were present in the lives of pharaohs and citizens alike, creating a more completely theocratic society than any other civilization of the ancient world. The truth behind Herodotus' statement that 'the Egyptians are more religious than any other people' is thus a broad one, encompassing literally hundreds of different gods and goddesses, temples seemingly without end, and a mythology that was surpassing in its richness and complexity.

Like the members of any other human culture the ancient Egyptians were driven to find meaning in existence, but for them this goal was attained in theological ideas which posited a myriad gods that were believed to have created the world and to be involved in every aspect of its existence and continuance. The number of deities worshipped by the ancient Egyptians was indeed staggering, and almost 1,500 gods and goddesses are known by name, though fewer are known in detail. To the modern viewer this panoply of seemingly countless deities – including animal, human, hybrid and composite forms – with their kaleidoscopic symbols and attributes often appears strange and confusing at best and quite unintelligible at worst. Yet closer examination reveals a world of interacting gods and goddesses whose myths and representations weave an amazing tapestry, often of unexpected intellectual and artistic sophistication.

The 'Great Royal Wife' and 'Mistress of the Two Lands', Nefertari, presents a libation to the goddesses (centre right to left) Hathor, Serket and Maat. 19th dynasty. Tomb of Nefertari, Valley of the Queens, western Thebes.

Our evidence for these deities is both ancient and extensive, comprising textual, architectural, representational and artifactual sources. Yet it is also surprisingly disjointed and fragmentary. Temples and tombs, the chief theatres for the enactment of religious ritual and the recording of religious beliefs, exist by the hundred and are the source of much of our knowledge of the ancient gods, though we lack temples from a number of periods and geographic areas. We learn also of Egypt's deities from the shrines, icons and other artifacts found in even the simplest homes at sites such as the ancient workmen's village at Deir el-Medina though, again, domestic settings are unfortunately underrepresented for many periods and areas. As a result of the uneven preservation of Egyptian sites and monuments, there are large gaps in the written texts at our disposal – leaving persistent questions regarding the gods and their worship. Nevertheless, the texts inscribed on the walls of Old Kingdom pyramids (which are the oldest religious writings in the world), and their later derivative texts, provide us with invaluable, if sometimes cryptic, evidence of the rich theological milieu of the ancient Egyptians.

Through the various sources at our disposal we know that some of Egypt's deities originated before the beginning of recorded time and survived to the very end of the ancient world – having been worshipped for fully three-fifths of recorded human history. Even when they were eventually replaced by later faiths, the gods of Egypt sometimes found new life, and their influence has persisted in many and remarkable ways – ranging from apparent precursors of minor religious motifs and stories to perhaps even the concept of monotheism itself.

7

But in ancient times, for the Egyptians themselves, the gods were far more than the sum of all their myths and images. The monuments and artifacts which have survived give only glimpses of the great power of the Egyptian gods. While they lived in the minds of the ancient Egyptians their influence was prodigious. For many if not most Egyptians, they were the breath of life itself and it is only to the extent that we understand these ancient deities that we can understand the nature of ancient Egyptian culture and society: the lives and hoped-for afterlives of the Egyptians themselves.

Chronology of the Rulers

The precise dates of the Egyptian dynasties and of individual reigns are still the subject of much scholarly debate. The dates employed here are based largely on the chronology developed by Professor John Baines and Dr Jaromir Málek and put forward in their *Atlas of Ancient Egypt*. The so-called Amarna Period encompasses the reigns of Akhenaten, Tutankhamun and Ay in the 18th dynasty. Only the rulers discussed in the text are listed here.

Late Predynastic	*c.* **3000** BC
Early Dynastic Period	
1st dynasty	**2920–2770**
Narmer; Aha; Djer; Den; Semerkhet	
2nd dynasty	**2770–2649**
Raneb; Peribsen; Khasekhemwy	
3rd dynasty	**2649–2575**
Djoser	2630–2611
Old Kingdom	
4th dynasty	**2575–2465**
Sneferu	2575–2551
Khufu (Cheops)	2551–2528
Khafre (Chephren)	2520–2494
Menkaure (Mycerinus)	2490–2472
5th dynasty	**2465–2323**
Userkaf	2465–2458
Sahure	2458–2446
Shepseskare	2426–2419
Djedkare-Isesi	2388–2356
6th dynasty	**2323–2150**
7th/8th dynasties	**2150–2134**
First Intermediate Period	
9th/10th dynasties	**2134–2040**
11th dynasty (Theban)	**2134–2040**
Intef II	2118–2069
Middle Kingdom	
11th dynasty (all Egypt)	**2040–1991**
Montuhotep III	1997–1991
12th dynasty	**1991–1783**
Senwosret I	1971–1926
Senwosret III	1878–1841?
Amenemhet III	1844–1797
Amenemhet IV	1799–1787
Sobekneferu	1787–1783
13th dynasty	**1783–1640**
Wepwawetemsaf	
Sobekhotep	
14th dynasty	
Probably contemporary with the 13th or 15th dynasty	
Second Intermediate Period	
15th dynasty (Hyksos)	
16th dynasty	
Contemporary with 15th dynasty	
17th dynasty	**1640–1532**
New Kingdom	
18th dynasty	**1550–1307**
Ahmose	1550–1525
Tuthmosis III	1479–1425
Hatshepsut	1473–1458
Amenophis II	1427–1401
Tuthmosis IV	1401–1391
Amenophis III	1391–1353
Akhenaten	1353–1335

Tutankhamun	1333–1323
Ay	1323–1319
Horemheb	1319–1307
19th dynasty	**1307–1196**
Ramesses I	1307–1306
Sethos I	1306–1290
Ramesses II	1290–1224
Merenptah	1224–1214
Siptah	1204–1198
Tawosret	1198–1196
20th dynasty	**1196–1070**
Sethnakhte	1196–1194
Ramesses III	1194–1163
Ramesses V	1156–1151
Ramesses VI	1151–1143
Third Intermediate Period	
21st dynasty	**1070–945**
22nd dynasty	**945–712**
Sheshonq II	?–883
23rd dynasty	*c.* **1070–712**
Osorkon III	873–745
24th dynasty	*c.* **724–712**
25th dynasty	**770–712**
(Nubian and Theban area)	
Late Period	**712–332**
25th dynasty	**712–657**
Shabaka	712–698
26th dynasty	**664–525**
Psamtik I	664–610
27th dynasty	**525–404**
Darius I	521–486
28th dynasty	**404–399**
29th dynasty	**399–380**
30th dynasty	**380–343**
Nectanebo I	380–362
Nectanebo II	360–343
Greek Period	**332–30**
Macedonian dynasty	**332–304**
Alexander the Great	332–323
Philip Arrhidaeus	323–316
Ptolemaic dynasty	**304–30**
Ptolemy I	304–284
Ptolemy III	246–221
Ptolemy IV	221–205
Ptolemy V	205–180
Cleopatra III	116–88
Cleopatra VII	51–30
Roman Era	**30** BC–AD **337**
Augustus	30 BC–AD 14
Tiberius	14–37
Diocletian	284–305
Byzantine Era	**337–641**
Theodosius	378–395
Valentinian III	425–455

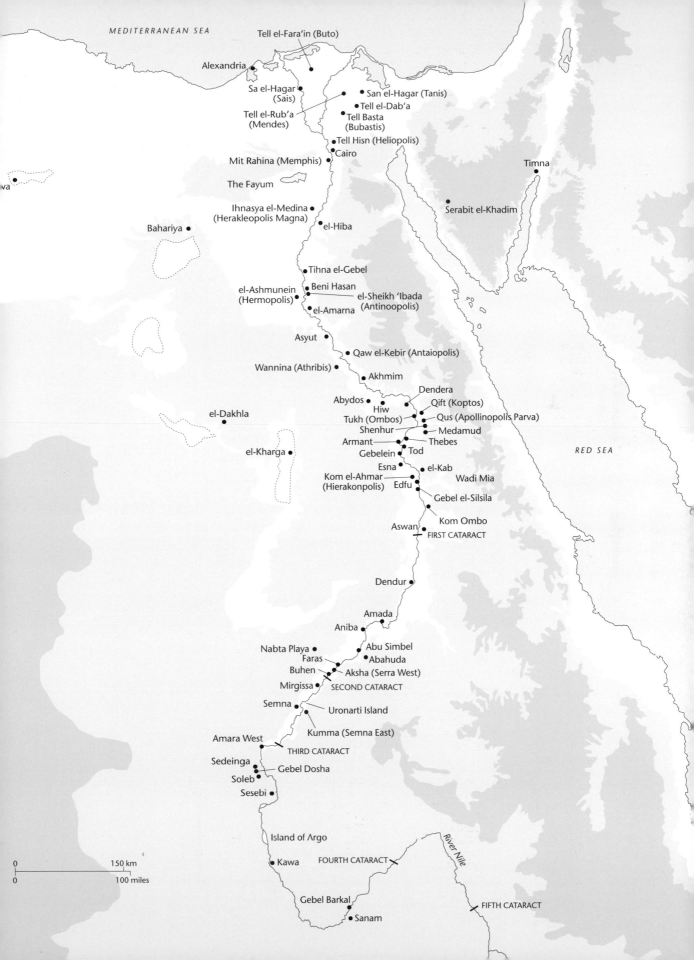

MEDITERRANEAN SEA

Tell el-Fara'in (Buto)

Alexandria

Sa el-Hagar (Sais)

San el-Hagar (Tanis)

Tell el-Dab'a

Tell el-Rub'a (Mendes)

Tell Basta (Bubastis)

Tell Hisn (Heliopolis)

Cairo

Mit Rahina (Memphis)

The Fayum

Ihnasya el-Medina (Herakleopolis Magna)

el-Hiba

Bahariya

Tihna el-Gebel

el-Ashmunein (Hermopolis)

Beni Hasan

el-Sheikh 'Ibada (Antinoopolis)

el-Amarna

Asyut

Qaw el-Kebir (Antaiopolis)

Wannina (Athribis)

Akhmim

el-Dakhla

Abydos

Dendera

Qift (Koptos)

Hiw

Tukh (Ombos)

Qus (Apollinopolis Parva)

Shenhur

Medamud

el-Kharga

Armant

Thebes

Gebelein

Tod

Esna

el-Kab

Kom el-Ahmar (Hierakonpolis)

Wadi Mia

Edfu

Gebel el-Silsila

RED SEA

Kom Ombo

Aswan

FIRST CATARACT

Dendur

Amada

Aniba

Nabta Playa

Abu Simbel

Faras

Abahuda

Buhen

Aksha (Serra West)

Mirgissa

SECOND CATARACT

Semna

Uronarti Island

Kumma (Semna East)

Amara West

THIRD CATARACT

Sedeinga

Gebel Dosha

Soleb

Sesebi

Island of Argo

River Nile

Kawa

FOURTH CATARACT

Gebel Barkal

FIFTH CATARACT

Sanam

Timna

Serabit el-Khadim

0   150 km

0   100 miles

The origins of religion in ancient Egypt, and of the gods themselves, go back to dimly distant prehistoric times which may lie forever beyond our grasp in terms of any full degree of understanding. Yet, although we have no contemporary records to explain the evidence of these earliest prehistoric periods, archaeology and even myths recorded in later times have afforded us significant clues relevant to the birth of Egypt's gods. The evidence reveals a culture whose deities came into being as an inherent part of the world and as such could live and die and mythically were doomed to the same apocalyptic fate as the universe itself – time, for the gods, as for all other aspects of creation, would eventually run out.

But the tenure of the gods was still one of cosmic proportions and Egypt's deities, like those of most other cultures, held great power. Nowhere is this more clearly seen than in the myths of creation in which the development of the world was told in varying forms at Egypt's great religious centres. These stories exhibit a surprising underlying consistency of belief in deities which, while one with the universe itself, formed, shaped and ruled the physical world according to their own transcendent power.

The great god Osiris (seated) attended by (from left to right) Horus, Thoth, Isis, Nephthys, Shu and Heka. According to Egyptian mythology, Osiris was one of only two deities who had come into being who would eventually remain after the dissolution of the world. Detail, coffin of Nespawershefy, 21st dynasty, c. 984 BC, western Thebes. Fitzwilliam Museum, Cambridge.

I   Rise and Fall of the Gods

Birth of the Gods

The genesis of the Egyptian gods goes far back into prehistoric times. These earliest beginnings occurred long before Egypt's existence as a nation state and the invention of writing, so we are forced to work with only non-written evidence, often from relatively uncertain contexts and settings. Although scholars of anthropology, prehistory and religion have struggled to analyze this formative stage in Egyptian religion, the available evidence remains difficult to interpret and is subject to differing opinions. Nevertheless, it would seem to suggest the presence of the concept of the sacred in the existence of apparent cult objects, in human and animal burials, and in areas where formal rituals appear to have been enacted. Whether such artifacts and sites actually reflect belief in a divine being or beings is unknown but, as various scholars have stressed, the care with which the dead were buried in the prehistoric period, and the afterlife belief implied by that care, certainly suggests that the necessary intellectual sophistication was present for such belief.

(Left) The 'Great White', an early baboon god from the Late Predynastic Period, c. 3000 BC. Egyptian Museum, Berlin.

(Above right) The River Nile made the unification of Egypt possible at an early date and spread the knowledge and veneration of local deities over much greater areas. Western Thebes viewed from Luxor.

(Opposite) The celebrated Narmer Palette, obverse (right) and reverse (far right), shows that numerous zoomorphic deities and their symbols existed by the end of the Predynastic Period. The palette also shows the formal carrying of divine standards in the upper register of the obverse. From Hierakonpolis, c. 3000 BC. Egyptian Museum, Cairo.

Spirit, fetish, totem and god

Like most early humans the prehistoric peoples who dwelt around the Nile seem to have been reverential towards the powers of the natural world – both animate and inanimate. The former seem to have taken precedence in Egypt, although the recurrent star images found on the Gerzeh Palette and other artifacts from the later Neolithic Period (3600–3300 BC) may indicate that an astral cult developed early in Egypt. However, the first clear divinities we find in Egypt's archaeological record are in most cases animal deities such as the cow and the falcon: gods which represented aspects of the cosmos, yet which doubtless were believed to hold sway over human occupations and lives. By the late prehistoric period we find evidence of animals – especially dogs (or jackals), gazelles, cattle and rams – which were buried in what appear to have been ritual contexts, and also representations of animals which may signify some kind of animism or fetishism (the idea that animals, like humans, possessed 'spirits' that must be respected and propitiated). If these zoomorphic images are not merely totems of tribal groups and do signify manifestations of the divine in some way, they represent a significant stage in the development of the Egyptian gods. The idea that the divine might be manifest in animal form is a vital prerequisite for the animals which are shown acting in entirely human ways and which are the major representations of the Egyptian gods at the end of the Predynastic Period. The celebrated Narmer Palette which dates to this time

of transition (c. 3000 BC) provides clear examples of this situation. On its reverse the palette shows a falcon holding a captive and on the obverse a bull breaking down a city wall and trampling an enemy figure. Long-necked mythical serpopards are also depicted, and on both sides of the palette – doubtless indicating their importance – twin images of a cow-headed deity fusing human and bovine features surmount these scenes. Here and in other artifacts of this period we doubtless have zoomorphic deities, and it would seem that a good many of them were already extant.

On the other hand, it is disputed whether deities in human form appeared in this early period or

Cattle Goddesses and Hunting Gods

Some of the earliest anthropomorphic images known from Egypt seem to fuse the human form with zoomorphic characteristics as in the curving, horn-like pose of the arms of this painted pottery female figurine from the Naqada II Period. Brooklyn Museum of Art.

In Egypt, cattle were particularly important in the development of religious belief. Recent study of the sites of Nabta Playa and Bir Kisseibain the Sahara to the west of the upper Nile Valley has shown that cattle were perhaps venerated long before domestication around 7000 BC. Horn cores of cows, placed on burials in Tushka in Nubia as early as 10,000 BC, suggest an association with afterlife beliefs and rituals, and this background fits well with the prevalence in dynastic Egypt of cow imagery associated with early goddesses such as Hathor, Nut and Neith. As Fekri Hassan has stressed, 'it is very likely that the concept of the cow goddess in dynastic Egypt is a continuation of a much older tradition of a primordial cow goddess or goddesses that emerged in the context of Neolithic cattle-herding in the Egyptian Sahara.' Hassan has also pointed out that as both the cow and woman gave milk, both shared an identity as a source of life and nourishment. The mothers who gave physical birth and sustenance – in human or bovine form – symbolized powers (such as the goddess Hathor) that brought the deceased back to life through spiritual rebirth. The burial pit with its food offerings was an image of the womb, and the contracted foetal position of the earliest surviving interments may have foreshadowed the desired rebirth. There is also evidence of very early male deities who seem to be associated with hunting and male fertility, and these gods may have been paired with the bovine goddesses in a parallel to the social conditions of the early Egyptian pre-agricultural, cattle-keeping and hunting cultures.

later. Crudely formed anthropomorphic figures of clay or ivory are found in the archaeological record of the Naqada Period and even earlier, but although they have been interpreted as deities, extensive study by Peter J. Ucko showed that a wide variety of uses and meanings of these figures is likely and none can be certainly accepted as representing a deity. By the beginning of the historical period we do have evidence of deities such as Min and Neith being worshipped in human form, although the concept of anthropomorphic deities seems to have been adopted only slowly in Egypt and was, in one sense, never complete, as Egyptian gods and goddesses frequently were viewed as hybrid forms with the heads or bodies of animals throughout Egyptian history. The goddess Hathor, for example, appears to have been one of the first deities to be given anthropomorphic form, but even she retained the horns of her sacred animal, the cow, and was frequently depicted in bovine form millennia after her appearance.

Primal and political needs

The development of the concept of individualized deities who held power over specific events and natural conditions is usually seen as concurrent with the development of the desire to gain some kind of control over the world and human vulnerability. In this the needs of early human societies were the same everywhere – and did not particularly change throughout history – though the immediate vulnerability of ancient humans to attacks by wild animals and the forces of nature may have gradually given way to the awareness of longer-term needs such as freedom from pain and want.

Once a central government arose around 3000 BC, perceived and real needs may have changed rapidly for the ancient population of the Nile Valley. National deities came into existence as well as the cult of the divine king; and as John Baines has pointed out, the emergence of monarchy and the resultant origin of the Egyptian state effectively transformed ancient religion by providing a new focus which unified its different goals and needs. Indeed, it might be said that from this point forward, the infancy of Egypt's deities had ended and more than 3,000 years of subsequent historical development would fail to radically change the underlying nature of Egyptian religion.

Rule of the Gods

It is one of the ironies of ancient Egyptian religion that although we must cope with a dearth of archaeological evidence regarding the origin of the gods, Egyptian texts of the later periods contain many clear yet often seemingly contradictory accounts of their mythic genesis, and rule of the cosmos. In recent years, many Egyptologists have come to feel that these varying accounts may not simply reflect the conflicting traditions of different cult centres, as has long been assumed, but can instead be seen as different aspects of an underlying understanding of how the world and its creator gods came into being. Certainly, there was no single, unified Egyptian myth of creation, but the major cosmogonies (stories of the origins of the universe) and theogonies (stories of the origins of the gods) associated with the most important cult centres may be more alike than is at first apparent.

Remains of a temple dedicated to the gods of Hermopolis and Heliopolis by Ramesses II at the site later called Antinoopolis in Middle Egypt. .

Latent power: the Hermopolitan view

At Hermopolis in Middle Egypt there existed a developed myth of creation by means of eight original deities – the so-called 'Ogdoad' or 'group of eight' who represented aspects of the original cosmos (see p. 77). Although most of the surviving textual evidence for this view of creation comes from the Ptolemaic Period, the ancient name of Hermopolis, Khemnu or 'eight town', is attested from the 5th dynasty (and may well go back earlier), showing the antiquity of the myth.

According to the Hermopolitan view the eight primordial deities existed in four pairs of male and female, each associated with a specific aspect or element of the pre-creation: Nun (or Nu) and Naunet, Water; Heh and Hauhet, Infinity; Kek and Kauket, Darkness; Amun and Amaunet, Hiddenness. These original 'elements' were believed to be inert yet to contain the potential for creation. James Hoffmeier has shown that interesting similarities exist between these elements and the conditions listed as immediately prior to the creation account in the biblical book of Genesis. In Egypt, however, the members of the Ogdoad were regarded as distinct divine entities and their names were grammatically masculine and feminine to reflect the equating of creation with sexual union and birth. They were

called the 'fathers' and 'mothers' of the sun god, since this deity was the focal point of ongoing creation in the Hermopolitan world view – as he was elsewhere.

Just as the beginning of the annual season of growth was marked in Egypt by the Nile's receding inundation and the emergence of high points of land from the falling river, so the Egyptians viewed the original creation event as occurring when the primordial mound of earth (see Tatenen) rose from the waters of the First Time. It was said that a lotus blossom (see Nefertem) then rose from the waters or from the same primeval mound; and it was from this flower that the young sun god emerged bringing light into the cosmos, and with it the beginning of time and all further creation.

The power of the sun god: the Heliopolitan view

Heliopolis, the chief centre of solar worship, produced a somewhat different mythic system built around the so-called Ennead (see p. 78) or 'group of nine' deities which consisted of the sun god and eight of his descendants. The Heliopolitan theologians naturally stressed the role of the sun god in their creation stories which focus, as a result, not so much on the inert aspects of preexistence but on the dynamic aspects of the resultant creation itself. The form of the sun god usually associated with this creation was Atum (see p. 98), who was sometimes said to have existed within the primeval waters 'in his egg' as a way of explaining the origin of the god. At the moment of creation Atum was said to have been born out of the primordial flood as 'he who came into being by himself', thus becoming the source of all further creation. The god next produced two children, Shu (air) and Tefnut (moisture), from himself. Several versions of the story exist, but in all of them Atum's children are produced through the exhalation of the god's body fluids or

(Above) One variant of the Great Ennead or 'group of nine deities' which here consists of (right to left) the sun god Re-Horakhty with Atum and his descendants Shu, Tefnut, Geb, Nut, Osiris, Isis and Horus. 18th dynasty. Tomb of Ay, western Valley of the Kings, western Thebes.

(Left) A god raises the disk of the sun from the earth into the heavens. Central to the Heliopolitan theology, the sun also played a role in all Egyptian creation accounts. Late Period papyrus. Egyptian Museum, Cairo.

mucus – either through the metaphor of masturbation, spitting or sneezing.

In turn, this first pair produced their own children, Geb (earth) and Nut (sky), who took their respective places below and above their parents, giving the creation its full spatial extent. Geb and Nut then produced the deities Osiris and Isis, Seth and Nephthys who viewed from one perspective represented the fertile land of Egypt and the surrounding desert, so that the key elements of the Egyptian universe were completed at this time. Frequently the god Horus, son and heir of Osiris and the deity most closely associated with kingship, was added to this group, thus supplying the link between the physical creation and societal structures. All these aspects, however, were viewed as simply extensions of the original coming into being of the sun god who lay at the heart of this world view and who was thus 'the father of all' and 'ruler of the gods'.

(Below) The air god Shu, assisted by other deities, supports the sky goddess Nut above her husband, the earth god Geb. 21st/22nd dynasty. Vignette from the Book of the Dead of Nesitanebtasheru. British Museum.

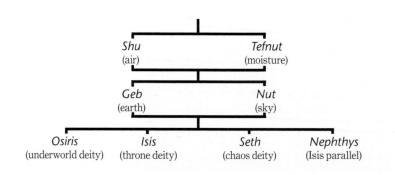

Shu (air)		Tefnut (moisture)
	Geb (earth)	Nut (sky)
Osiris (underworld deity)	Isis (throne deity)	Seth (chaos deity)	Nephthys (Isis parallel)

The power of thought and expression: the Memphite view

While the scholars of Heliopolis focused mainly on the emergence and development of the sun god, Atum, the priests of nearby Memphis looked at creation from the perspective of their own god Ptah. As the god of metalworkers, craftsmen and architects it was natural that Ptah was viewed as the great craftsman who made all things. But there was also another, much deeper, link between Ptah and the creation of the world which set the Memphite view of creation apart. The so-called Memphite Theology which is preserved on the Shabaka Stone in the Egyptian collection of the British Museum reveals this important aspect of the Memphite theological system. While the inscription dates to the 25th dynasty it was copied from a much earlier source, apparently of the early 19th dynasty, though its principles may have dated to even earlier times. The text alludes to the Heliopolitan creation account centred on the god Atum, but goes on to claim that the Memphite god Ptah preceded the sun god and that it was Ptah who created Atum and ultimately the other gods and all else 'through his heart and through his tongue'. The expression alludes to the conscious planning of creation and its execution through rational thought and speech, and this story of creation *ex nihilo* as attributed to Ptah by the priests of Memphis is the earliest known example of the so-called 'logos' doctrine in which the world is formed through a god's creative speech. As such it was one of the most intellectual creation myths to arise in Egypt and in the ancient world as a whole.

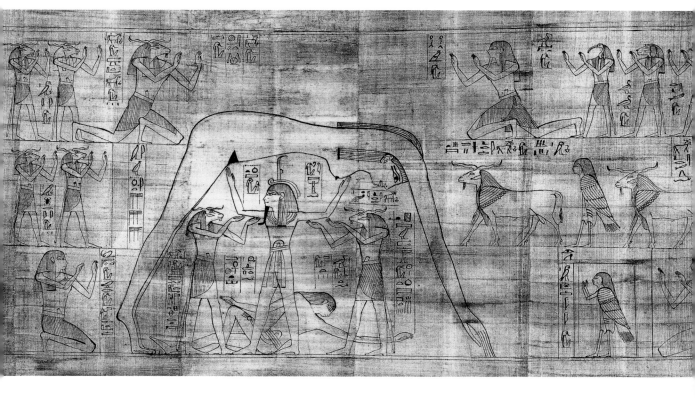

It lies before, and in line with, the philosophical concepts found in the Hebrew Bible where 'God said, let there be light, and there was light' (Genesis 1:3), and the Christian scriptures which state that 'In the beginning was the Word [logos]…and the word was God…all things were made by him…' (John 1:1, 3). Like Atum, however, Ptah was also viewed as combining male and female elements within himself. This is seen in early texts, and in the latest period of Egyptian history the name of the god was written acrophonically as *pet-ta-heh* or p(et)+t(a)+h(eh) as though he were supporting the sky (*pet*) above the earth (*ta*) in the manner of the Heh deities (see p. 109), but also bridging and combining the female element of the sky and the male element of the earth in the androgynous manner of the primordial male-female duality Ptah-Naunet.

(Above) The Shabaka Stone bears an inscription which is our main source of knowledge of the creation myth developed by the priests of Ptah at Memphis. The stone, which was later used for grinding, dates to the 25th dynasty, c. 700 BC. British Museum.

(Left) The god Ptah who was said to have brought forth the world through thought and creative speech. Graeco-Roman Period. Decorated block, Karnak.

Mythic variants

As much as these three systems of cosmogony and theogony differ in their details and in the stress placed upon differing deities by their own cults, it is clear that they all share a similar approach to creation. Although the differing approaches were apparently never combined into one unified myth, stories existed for many of the individual myths which fitted into the same overall framework. In the stories stressing the solar origin of creation, for example, we find variants which proclaimed that the sun god came into being as a hawk or falcon (see p. 205) or as a phoenix (see p. 212), in the form of a child (see p. 133), a scarab beetle (see p. 230) or some other creature, but these all originated from the primeval waters or from the mound which rose from them. There are also variants of the manner in which the monad (the prime, indivisible entity) is said to have produced the rest of creation – a Middle Kingdom text found on coffins at el-Bersheh states of the 'All-lord': 'I brought into being the gods from my sweat, and men are the tears of my eye'; but these do not differ radically from those of Heliopolis considered above. To some extent all these stories appear as kaleidoscopic variations of core mythic elements, and may indicate an effort on the part of the Egyptian theologians to incorporate deities which had arisen in different parts of Egypt, or at different times, into existing mythic frameworks. It is often the nature of the creator deities and the basis of their power which is at issue in the varying stories of the origin and rule of the gods.

Decline of the Gods

Despite his divinity, the death of the god Osiris plays a central role in Egyptian mythology. He is mourned by his sisters Nephthys and Isis as he lies on a funerary bier in this detail of a Roman Period gilt coffin. Graeco-Roman Period, c. 1st century BC. Metropolitan Museum of Art, New York.

The Egyptians' ideas of the origin and nature of the cosmos help us to understand the ultimate decline of their deities – for the inherent vulnerability of the gods is an integral part of Egyptian mythology and one which has important ramifications for our understanding of the ancient religion. Perhaps as Egypt's gods were progressively anthropomorphized they increasingly took on the weaknesses and limitations of their human subjects. However, according to Egyptian theological speculation, the gods themselves could, and would, eventually die – though the evidence for this must be carefully assessed and understood in context.

Even gods can die

A number of Egyptian texts show that although the gods were not considered to be mortal in the usual sense, they could nevertheless die. This is clearly implied in the so-called 'Cannibal Hymn' of the Pyramid Texts, and is of great importance in the development of even some of the greatest cults of Egyptian religion – particularly those of the netherworld god Osiris and the sun god Re. Although the Egyptian texts do not ever specifically say that Osiris died – almost certainly because such a statement would be believed to magically preserve the reality of the god's death – they, and later Classical commentators, do clearly show that Osiris was slain at the hands of his antagonist Seth, and was mummified and buried. The great sun god Re was thought to grow old each day and to 'die' each night (though for the same reason, specific mention of the god's death is not found), and then to be born or resurrected each day at dawn. This concept is clearest in late evidence such as texts found in the temples of Ptolemaic date, but it was doubtless an

idea long speculated on by the Egyptians and is implicit in many of the representations and texts found in New Kingdom royal tombs. It is also found in several Egyptian myths which describe the sun god as immensely old and clearly decrepit. One spell from the Coffin Texts includes an overt threat that the sun god might die (CT VII 419), showing that the idea of his demise extends at least as far back as Middle Kingdom times.

Divine demise

The principle of divine demise applies, in fact, to all Egyptian deities. Texts which date back to at least the New Kingdom tell of the god Thoth assigning fixed life spans to humans and gods alike, and Spell 154 of the Book of the Dead unequivocally states that death (literally, 'decay' and 'disappearance') awaits 'every god and every goddess'. Thus, when the New Kingdom Hymn to Amun preserved in Papyrus Leiden I 350 states that 'his body is in the west', there can be no doubt that this common Egyptian metaphorical expression refers to the god's dead body. Scholars such as François Daumas and Ragnhild Finnestad have shown that there are clues in late Egyptian temples that the innermost areas were regarded as the tombs of the gods. There are also various concrete references to the 'tombs' of certain gods with some sites – such as Luxor and western Thebes – being venerated as such from New Kingdom times at least. But all this evidence must be viewed in its proper context, for death need not imply the cessation of existence. From the Egyptian perspective life emerged from death just as death surely followed life and there was no compelling reason to exempt the gods from this cycle. This idea was aided by the fact that the Egyptians

distinguished two views of eternity: eternal continuity (*djet*) and eternal recurrence (*neheh*). This is clear in statements such as that found in the Coffin Texts, 'I am the one Atum created – I am bound for my place of eternal sameness – It is I who am Eternal Recurrence' (CT II 31). The gods could thus die and still remain in the ongoing progression of time. As Erik Hornung has stressed, the mortality of Egyptian gods 'enables them to become young again and again, and to escape from the disintegration that is the inevitable product of time'.

The end of time

Ultimately, a final end did await the gods. In Egyptian mythology it is clear that only the elements from which the primordial world had arisen would eventually remain. This apocalyptic view of the end of the cosmos and of the gods themselves is elaborated upon in an important section of the Coffin Texts in which the creator Atum states that eventually, after millions of years of differentiated creation, he and Osiris will return to 'one place', the undifferentiated condition prevailing before the creation of the world (CT VII 467–68). In the Book of the Dead this 'end of days' is even more clearly described in a famous dialogue between Atum and Osiris in which, when Osiris mourned the fact that he would eventually be isolated in eternal darkness, Atum comforted him by pointing out that only the

(Left) The god Osiris, wrapped in a mummy's bandages, stands beside a stylized tomb. Detail of coffin decoration. 21st dynasty. Egyptian Museum, Cairo.

(Below) Neheh (recurrent time) and Djet (continuous time) personified as a god and goddess representing differing aspects of eternity in ancient Egyptian thought. Detail, outer shrine of Tutankhamun. Egyptian Museum, Cairo.

two of them would survive when the world eventually reverted to the primeval ocean from which all else arose. Then, it is said, Atum and Osiris would take the form of serpents (symbolic of unformed chaos) and there would be neither gods nor men to perceive them (BD 175). Despite their seemingly endless cycles of birth, ageing, death and rebirth, the gods would finally perish in the death of the cosmos itself, and there would exist only the potential for life and death within the waters of chaos.

Twilight of the gods

Historically, a veritable Götterdämmerung also awaited the Egyptian gods. The eventual rise of Christianity and later of Islam spelled doom for the old pagan religion, but it did not die easily. In AD 383

pagan temples throughout the Roman Empire were closed by order of the Emperor Theodosius and a number of further decrees, culminating in those of Theodosius in AD 391 and Valentinian III in AD 435, sanctioned the actual destruction of pagan religious structures. Soon most of Egypt's temples were shunned, claimed for other use, or actively destroyed by zealous Christians, and the ancient gods were largely deserted. But signs of their tenacity are evident in many historical records.

Isis-Aphrodite, a form of the ancient goddess widely worshipped in the Roman Period. Isis was one of the last of Egypt's deities to survive historically. University of Leipzig Museum.

As late as AD 452, under a treaty between the Roman government and native peoples to the south of Egypt, pilgrims travelled north to the temple of Philae and took from there the statue of the goddess Isis to visit her relatives, the gods in Nubia. This situation was remarkable, as Eugene Cruz-Uribe has stressed, because it occurred at a time when Roman law had prohibited the worship of the old cults and officially endorsed Christianity as the only religion of Egypt and the Empire.

Clearly, in at least this outpost, and perhaps in others, and through secret worship, the old deities hung on for a time. By AD 639 when Arab armies claimed Egypt they found only Christians and the disappearing legacy of ancient gods who had ruled one of the greatest centres of civilization for well over 3,000 years. Yet, while the old gods had almost vanished, they left influences which would persist for thousands more years, as the Epilogue to this book shows.

The temple of Isis at Philae was one of the last strongholds of Egyptian paganism, functioning long after most temples had been closed by imperial decree.

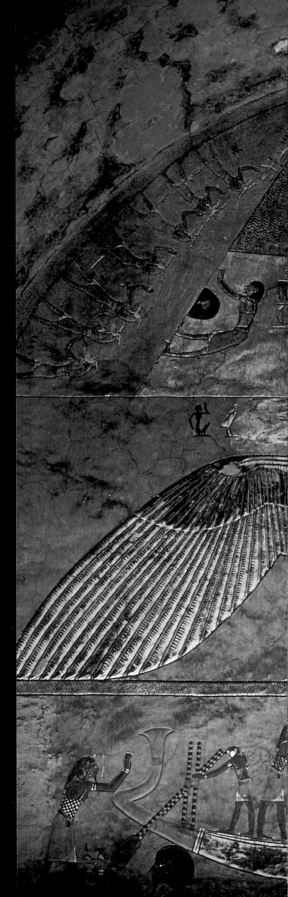

'Secret of development but glittering of forms,
wonderful god of many developments
All gods boast in him,
in order to magnify themselves in his perfection…'

Papyrus Leiden I 350, trans. by James Allen

The nature of the gods is one of the most fascinating yet complex aspects of ancient Egyptian religion, for the very concept of 'god' had a much broader meaning in this civilization than in many others. The deities of Egypt had both human and elevated qualities, the latter often masked by strange animal appearances and seemingly bizarre roles, yet they commanded sometimes surprising heights of religious development.

There is no doubt that the ancient Egyptians honoured literally hundreds of deities. Was there, however, beneath this rampant polytheism, a recurrent insight leading towards an understanding of a unity among gods, a primitive idea of the manifestation of one god in many, or even true monotheism itself? Scholars have debated this question for generations, and only recently have convincing answers begun to take shape.

The daily birth of the sun god from the concluding representation of the Book of Caverns. The solar deity is shown in different aspects of his nature – as a sun disk, child, scarab, and ram-headed bird. 19th dynasty. Tomb of Queen Tawosret, Valley of the Kings, western Thebes.

II Nature of the Gods

Forms of the Divine

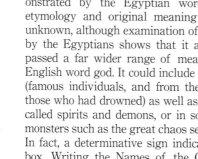

The ancient Egyptians visualized their gods and goddesses in manifold ways, and this is demonstrated by the Egyptian word *netcher*, the etymology and original meaning of which are unknown, although examination of the word's use by the Egyptians shows that it actually encompassed a far wider range of meanings than the English word god. It could include deified humans (famous individuals, and from the 30th dynasty, those who had drowned) as well as what might be called spirits and demons, or in some cases even monsters such as the great chaos serpent Apophis. In fact, a determinative sign indicating 'god' (see box, Writing the Names of the Gods) could be added to the name of any unusual or exotic creature and even the Egyptians' hieroglyphs were themselves sometimes regarded as 'gods'.

Gods, spirits, demons and *bau*

In addition to their major gods and goddesses, the ancient Egyptians also believed in various other types of supernatural beings which are often included in the category of minor deities. Even the earliest religious writings are peopled with frightening creatures (especially underworld monsters and demon-like beings) and throughout ancient Egyptian literature we find references to demons and spirits which seem to be similar to the djins and afrits of Arab culture. The ghosts or spirits of the deceased were also feared by the Egyptians and were known as *akhu*, a term which itself was also used of demons in the later periods. But the most feared, or at least most commonly feared, beings were the messengers and *bau* of deities. *Bau* were

manifestations or emanations of a god. Often they occurred in groups and seemed quite generic, but they were also linked with specific deities which, when offended, sent their *bau* to punish or trouble the offender. Magicians used their most potent spells and conjured the images of the most bizarre and frightening beings to combat these *bau* and hold them at bay.

Appearance of the divine

Despite the fact that the Egyptian pantheon appears to the outside observer to be filled with a veritable menagerie of gods, goddesses and other beings in an almost mindless variety of manifestations, for the most part Egyptian deities were conceived in logical types consisting of human (anthropomorphic), animal (zoomorphic), hybrid, and composite forms.

Generally, the so-called 'cosmic' gods and goddesses of the heavens and earth such as Shu, god of the air, and Nut, goddess of the sky, were anthropomorphic in form, as were 'geographic' deities or those representing specific areas such as rivers, mountains, cities and estates. Certain others, not fitting these categories – some of them very ancient, such as the fertility god Min – also took human form, as did deified humans such as deceased kings and other notables.

Zoomorphic deities were also common throughout Egyptian history. Perhaps the most ancient deity known in Egypt took the form of the falcon, and the worship of animals as representative of deities was especially prevalent in the latest periods. Gods associated with specific animal species were viewed as male or female according to their apparent or perceived characteristics. Male deities often took the form of the bull, ram, falcon or lion; and female deities were often associated with the cow, vulture, cobra or lioness.

'Hybrid' or more accurately 'bimorphic' half-human and half-animal deities existed in two forms

(Below) Knife-wielding demons and demi-gods. Detail of funerary papyrus, Ptolemaic Period. Egyptian Museum, Cairo.

(Opposite right) The human-headed, leonine-bodied sphinx personifies one form of 'hybrid' deity in which a human head is fused with the body of an animal. Sphinx of Amenemhet II. 12th dynasty. Louvre, Paris.

(Opposite far right) Osiride pillars, such as those within the temple of Ramesses II at Abu Simbel, provide an example of deities which take anthropomorphic form. Such deities tend to be infrequently depicted in non-human forms.

The Egyptian word *netcher* or 'god' was usually written by means of one of a number of hieroglyphic signs which were added as 'determinatives' or group indicators at the end of names of deities, as well as being used alone. One of the commonly used signs found from Old Kingdom times was a seated divine figure (see illustration 1) which could be male or female and thus was used specifically for gods and goddesses. Variants of this sign which signified individual deities (in a few cases standing or depicted in some other position) were also used, especially in the New Kingdom and later periods. From much earlier times the word 'god' could also be written by means of a hieroglyph depicting a falcon (2) – sometimes on a perch – doubtless indicative of the great antiquity of many of the falcon gods of Egypt. The most commonly used sign for god,

however, which was also very ancient, resembles in its developed form a flag atop a pole (see illustration 3) – the symbol of divine presence which fronted Egyptian temples and shrines back to predynastic times. As John Baines has shown, this sign has a complex history and may have developed as a means of signalling the presence of a deity without having a narrow, individual meaning associated with a specific divine power. Very late in Egyptian history the hieroglyph of a star (see illustration 4) could also be used to write the word god, but this is found only from the Ptolemaic Period on. All these signs could be written twice for dual numbers or three times for the plural 'gods' and sometimes in even larger numbers such as three groups of three signifying an ennead or group of nine gods: a writing which could also connote a 'plurality of plurality' or 'all the gods'.

– having the head of either a human or an animal and the body of the opposite type. Evidence for the former dates to at least the 4th dynasty with the sphinx as a human-headed animal, and on the 3rd-dynasty stela of Qahedjet (in the Louvre) a hawk-headed anthropomorphic god is the earliest known example of the latter type. The head is consistently the original and essential element of these deities, with the body representing the secondary aspect. Thus, as Henry Fischer pointed out, 'a lion-headed

The lion-headed goddess personifies the most common type of 'hybrid' or bimorphic deity in which the head of an animal is fused with an anthropomorphic body. Graeco-Roman Period. Dakka Temple, Nubia.

goddess is a lion-goddess in human form, while a royal sphinx, conversely, is a man who has assumed the form of a lion'.

Composite deities differ from the hybrid forms by combining different deities or characteristics rather than representing an individual god in a particular guise. They may be made up of numerous zoomorphic or anthropomorphic deities, and range from baboon-hawks or hippopotamus-serpents to multiple-headed and -armed deities combining as many as a dozen different gods. Despite their bizarre appearances, there remains a certain logic to many of these polymorphic deities as seen, for example, by comparing the fearsome Ammut and the more benign Taweret: both are part hippopotamus, crocodile and lioness, but fused to very different effect.

A fixed iconography for a given god was uncommon, and some appear in several guises – Thoth was represented by both the baboon and the ibis and Amun by the ram or the goose. However it is rare for a deity to be found in human, animal and hybrid forms, for example the sun god Re was depicted as a falcon or a human with the head of a falcon but not usually in purely human form. There

Ram-headed scarab beetle and four-headed ram 'wind deities' provide examples of the kaleidoscopic manner in which the Egyptians produced composite deities. Ptolemaic Period, temple of Deir el-Medina.

are some exceptions – the goddess Hathor could be represented in fully human form, as a cow, as a woman with the head of a cow, or as a woman with a face of mixed human and bovine features.

Divine identities

Ultimately it must be remembered that the various representations of the gods do not reflect the Egyptian concept of what their deities actually looked like. Their assigned forms were merely formalities, giving visible, recognizable appearances to deities that were often described as 'hidden', 'mysterious' or even 'unknown'. The physical form allowed cultic or personal interaction with deities, but their real identity was to be found in their own individual roles and characters, which were usually far broader than could be delimited by physical images or representations. Although many deities

(Far left) Faience amulet of Taweret depicts the goddess in the composite form of a hippopotamus with the paws of a lion and tail of a crocodile. Third Intermediate Period, 21st–24th dynasty. Harer Collection, San Bernardino.

(Left) The Ammut or 'eater of hearts' fused various dangerous creatures into a fearsome composite deity of afterlife punishment. Graeco-Roman Period papyrus. Egyptian Museum, Cairo.

Crouching deity in the hieroglyphic pose for 'god'. The Egyptians often used such generic images of deities – sometimes specified by name and at other times anonymous – to represent the idea of divinity, as the forms assigned to deities were not necessarily believed to depict their true appearance. Detail, painted coffin, 12th dynasty. Egyptian Museum, Cairo.

had clear associations, such as that of Re with the sun, different deities could share the same associations – Atum, Re, Khepri, Horakhty and several other gods were all associated with the sun, for example. Conversely, many deities were associated with more than one characteristic. Most of the more important gods and goddesses had many different names showing their multiple identities – and some, such as Neith and Hathor, fulfilled several distinct roles, often without exhibiting any single identity which could be said to be clearly 'primary'. Generally, and often as a result of fusion of lesser deities, the greater the deity the wider the range of his or her associations and identities.

The characters of individual deities and their relationships with humanity could be widely different. Some deities were viewed as particularly helpful to humans. Thoth, Horus and Isis were all called *sunu* or 'physician', for example, due to their healing powers. But while many gods and goddesses were viewed as benevolent, others were regarded as being inimical towards humanity. Even some of those who were generally regarded as benevolent could be ambivalent in nature. This was especially true of female deities. Hathor, for example, was worshipped as a goddess of love, music and celebration, but she was also mythically typecast as a raging destroyer of humanity. In some cases deities exhibited different forms according to aspects of their nature, so that in her usual placid role the goddess Bastet appeared in the form of the cat, and in her more ferocious role in the guise of a lioness. Such ambivalence is not rare among the Egyptian gods, and it is sometimes difficult to ascertain whether certain deities were worshipped despite or because of their potential hostility. Like their own

human subjects, the Egyptian gods could eat and drink (sometimes to excess), they could work, fight, think, speak and even cry out in despair. They could interact well or poorly and could exhibit anger, shame and humour – often exhibiting distinctive personality traits as part of their identities.

Time and change

While every area of Egypt doubtless originally had its own god or goddess, many deities developed other regional associations through time – sometimes rising to the status of regional or national gods. The reverse could also occur, and some deities such as the god Montu eventually lost much of their area of influence and finally held revered but fairly limited local status. Although the area of origin of a deity often became the location of that god or goddess's chief cult centre, this was not always the case. While the centre of worship of the great god Amun was located at Thebes, for example, it seems that he was not himself of Theban origin.

Change could also affect the organization of gods. As time progressed, many of the cults of the major deities were organized into family triads of a 'father', 'mother', and 'son' – as with Amun, Mut and Khonsu at Thebes; or Ptah, Sekhmet and Nefertem at Memphis. This development effectively strengthened the position of some deities and meant that others, not included in important temple 'families', tended to be relegated to less important status and were less likely to receive cultic service.

Even the character or nature of deities could change with time, and perhaps the most dramatic example of this is found in the god Seth, whose perceived nature, popularity and importance fluctuated widely in different periods. The process of change often occurred in one of two ways – through the assimilation of a less important deity by a greater one or, more rarely, by the assimilation of a characteristic of a great deity by a lesser one. The god Osiris provides an excellent example of the first situation, as he took on many epithets and characteristics from deities which he assimilated during the wide-ranging spread of his cult. On the other hand, the often superlative role played by solar theology in Egyptian religion led to the association of many lesser deities with the sun god or solar characteristics. The phenomenon is especially noticeable in later periods, and in temples of the Ptolemaic Period we find Hathor, Isis, Horus, Khnum and other deities praised not only as the children of the sun god but also as solar deities in their own right with clear solar epithets and iconographic attributes. Egypt's gods were thus susceptible to change through time regarding their very natures as well as their relative importance.

The god Amun-Re (seated), with Mut (far left) and Khonsu (far right), grants endless jubilees to Ramesses III. While Amun rose to national prominence as a Theban god, he did not necessarily originate in the Theban area. Many deities underwent changes in the location and extent of their worship. 20th dynasty. Mortuary temple of Ramesses III, Medinet Habu, western Thebes.

Falcon-headed crocodile deity from Naqa, Upper Nubia. Although such deities seem to have been first worshipped in Egypt, the particular iconography of this god with human hands and leonine rear legs shows subtle changes which occurred with its assimilation into the Meroitic culture.

Manifestations of the Gods

God as many gods

In the Egyptian texts the gods are often said to be 'rich in names', and the multiplicity of names (and therefore manifestations) exhibited by individual deities provides an important example of the principle whereby one god may be seen as many. In the New Kingdom text known as the Litany of Re the solar god is identified in 'all his evolutions' as 75 different deities – including not only common forms of the sun but also female deities such as Isis and Nut. Osiris received prayers and litanies of praise under many names, and the mythological story explaining how his body was torn into pieces and scattered throughout Egypt provides an example of how one god could become many. Yet this example is unique and such a physical explanation for multiple instances and locations of a deity was not necessary for the application of the principle. In the Ptolemaic temple of Edfu we find that the goddess Hathor is represented by as many forms as there are days in the year (and each of these is actually named as two variant forms), but there seems to have been no mythic backdrop to this situation which would have required the Egyptians to posit many independent forms of the goddess. Perhaps the ultimate example of the multiplicity of divine names is to be found in the great god Amun, who was given so many names that the number was said to be unknowable.

Another aspect of the multiple names of individual gods can be seen in those cases where a given deity was regarded as the *ba* or manifestation of another. Of the god Khnum, for example, it was often said that he was the '*ba* of Re' or of Osiris

and so on, so that a given deity was not only associated with another, but also took on further names and identities in this manner. As several scholars have pointed out, the form, name and epithets of Egyptian deities seem to have been variable almost at will, and are often interchangeable with those of other deities. But while it could be argued that in almost all these cases the various names and manifestations of deities are simply forms of the same underlying god or goddess, individual deities were manifest in often increasingly diverse ways showing a basic Egyptian predilection for the concept of one god as many.

Pantheism

Pantheism, the related idea that identifies all aspects of the universe with a god, is a concept that has appealed to a number of Egyptologists since the latter part of the 19th century. These included scholars of the stature of Edouard Naville and James Henry Breasted, who felt that solar pantheism was an important part of ancient Egyptian religion. Yet, more recently several Egyptologists have shown that Egyptian religion exhibits clear traits that deny this equation. These are the self-imposed limitation of Egyptian religion, which clearly did not try to deify every aspect of creation, and limitations in the number and types of forms that even the greatest gods are said to take. As Erik Hornung has written, 'Amun may appear in the most various forms, but never as the moon, a tree, or a stretch of water', and this list may be extended considerably. In fact, as Marie-Ange Bonhême has put it, the boundaries of the individuality of the Egyptian gods 'forbids certain manifestations so as to prevent a progression toward complete pantheism'; and although the vast number of deities found in Egyptian religion may be reminiscent of pantheism, the resemblance is superficial, as Hornung rightly claims. For the Egyptians the creator god may have manifested himself in his creation, but he was certainly not absorbed by it.

Many gods as one

The ancient Egyptians seem to have formed groups among their deities since very early times. Although we cannot tell if the various deities depicted together on Pre- and Early Dynastic palettes and other artifacts were intended to represent groups of any kind, this might have been the case in some instances. However, by the time of the Pyramid Texts of the Old Kingdom the grouping of gods and goddesses into enneads of nine (though sometimes more or fewer) deities is fully established, as is the grouping of the Souls of Pe and Nekhen, or the Souls of Pe and Heliopolis and the 'Followers of Horus'. Even before the formulation of these groups there seems to have existed a very early grouping of gods called simply the *khet* or 'body' – this is found in the Pyramid Texts (PT

Variant, individual forms of the sun god Re from the 'Litany of Re' inscribed in New Kingdom tombs exemplify the differentiating aspect of Egyptian theology. 18th dynasty. Tomb of Tuthmosis III, Valley of the Kings, western Thebes.

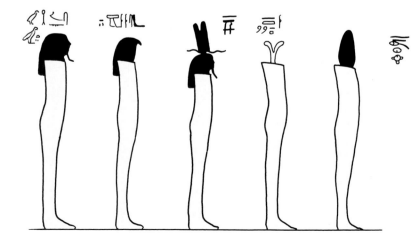

1041) but is probably much older, as it may be seen in the names of several early monarchs beginning with the 1st-dynasty king Semerkhet.

Many other smaller groups of deities such as the various triads, tetrads, pentads, hexads, hebdomads and ogdoads (see p. 74–79) were also formed, but there is no clear pattern in the development of these groups and certainly no gradual movement toward smaller groupings which might indicate some kind of preliminary progression toward monotheism. In the same manner, although the number three was utilized by the Egyptians to signify a closed system which was both complete and interactive among its parts, the many triads of deities which developed in Egyptian religion were in no way directly comparable to the Christian idea of the trinity. Egyptian groups of three deities were usually linked in a father-mother-child union, but this was never expressed as a unity, and each

member of the triad preserved his or her distinct individuality as a separate deity.

Syncretism

There is, nevertheless, a good deal of evidence for the Egyptian practice of linking or bringing together different deities into the body or identity of a combined god or goddess (sometimes, though not always, with 'composite' form). This was accomplished in several ways, most commonly through the linkage of the deities' names, creating composite gods such as Atum-Khepri, Re-Horakhty, and Amun-Re. Some of these syncretisms may be seen as simple combinations of similar deities or even different aspects of the same god – Atum-Khepri combined the evening and morning manifestations of the sun and Re-Horakhty formed a composite of two other important aspects or forms of the solar

The solar god Re-Horakhty blesses a female worshipper with flower-like rays. The combined Re and Horakhty were joined into a new and powerful deity through a strong unifying or syncretistic trend in Egyptian religion. Stela of Tanetperet, Thebes, 22nd dynasty. Louvre, Paris.

(Above) The great god Amun-Re (left), seen here receiving the gift of 'meret chests' from Ramesses II, represented the syncretism of two very different deities through the linking of the most powerful visible and invisible forces in the Egyptian cosmos. 19th dynasty. Temple of Amun, Karnak.

(Left) Symbolic representation of the syncretism of multiple deities. Decorated blocks, Graeco-Roman Museum, Alexandria.

deity. In other cases, syncretism involved the linking of deities of very different natures, as with Amun-Re in whom the Egyptian theologians wished to combine Amun and Re to unite the greatest visible and invisible powers of the world. The practice could also reflect the association of a local deity with one of the greater gods (as with Sobek-Re or Khnum-Re); often, as Hermann Junker first pointed out, the name of the local god is placed before that of the external, and usually greater, god. In these cases the power and standing of the major god were shared with the lesser deity, though the arrangement also accorded more power to the external god in the local sphere. The process could also bring together three, four or even more deities, as in the case of the syncretism of Ptah, Sokar and Osiris into one consummate funerary deity, or the form Harmachis-Khepri-Re-Atum, which brought together major solar-related gods. The same process could also unite foreign deities with Egyptian ones as with the Asiatic-Egyptian Anat-Hathor and the Meroitic-Egyptian Arensnuphis-Shu, as well as the great Ptolemaic hybrid deity Serapis who brought together Osiris, Apis, Zeus and Helios.

(Right) Amun-Min linked the powerful god Amun with the fertility deity Min in a manner which strengthened the creative and procreative nature of Amun and gave ascendancy to Min. 19th dynasty. Temple of Amun, Karnak.

The purpose of syncretisms such as these was doubtless not to simply combine conflicting or competing deities, as was assumed by many early Egyptologists. In many cases there clearly was no prior conflict between syncretized deities, and there is frequently no reason why the two or more united deities should not have been simply worshipped side by side, as Horus and Sobek were at Kom Ombo in the Ptolemaic Period or, in fact, as a great many of Egypt's deities were worshipped in multiple chapels in temples throughout the land from much earlier times. Rather, it is as if the Egyptians were acknowledging the presence of one god or goddess 'in' another deity whenever that deity took on a role which was a primary function of the other. But this indwelling does not mean that one deity was subsumed within another, and nor does it indicate that the two deities became identical or that there was also an underlying movement towards monotheism involved in the process. Erik Hornung has shown that, properly understood, syncretism does not isolate but rather links different deities and often the process effectively creates a third god where there were originally only two.

The syncretistic image of Osiris-Re supported by Nephthys and Isis and explained as 'Osiris "resting" in Re and Re "resting" in Osiris'. 19th dynasty. Tomb of Nefertari, Valley of the Queens, western Thebes.

Egypt and Monotheism

In the 19th century a debate arose among Egyptologists which was to rage for many years and which is still not entirely over. The debate has centred around a fundamental aspect of Egyptian religion: were the ancient Egyptians at all times polytheists or were there times or even ongoing trends in which Egyptian religion moved slowly but inexorably towards monotheism?

Believers in One god or Many

In his early 1930s work *The Dawn of Conscience*, the American Egyptologist James Henry Breasted argued that the religion of the heretic 18th-dynasty pharaoh, Akhenaten – who attempted to do away with most of Egypt's traditional gods and to replace them with the worship of the solar disk or Aten

Tuthmosis III (at left) offers incense and libation before Amun, the Theban god who rose to national pre-eminence during New Kingdom times. 18th dynasty. Chapel of Tuthmosis III from Deir el-Bahri. Egyptian Museum, Cairo.

(see p. 236) – was nothing less than a direct precursor of the Judeo-Christian-Islamic monotheism of later history. From 1934 the German Egyptologist Hermann Junker went even further, suggesting that Egyptian religion had, in fact, originally been monotheistic and had only eventually degenerated into a morass of separate cults after the founding of the Egyptian state. Although the argument for this kind of primitive monotheism and the idea of a single, transcendent deity has long been discarded, the idea that the Egyptians did gradually develop monotheistic ways of thought has been more abiding. Some scholars have seen the successive rise of pre-eminent deities such as Re, Osiris and Amun as precisely this kind of development. Others have felt that the Egyptian word for god, *netcher,* used without reference to any particular god (especially common in Egyptian 'wisdom literature' or 'instructions' and in personal names that combined the word god with another element) also demonstrated the idea of an underlying single god in Egyptian religion. In an influential work published in 1960 Siegfried Morenz drew these arguments together in support of the idea that behind the nearly countless deities of the Egyptian pantheon there was, historically, among at least some Egyptians, a growing awareness of a single god.

But another side to the story appeared with the publication of an incisive study by Erik Hornung in 1971. Hornung systematically examined this question, and found no evidence for an ongoing movement towards monotheism. Of central importance, he argued that the word 'god' in Egyptian usage never appears to refer to an abstract deity of higher order than other gods but is rather a neutral term which can apply to any deity, or as Hornung expressed it, 'whichever god you wish'. In the same manner, personal names such as Mery-netcher, translated as 'whom god loves', could mean any god and may be found with many specified parallels such as 'whom Ptah loves'. From this perspective the various expressions of syncretism or the 'indwelling' of one deity in another do not present evidence of a move towards monotheism. While worshippers may have elected to venerate a given god above all others, this is merely henotheism, a form of religion in which the other gods remain. Finally, while it is true that at given times we find a supreme god at the head of the Egyptian pantheon, the other gods remain, the qualities of the supreme being are not limited to any one god, and even within the same period of time we find many gods being called 'lord of all that exists' and 'sole' or 'unique'. According to Hornung, only the 'heretic' Akhenaten clearly insisted upon an approach which affirmed One god to the exclusion of the Many.

Other scholars have looked at the context of Akhenaten's religious 'revolution' differently, however. In his 1997 work *Moses the Egyptian,* for example, Jan Assmann has pointed out that

Painted limestone stela depicting Akhenaten and Nefertiti with infant princesses. The disk of the solar Aten shines on the royal family in an expression of what was essentially a closed theological system. 18th dynasty. Egyptian Museum, Cairo.

the various creation accounts developed by the Egyptians, and the ongoing process of syncretism, reflect two fundamental but different approaches to the paradox of 'the One and the Many' inherent in all ancient Egyptian religion. Assmann has characterized these divergent viewpoints as one of *generation* – by which the One produces the Many (as seen in Egyptian creation accounts), and one of *emanation* – in which the One is present in the Many (as seen in syncretism). These viewpoints existed concurrently in Egypt throughout most of the Dynastic Period, but in the religion of Akhenaten the concept of the emanation of the god Aten is not to be found. It is through generation alone that the Aten recreates the world and all that is in it. In this view, although visible and in that sense immanent in his creation, the Aten also transcended it in the manner found in true monotheism.

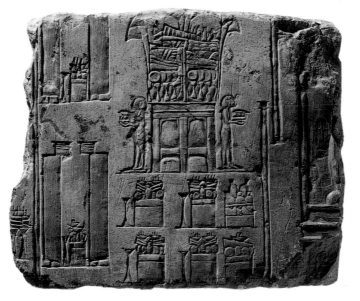

Part of the Great Aten Temple at Akhetaten (Amarna) represented on a talatat block found at el-Ashmunein. The great altar at the top is flanked by statues of the king bearing offerings in another expression of the carefully delimited nature of Aten worship. 18th dynasty. Egyptian Museum, Cairo.

(Below) The 'Restoration Stela' of Tutankhamun documenting the return to orthodox Egyptian religion and the restitution of the god Amun after the Amarna Period. Discovered in the temple of Amun at Karnak. Egyptian Museum, Cairo.

Believers in the Many and the One

More recently, James Allen has suggested a synthesis of the two opposing views of Egyptology regarding Akhenaten's monotheism. One approach (accepted predominantly by earlier Egyptologists) views Akhenaten's ideas as derivative of concepts present in Egyptian religion long before that king's reign, and the other (championed by Erik Hornung) sees Akhenaten's religion – especially his monotheism – as a radical innovation without any precedent whatsoever. Allen accepts evidence from both sides and provides a new perspective. While stressing that Hornung is certainly right in pointing to the distinction between Akhenaten's monotheism and earlier Egyptian understandings of god, Allen has shown that what was radical about Akhenaten's theology was not its proclamation of the oneness of god but its insistence on *exclusivity*. The polyvalent logic of Egyptian thought could easily allow an appreciation of the underlying oneness of god to coexist with traditional Egyptian polytheism. He suggests, in fact, that the best evidence for this is actually the phenomenon of syncretism which 'unites the view of god as simultaneously Many and One'. This is not to say that Egyptian religion was essentially 'monotheism with a polytheistic face' – and the perception of god as essentially One may perhaps have been limited to a few Egyptian theologians at any one time. But maybe for even ordinary Egyptians the experience of god could have been to some extent monotheistic – while they continued to view the world in polytheistic terms, they also identified their uniform notion of 'god' with a particular god in specific situations.

The advantage of this view is that while it accepts Hornung's valid criticism of many individual pieces of proof of Egyptian monotheism, it nevertheless allows evidence as to the attitude that does seem to lie beneath many Egyptian writings, such as those found in the so-called Wisdom Texts. As Allen has written, 'The authors of these texts are not espousing a particular theology; they are giving expression to their appreciation of humanity's relationship to the divine in general – not "this god" as in polytheism, or "the god" as in

The Concept of Transcendence

The question of whether the ancient Egyptians ever believed in the concept of monotheism contains within itself another question – whether they developed the idea of a transcendent deity. Earlier sweeping affirmations in this regard have not stood the test of time and scholarly analysis, but the idea of transcendent divine ability – especially as manifest in the transcendence of space and time – may still be reflected in some of the Egyptian evidence.

As early as the Instruction for Merikare (apparently composed in Middle Kingdom times) we find the expression 'the god knows every name', indicating perhaps the idea of an omniscient god. By late New Kingdom times we find instances of the great god Amun being viewed in a manner which could indicate belief in his transcendent ability. One text states that 'Amun hears the prayer of one who calls to him, in a moment he comes from afar to the one who cries out to him'. A few other texts seem to echo this same attitude. While they may indicate only that Amun was being viewed as acting on a grander and wider scale than had been common before Ramessid times, there is no firm indication that the concept of transcendence was not involved. Certainly the Egyptian gods did not ultimately transcend time – as was seen in Part I – because like their human counterparts they were subject to old age and eventual demise. Nor could they fully transcend space, as they could not penetrate the outer regions beyond the created cosmos which Egyptian mythology explicitly states is uninhabited by the gods, or those regions of the Duat where the light of the sun god does not penetrate. Yet, despite these facts, it is possible that from the Egyptians' perspective, there was an idea of relative – if not absolute – transcendence in the religion of the late New Kingdom. The few texts which address the subject do seem to show that Amun was viewed as transcending space *within* the world in which the gods were created and functioned. We may also find, with the same god, texts which intimate the god's transcendence of even the bounds of the Egyptians' mythical cosmos. Papyrus Leiden I 350 says of Amun:

'He is hidden from the gods, and his aspect is unknown. He is farther than the sky, he is deeper than the Duat…'

In this text the 'unknowable nature' of Amun is the main issue which is stressed, yet the expression 'He is farther than the sky, he is deeper than the Duat' seems to indicate a view of the deity's transcendence

The god Amun came to be revered as a deity whose nature included a transcendent aspect close to that of the monotheistic god of Judaism, Christianity or Islam. Detail, statue of Amun from Thebes. Luxor Museum.

of the cosmos itself and is not essentially different from the sentiment of the biblical Psalmist, long regarded by scholars as reflecting the transcendent omnipresence of the Hebrew God:

'Where shall I go from your spirit? Or where should I flee from your presence?
If I ascend up into heaven, you are there; If I make my bed in hell, behold you are there.'

Psalm 139:7–8

It is also possible to view the nature of Akhenaten's Aten as being transcendent in certain ways (see p. 236) and the fact that in the Late Period the solar ram was said to have not only four heads, but also 777 ears and millions of eyes, shows the idea of the greatly enhanced senses of the god in a practical, mythical manner. While this does not prove omniscience, it is not essentially different from the theological developments of later history which posit the idea of a God who sees even the smallest event.

henotheism, but simply "god".' From this perspective, the Egyptians were in a sense both polytheists and monotheists, and the religion of Akhenaten may have had certain precedents in formal theology and even in popular attitudes which amount to the idea of god in the singular. Rather than its radical focus on one god, however, it was a dogmatic exclusiveness that set the religion of Akhenaten apart and that ultimately made his theology unacceptable to most ancient Egyptians. It would only be with the eventual rise of Judaism, Christianity and Islam that such exclusivity in the worship of the One would take hold, and in so doing, would historically spell the end for Egypt's Many.

The ancient Egyptians believed that the stability of the created world
had to be carefully preserved through the upholding of their deities –
for it was the care and sustenance of the gods and the maintenance of
cosmic balance which kept chaos and non-being from encroaching
upon and overwhelming the world. Thus, the Egyptian concept of
religion centred far more upon individual and collective service of the
gods and upon right actions than on abstract theological ideas, creeds
or tenets of belief.

Collective worship of the gods involved constant service through
the daily cleansing, clothing, feeding and entertainment of their
images in formal temple settings as well as in a myriad festivals,
rituals and mysteries. At a personal level, individuals in all sections of
society had access to the gods which developed, especially in the later
periods of Egyptian history, into a close relationship with the divine
and eventually to the concept of personal salvation itself.

*Offering-bearers present bread, beer, vegetables, meat, papyrus, flowers and other gifts
to the* ba *of Ptah-Sokar-Osiris. Tomb of Kheruef. 18th dynasty. Western Thebes.*

III   Worship of the Gods

Care of the Gods

From the very establishment of the ancient Egyptian state around 3000 BC, religion developed along two separate paths – which often ran in very different directions. On the one hand, individual veneration of the gods continued to develop its own stresses and focal points (which are considered in the next section). On the other hand, the founding of the monarchical state enhanced the development of state-favoured and subsidized cults which served the gods formally.

Houses of the gods

Unlike the gods of the ancient Greeks and some other cultures, Egyptian deities did not readily mix with their human subjects, and their interaction was usually found in specific contexts and areas, the most important of which was the temple. From the small reed huts of predynastic times to the towering stone structures of the New Kingdom and later periods, temples were the focal points of individual population centres and of Egyptian society as a whole. Unlike modern cathedrals,

(Right) The mortuary temple of Ramesses III at Medinet Habu, western Thebes. Although used during the king's lifetime, such royal mortuary temples were designed for the ongoing care of the deceased and divine king.

(Far right) Inner sanctuary and shrine of the temple of Horus at Edfu. Ptolemaic Period.

(Below) Female fecundity deity bearing stylized tray of offerings symbolically supplies the needs of the gods. Graeco-Roman Period. Temple of Montu, Medamud.

(Below right) Divine personification of 'United with Eternity', the mortuary temple of Ramesses III. 20th dynasty. Medinet Habu, western Thebes.

churches, synagogues, mosques and other religious structures, however, Egyptian temples were not primarily designed for the worship of the gods. Worship could and did take place within them, but they primarily functioned as complex symbolic models of the cosmos, as interfaces between the physical and supernatural worlds, and as 'houses' of the gods for their care and provision – functions which overlapped to a considerable degree. Even though some deities had no temples of their own and others were not even represented as subsidiary deities in any temple, in a sense they were all represented by the temples, which functioned to preserve cosmic order and thus the gods themselves.

The physical form of the temple was shaped to this purpose. Sacred sites were ringed by *temenos* walls designed not only to exclude the profane but also to symbolically and even physically keep external unrest and chaos at bay. The outer temple walls defined an area not only sacred in the religious sense but also representative of the very sphere of life and order which existed within the infinite chaos posited by Egyptian cosmography. The architectural programme and decoration of the temple proper furthered this model. Its axial processional way symbolized the path of the sun, and its darkened inner sanctuary acted as a physical metaphor for both the darkness of night out of which came rebirth and the darkness of initial creation out of which sprang life and order in the beginning. These detailed cosmic models functioned like exquisite and perfectly regulated time pieces with the work of the king, and of the priests who represented him, providing the power to run them through the mystery of cultic service.

Temple service

The service and care of the gods was thus paramount not only to the Egyptians' sense of religious responsibility toward their deities but also to the continuation of existence itself. This was effected through the practice of rituals which supported the gods so that they in turn might be able to preserve and sustain the world. In fact, Dimitri Meeks has shown that a single common feature shared by the various beings called 'gods' by the Egyptians is that they were the recipients of ritual. These rituals were of many types but are most easily classified on a temporal basis. Viewed this way we may differentiate the daily ritual service of the gods which tended their basic needs; the occasional but regular rituals which were part of the recurrent festivals of the temple calendar; and finally, the non-regular rituals which were performed only on special occasions or under special circumstances. Rituals of the third class were naturally the least commonly enacted and are rarely depicted in temple scenes, while those of festival and daily rituals decorate the walls of many Egyptian temples. In virtually all cases, however, temple depictions of ritual service do not reflect the reality of the ritual but are rather an idealized representation in which the king and deity are the sole participants. Even in scenes where priests are represented – as in depictions of processions – they are clearly ancillary to the figure of the monarch, for the most fundamental aspect of temple service during the pharaonic period was that in theory, and hence symbolically, it was the king himself who performed all major actions of the service of the cult. This aspect of temple function was rooted in the mythic reality of the king as legitimate descendant and heir of the gods – concepts which will be examined later. However in actual practice it was, of course, the priests who acted as the king's surrogates and who usually performed the rituals involved in the care of the gods.

Amenophis III offers incense and a libation over a richly laden altar. 18th dynasty. Luxor Temple. Although usually represented by the priesthood, it was both a prerogative and a responsibility of the Egyptian king to supply the ongoing needs of the gods.

43

Images of the gods

The object of this service was the divine image, for the statue of the deity housed within the sanctuary of the temple was the focal point of the entire cult. As a result, the amount of work dedicated to the production of divine images was often considerable and the results doubtless awe-inspiring.

Although they were not considered to be the gods themselves, statues of gods and goddesses were believed to house the spirits or manifestations of the deities, and because of this they were treated as though they were alive. Divine images were taken from their shrines each day and washed, dressed in clean clothes, adorned with precious ornaments and censed. They were given offerings of food and drink – usually wine, milk or water – and then returned to their shrines. The distinction between the medium of the statue and the separate identity of the deity is clear in textual sources, however:

'The God of this earth is the sun in the sky.
While his images are on earth,
When incense is given them as daily food,
The lord of risings is satified.'

The Instruction of Any

The divine image was not only treated reverentially but was also the recipient of considerable gifts. For

Creating Bodies for the Gods

Cult images of the gods were produced from only the most permanent or symbolically significant materials, and the production of a divine statue was considered as an act of creation accomplished by human craftsmen with the help of the gods themselves. There was thus something of the supernatural about the divine image even from its initial design and fashioning at the craftsmen's hands. Mythologically, the skin of the gods was said to be of pure gold so divine images were often gilded or made entirely with the precious metal. Their hair was said to be like lapis lazuli so this semi-precious stone was often inset into statues of deities to signify their hair and eyebrows. Symbolic connections were also made with the deity by means of the materials used in its image – lunar deities, for example, often being inset with silver, which signified the moon. The connection between the image and the deity it represented was made total, however, through the rite of the 'opening of the mouth'. This ritual symbolically removed all traces of human origin from the image and instilled it with the emanation of the deity. At this point the image was believed to become the invisible deity's visible body on earth. As such it 'lived' and fulfilled the function not only of an intermediary but as the very nexus of interaction between this world and beyond.

'Opening of the mouth' scene, Tomb of Inherkha, Thebes.

example, Amenophis Son of Hapu, chief steward of Amenophis III, records that he donated 1,000 animals to a statue of the king. Royal gifts to the gods were even more prodigious, of course, and were often recorded in representations of the king presenting his gifts before the image of the deity to whom they were made.

On festival days or other special occasions the images of the gods were often placed in portable barques which were carried upon the shoulders of the priests and taken in procession to significant sites. These were often the temples of other deities, or their own outlying temples where the deity would simply take up temporary occupancy for the duration of the festival or special event.

Festivals, rituals and mysteries

The festivals of the deities provided the structural framework for many of the important rituals focusing on the gods and on cultic or cosmic renewal. 'Festival calendars' or lists of ritual activities were inscribed on the walls and doorways of temples and often included the offerings to be made not only in the regular daily service but also on all the particular high days celebrated in the temple's cult.

Renewal is particularly important in these festivals as their purpose was ultimately directed to the same kind of rejuvenation or rebirth achieved each day in the constant solar cycle. Thus, one of the rituals performed on New Year's Day – also called 'the birth of Re' – and most fully recorded in Ptolemaic times involved carrying the statues of deities up to the temple roof. Here the god or goddess could see and be united with the rising sun in a moment of shared rebirth. Many of the same rituals and religious performances were enacted on a number of key festivals such as those of the first day of the first month (New Year) and the first day of the fifth month (celebrating the rebirth of Osiris). Some festivals had their own particularly focused meanings, of course, but renewal or rebirth was a predominant theme in a great number of them.

The power of the gods was also tapped and order maintained by means of rituals utilized on unscheduled special occasions. This could be the kind of ritual employed in the 'opening of the mouth' ceremony in order to animate a temple statue or it could be one with much wider application. The goddess Sekhmet, for example, was regarded as a potential bringer of plague and disease who sometimes had to be propitiated and her priests were often skilled in medicine. Placation could be accomplished through large-scale magico-religious rituals performed in the temples as well as through more focused rituals directed at individual sufferers. Thus rituals for the care of humanity ultimately also served to care for the gods.

Many aspects of the daily service, festival and special rituals were described by the Egyptians as 'mysteries' (Egyptian *shetau*). In fact, by virtue of

its supernatural basis, any ritual might be said to be a mystery. More particularly, any part of a ritual which was conducted privately, beyond the view of the people at large, was given this name because it was also hidden and part of the secret knowledge of the priests and others who were skilled in its performance. A general atmosphere of secrecy was developed by the priesthoods as time progressed, but in reality the same priests sometimes performed similar rituals – such as the 'opening of the mouth' – in both hidden and open settings, and the boundaries between formal temple ceremonies and private ritual were probably blurred to some degree.

The divine barque of Amun, carried by priests and led by the king, in ritual procession. Shrine of Philip Arrhidaeus, c. 323 BC, temple of Amun, Karnak.

Procession with fattened bulls and offerings for the great Opet festival. 19th dynasty, Luxor Temple.

Popular Religion and Piety

Although the common people played little or no active part in the formal rituals conducted by the official cults, they had their own opportunities and avenues for worship of their deities. Herodotus' often quoted statement that the Egyptians were 'religious beyond measure...more than any other people' seems to have applied not only to the great temples with their multitudes of priests and elaborate service of the gods, but also to the piety of many ordinary people. But achieving a fuller assessment of popular religion in ancient Egypt is made difficult by a number of factors. As John Baines has stressed, on the one hand, the archaeological record is incomplete since far less is known of the religious practices of people living in towns, villages and rural areas than about the formal worship that took place in the cult temples of gods and kings. On the other hand, the archaeological record itself can be somewhat misleading. While a great deal of the ancient Egyptian material which has survived is religious in nature, the bulk of it was produced by and for the society's elite – the royal and noble families. Their religion was not necessarily the same as that of the common people, however, and in some cases it was clearly different. We do not know to what degree religious piety was present throughout Egypt's various social classes or to what extent this situation changed over time. Nevertheless, despite these difficulties, a fair amount is known about popular religion – at least in certain areas and times – and we can only presume that what is known is indicative of the broader picture.

Access to the gods

In the earlier periods of Egyptian history there was often no clear distinction between the priesthood and other members of society, as temple service was conducted by individuals who, after their assigned rotation of duties, returned to secular work in their communities. However, in New Kingdom and later times when the priestly offices became professional and largely hereditary ones, the situation changed considerably, and we find a much greater gap between the population at large and those involved in formal service of the gods. Lay individuals could place votive offerings in the outer areas of temples, but the chief occasions during which they could approach the gods were public festivals. At these times lay people might witness the procession of a deity, although it would be from a decorous distance

and usually the actual image of the god would not be visible to them. Those outside the priesthood had access to 'hearing ear' shrines placed in the outer walls of many temples, and the colossal statues in front of their pylons were also readily accessible to the people as mediators of their prayers. In some temples the gods could also be approached through oracles which would answer important questions, and common people also had some access to the gods in legal matters. This was sometimes accomplished through specific movements of the god's portable shrine barque while it was being carried in procession, when questions were addressed to the deity. Though we do not know how commonly this type of oracular manifestation occurred or how widely it was accessible, it is probable that such guidance of the gods was sought when the courts were not able to settle a matter.

Another way in which the common people had access to the gods was through dreams. For Egyptians, the sleeper temporarily inhabited the world of the gods, and dreams could thus often involve contact with the gods. The best-known examples of this are found in the records of New Kingdom monarchs such as Tuthmosis IV to whom the Great Sphinx spoke as a god in a dream, but even the most humble commoner could dream of deities in the same manner. Magical texts describe the meanings of many such dreams which might be experienced, and we have ample evidence of dreams being actively elicited as means to understanding the will of the gods.

Finally, we must not rule out other forms of perception, for the Egyptian gods could also be sensed through their fragrance, through sounds and in other such ways. For the ancient Egyptian even the wind felt on a person's face might be perceived as the breath of a god or the passage of the air god Shu. We should not altogether discount the perceived ability of the Egyptians to encounter their gods in everyday contexts, although these may have been viewed as of relatively less importance than the potential for interaction with the divine found in the houses of the gods.

Gifts to the gods

Pious visitors to temples donated perishable offerings such as food, drink or flowers as well as non-perishable gifts dedicated to the gods ranging from simple trinket-like objects to finely carved and painted statues and votive stelae. These latter items represent the most important votive gifts found in archaeological contexts.

Statues given as gifts to the gods or placed worshipfully before them were produced in large numbers in many periods. Most of the statues to have survived from ancient Egypt are in fact votive pieces donated to the gods by kings, nobles, priests and various officers of the state, and even as collective gifts from cities and towns. Such votive statuary usually comprised individual or group figures of gods, sometimes with the inclusion of an intermediary royal or priestly figure, and these divine images could range from individually crafted works to mass-produced figures of gods and goddesses utilized by the less wealthy. In the Late and Ptolemaic Periods the private donation of votive bronze statues grew tremendously, and the development of casting techniques led to the production of countless metal images of deities and sacred animals for devotional purposes and as offerings to temples and shrines.

Votive stelae were of different types, though many bore texts requesting favours from the gods and sometimes gave thanks for their help when it seemed that a request had been granted. The styles of such stelae varied geographically and changed over time but usually depicted the donor, sometimes together with members of his or her family, worshipping the deity to whom the stela was dedicated.

(Left) Statue of worshipper presenting votive of Mut, Amun and Khonsu. New Kingdom. Egyptian Museum, Cairo.

(Right) Gilded statuette of Osiris. 24th–25th dynasty. Roemer and Pelizaeus Museum, Hildesheim.

Painted wooden 'ear stela' of Bai with three pairs of ears representing divine hearing of the worshipper's prayer. From Deir el-Medina. Ramessid Period. Egyptian Museum, Cairo.

deceased and a 'personal piety' movement began to develop, eventually resulting in more direct divine access for the common people – perhaps in contrast to the increasingly hereditary and professional nature of the priesthood. Thus, by New Kingdom times, in addition to the great temples staffed by courses of priests there were numerous small local shrines in which prayers could be offered or votive offerings left for the deity to whom the shrine was dedicated. In the workmen's village of Deir el-Medina in western Thebes there were shrines of this type honouring Amun, Hathor, Ptah, Thoth, Isis, Osiris, Anubis and other gods as well as certain deities of foreign origin such as Astarte and Qadesh. A shrine to Hathor excavated there provides an example of one apparently receiving the veneration mainly of women.

These local shrines show evidence of a good deal of use, but it appears that the religion of many Egyptians may have been dominated by the veneration of personal or local gods honoured in even smaller household shrines. Homes excavated at Deir el-Medina contained niches in which were kept the images of departed relatives and also of household deities – most commonly the god Bes and the goddess Taweret. These deities had the power to ward off evil, appearing on plaques or as amulets which were attached to household objects or worn on the person. While such plaques and amulets may be considered apotropaic or protective magic rather than worship *per se*, the two can hardly be separated, as the Egyptian gods figured prominently in all types of magical rituals and procedures aimed at procuring desirable conditions or avoiding undesirable ones. The wish to control or tap the supernatural powers of the cosmos was pervasive in the religions of the ancient world and Egypt was certainly no exception, for its vast pantheon provided a rich realm of possible allies in the practice of religious magic.

In New Kingdom times in particular, such stelae also often depicted one or more large pairs of ears as symbolic listening devices to ensure that the supplicant's prayers were 'heard' by the god. Such 'ear' stelae may be almost completely covered with these depictions or decorated with the representation of a single, huge, pair of ears – presumably increasing the 'auditory' effectiveness of the stelae.

Private worship and personal piety

From the Middle Kingdom onwards we find stelae showing the direct worship of Osiris by the

(Left) Worker's house at Deir el-Medina showing an architectural feature which may have served as both a bed and a domestic altar. 18/19th dynasty. Western Thebes.

(Right) Interior staircase of the Ptolemaic temple of Hathor at Dendera. The Egyptians presented offerings at such formal temples as well as at more modest local and household shrines.

Relationships with the Divine

It is in the writings of the Egyptians themselves that we gain our deepest insights into their attitudes towards their religion and to the gods. There is a considerable body of textual evidence to support the contention that for many Egyptians their personal religious outlook and belief in the gods extended well beyond mere superstition. To be sure, it is possible to see selfish and transitory human needs and desires beneath many of these texts, but the level of personal piety often appears high. Of particular value in this regard are texts found at Deir el-Medina. While the inhabitants of the ancient village of this site – the workmen and artisans who constructed the royal tombs of the New Kingdom – may not have been entirely typical of Egyptian society the texts they left do provide fascinating insights into non-formal religion and especially into the relationships of the Egyptians with their gods. But these texts are not our only written evidence.

The remains of tombs, temples and dwellings at the workmen's village at Deir el-Medina, western Thebes, a key site for our knowledge of ancient Egyptian religion and everyday life.

From even earlier periods we find texts of sincere gratitude for answered prayers, hymns and paeans of praise, and texts which request the help of the gods in humble but eloquent ways. Such, for example, is a prayer of the 11th-dynasty monarch Intef II asking for protection through the darkness of the night and for the continued gift of life. While the text is a formal one from Intef's tomb stela, it is remarkable in the personal nature of its invocation:

'Will you depart, father Re, before you commend me?
Will sky conceal you before you commend me?
Commend me to night and those dwelling in it,
So as to find [me among your adorers], O Re,
Who worship you at your risings,
Who lament at your settings.
May night embrace me, midnight shelter me
By your command, O Re…'

From a stela of Intef II, trans. by Miriam Lichtheim

A merciful and personal deity

Personal piety appears to have reached a high point in New Kingdom times – when it was believed that the gods could forgive human sins – and is perhaps most clearly seen in the so-called 'penitential texts' which have survived to us from Deir el-Medina. These range from formal compositions inscribed on carved stelae to simple graffiti and include inscriptions dedicating them to Amun, Ptah, Hathor,

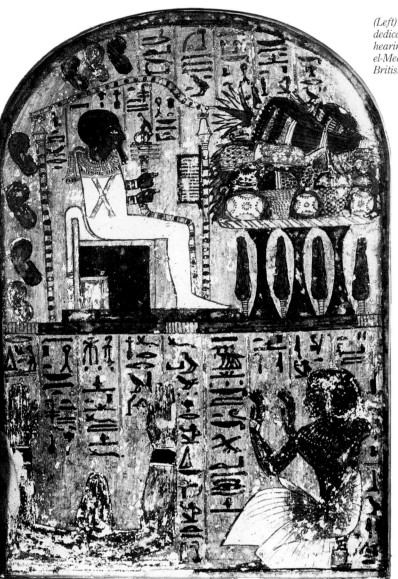

(Left) Stela of Penbuy,
dedicated to Ptah, with prayer-
hearing ears, from Deir
el-Medina. 19th dynasty.
British Museum.

(Below) The Egyptians wished
to continue their relationship
with the gods in the afterlife.
Painted amulets on cartonnage
mummy case of the Lady
Tentqerel. 22nd dynasty.
Egyptian Museum, Cairo.

Meretseger and other deities. In a good number of cases they demonstrate that – at least by New Kingdom times – the extent of the personal relationship possible between the common people of Egypt and even the greatest gods was considerable. Some of these texts preserve penitential inscriptions of considerable beauty not unlike that attained in some of the more famous Hebrew psalms. The votive stela of Nebre, for example, includes the following poignant words which underscore the Egyptian belief in the awareness and mercy of his god.

'You are Amun, the Lord of the silent,
Who comes at the voice of the poor;
When I call to you in my distress,
You come to rescue me,
To give breath to him who is wretched,
To rescue me from bondage…

Though the servant was disposed to do evil,
The Lord is disposed to forgive.
The Lord of Thebes spends not a whole day in anger,
His wrath passes in a moment, none remains.
His breath comes back to us in mercy,
Amun returns upon his breeze…'

Votive Stela of Nebre, from Deir el-Medina

In the final era of Egypt's ancient history the supreme position of Isis and the wide range of her cult appear to have been due, to a very large degree, to the personal relationship of the goddess with her followers and the promise of salvation which was tied to this bond. Often this personal relationship with the deity is seen as purely a development of the Graeco-Roman era, but its precedents in Egypt are clear and provided a fertile ground for the eventual development of Isis worship as a road to personal salvation in later times.

The ideology of kingship was nowhere more highly developed in the ancient world than in Egypt; and perhaps at no time in human history was it more deeply intertwined with religious beliefs. To a good degree Egypt's gods cannot be understood without reference to the Egyptian institution of kingship. On the one hand the living king served as a bridge between the gods and humanity and could himself be deified to a certain degree, and on the other hand deceased kings were regularly deified as they sought to continue their kingship as gods.

Kingship also entered the divine sphere in an even more fundamental way. The institution was such an integral part of the Egyptians' view of their society that it was held to be as essential to divine society as the gods. In a classic example of humans creating gods in their own image the Egyptians organized their deities according to the pattern of their own monarchical society – a fact which holds a number of ramifications for our understanding of Egyptian religion and of the gods themselves.

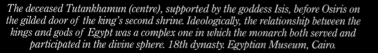

The deceased Tutankhamun (centre), supported by the goddess Isis, before Osiris on the gilded door of the king's second shrine. Ideologically, the relationship between the kings and gods of Egypt was a complex one in which the monarch both served and participated in the divine sphere. 18th dynasty. Egyptian Museum, Cairo.

IV   Kingship and the Gods

Between Gods and Men

Once Egypt had been united and a central government established, the cult of the living king seems to have been developed in addition to the cults of local and national deities. This fact tends to be taken for granted, but we know very little about how this situation came to be, and if or to what extent the early king was viewed as divine in his lifetime. Even in the later historical periods when evidence is clearer and more plentiful, there is disagreement among scholars as to the degree to which the Egyptian king was regarded as human, divine, or as both.

Kingship and divinity

That the living Egyptian king was viewed as divine certainly appears possible. In representations the king is far larger than his human subjects and on the same scale as the gods themselves. Not only were monarchs said to be 'like' (Egyptian *mi*) or the 'image of' (Egyptian *tiet*, or *tut*) various deities, but the word *netcher* or 'god' was also frequently used as an epithet of kings. The formal titulary of the Egyptian king also spelled out his relationship with several key deities, indicating that he was not only viewed as the son of Re during his lifetime (from the 4th dynasty on), but also as the living manifestation or image of the falcon god Horus (perhaps from the beginning of the Dynastic Period). There are other important lines of evidence for this point of view. The myth of the king's divine birth, for example, was developed in the New Kingdom but was apparently not something invented by Hatshepsut, as is sometimes stated, and seems to have existed since at least Middle Kingdom times. Even before this, the underlying purpose of the complex genealogy of the gods constructed by the priests of Heliopolis may have been as much to establish the divine lineage and nature of the king as to establish the order of creation, a fact seen by Rudolf Anthes as early as the middle of the last century. As a result of this type of evidence

The gods Thoth and Horus pour water over the king in a ritual lustration. Temple of Horus, Edfu. Theologically, the Egyptian king stood between humanity and the gods in his monarchical role.

Henri Frankfort, in his important study *Kingship and the Gods*, and a good many other scholars, have believed that the pharaoh's rites of coronation and accession elevated him to identity with the gods.

On the other hand, this may not be the only conclusion that can be drawn from the sources which provide our information on Egyptian kingship. There is no doubt whatsoever that the living king was regarded as subservient to the gods and that in theory, and to some degree in practice, every king acted as their servant in the enactment of temple rituals. The evidence considered above may also be viewed in different ways. The frequent identification of the king with various deities could often be little more than hyperbole. Marie-Ange Bonhême has also recently pointed out that while the king's formal names may indicate an aspect of divinity in the monarch, they do not clarify the 'degree of divinity' which is involved. As early as 1960, Georges Posener showed that the image of the living pharaoh as a god-king is perhaps exaggerated by the royal and religious sources which aim to heighten the divine aspect of kingship. In popular literature and texts the Egyptian king is hardly portrayed as a god. He cannot work the miracles of his wise men and is certainly neither omniscient nor invulnerable in the way we would expect if he were truly regarded as divine. From this perspective it would seem that it was not the king who was honoured as a god but the incarnate power of the gods that was honoured in the king.

A divine duality

The truth is probably to be found in a balance of these views. From the human perspective the Egyptian king was viewed as one of the gods – he is called such and depicted along with other gods in divine scenes. On the other hand, it could be said that from a divine perspective the king was still

(Left) The god Amun, attended by the birth-related goddesses Serket and Neith, impregnates Queen Mutemwia, mother of Amenophis III. 18th dynasty. Luxor Temple.

(Below) Hatshepsut, accompanied by Tuthmosis III, offers to a divine image of herself. 18th dynasty. Decorated block, Chapelle Rouge, Karnak.

human and was, of course, subject to human frailties and mortality. This dual nature of the living king – human and divine – seems to be implicit in the *serekh*, the device in which the king's name was written from early times (showing the god Horus atop the royal palace), and in the royal titulary which was drawn up at the king's accession from Middle Kingdom times. The *nesut-bit* or 'King of Upper and Lower Egypt' title preceded the king's formal throne name, and has long been interpreted as signifying only rulership over Upper and Lower Egypt. But it may refer, in fact, to the divine identity of the king in general (*nesut*) and the current human holder of the office in the line of kingly succession (*bit*). Beginning with Siegfried Morenz, a number of scholars have shown that the dual nature of the king may also be seen in contrasting *nesut* with another Egyptian word relating to kingship – *hem,* usually translated 'majesty'. The first word, *nesut,* refers to the divine power held by the king and used in the exercise of kingly roles, whereas the second word, *hem,* really refers to the idea of the individual in whom the divine power is incarnate. These two terms were sometimes used together (*hem en nesut*) meaning something like 'the incarnation of (divine) kingship'.

Accepting this duality amounts to a view of Egyptian monarchical ideology which understands the king as being in effect both human and divine during his lifetime. This apparent contradiction would have hardly been seen as problematic by the ancient Egyptians, whose theological systems contained many such enigmas. The apparent contradiction was resolved practically in the duality of the king's role – in essence, the nature of the Egyptian king depended upon the situation. The king represented the gods to his people as a god, and also the people of Egypt to the gods as a human. Theologically neither the divine nor the human realm could function without him.

Black granite statue of Ramesses II, the great pharaoh whose images and works strive to personify the ideal of divine kingship, and who was declared divine in his own lifetime. 19th dynasty. Egyptian Museum, Turin.

Deified in life

Despite the human-divine duality inherent in the reign of most Egyptian pharaohs there were instances when living kings do seem to have been declared fully divine within their own lifetimes. This was not the result of arbitrary theological or royal decree, however, and it seems clear that such kings usually 'earned' their immortality through long and successful reigns. The clearest evidence for this comes from the New Kingdom; although the exact details of the situation are not always clear, the living deification of Amenophis III and Ramesses II are relatively well attested. In the case of Amenophis III, we find that towards the end of his reign this king began the increasing solarization of Egypt's major cults and of his own kingship. According to the reconstruction of events by Raymond Johnson and others, at the time of his Sed jubilee celebrated in the 30th year of his reign the king declared himself deified and merged with the solar disk as the Aten or as Re-Horakhty. From this time we find the king taking divine prerogatives in his representations such as those showing him with the curved beard of the gods, with the horns of Amun and wearing the lunar crescent and sun disk or presenting an offering before a statue of himself. Even here, however, the evidence of royal deification may not be what it appears on the surface. Betsy Bryan has pointed out that Amenophis may not have intended by his own deification to have transcended kingship on earth permanently and that the cultic and political uses of a divine ruler could have been limited to prescribed occasions such as the king's Sed festival.

Representations of living deified kings in the presence of deities show a level of equality which transcends that found in normal scenes of the king among the gods. In the inner shrine of the great rock-cut temple of Abu Simbel, for example, the deified Ramesses II had four statues cut to represent

The sanctuary of the mortuary temple of Ramesses II at Abu Simbel holds seated statues of the gods Ptah, Amun, Ramesses and Re-Horakhty. Here, the figure of the king represents not only the god Osiris, but also Ramesses himself as god. 19th dynasty.

divine son of the god Aten, others have seen him as a member of a kind of divine triad which also included his queen Nefertiti. More recently, a number of Egyptologists have pointed out what appear to be associations with traditional Egyptian solar theology even within the Amarna Period. Eugene Cruz-Uribe has shown that just as Amenophis III may have been equated with the Aten, and his queen Tiye with Hathor, complex parallels may have been promulgated which suggested the equation of the living Akhenaten with the god Shu, Khepri and other solar deities, Nefertiti with Tefnut, and possibly, a royal daughter with the goddess Maat.

(Right) Statue of a statue of Amenophis III displays the king as a god and, on its rear face, the image of the human king prostate before the god Amun. Luxor Museum.

Akhenaten and his family present offerings to the Aten. The nature of Akhenaten's place in his own religion is not fully understood, but it seems that he and his family may have played some kind of divine role before his subjects. Limestone balustrade from el-Amarna. Egyptian Museum, Cairo.

Ptah, Re-Horakhty, Amun-Re and himself, seated side by side. That the king is not simply depicted in the company of the gods is clear as the figures are shown as incontrovertible equals. It has even been suggested that in this group the king might be represented as an embodiment or manifestation of all these national gods. We can only be sure that in some circumstances the living Egyptian king could be declared divine in a manner which transcended the aspect of divinity which was taken on at the coronation. Whether this deification of the living monarch equalled that accorded deceased kings in permanency or in degree we may never know.

The nature of Akhenaten is also of particular interest in regard to the question of monarchical divinity but is difficult to ascertain. While some scholars have seen this king as taking the role of

Divine Royal Statues

Statues of Egyptian kings functioned as integral parts of divine cults, often serving as intermediaries between the people and the gods within or at the entrances to temples and also – especially in later New Kingdom times – sometimes being regarded as divine themselves. Statues such as the titanic figure of Ramesses II set up in western Thebes – which was the subject of Shelley's poem 'Ozymandias' – were given special names, could own land, had their own attendant priesthoods, and were venerated as gods in their own right. A group of artifacts known as the Horbeit Stelae throw particular light on this phenomenon. The stelae, which were found in the eastern Delta near the modern Qantir, come from the region of Ramesses II's chief Delta residence and attest to the presence of a cult of several colossal statues of the king in that area. One of these stelae (that of Seti-er-neheh) depicts a statue of the deified Ramesses II along with the great gods Amun and Ptah in a manner which makes the importance of the statue unmistakable. Another stela (that of the military commander Mose) depicts Ramesses II in a unique manner. In its lower register the stela shows a colossal seated statue of Ramesses next to a smaller figure of the king (which is apparently intended as a divine manifestation of the statue) giving gifts to Mose. The statue and its manifestation both share the same name and show the divine nature of the deified king's image.

Of great interest for our understanding of ancient Egyptian theology are scenes which have survived to us of kings presenting sacrifices to deified statues of themselves. An example is found in the representation of Amenophis III offering to an image of himself in his temple at Soleb. Such depictions are based on the concept of dual (earthly and heavenly) roles played by the gods themselves. Beginning in the Old Kingdom we find evidence for the idea of deities being manifest both in the heavens or 'beyond' and in the physical sphere on earth, just as the living king was himself a manifestation of the earthly Horus as opposed to the god Horus in the heavens. Thus, a king deified in his own lifetime – within the physical sphere – could sacrifice to his own self as a deity in the spiritual sphere.

Stela of Seti-er-neheh shows the god Amun-Re (top left) before Ptah and a statue of the divine Ramesses II, 'Montu of the Two Lands'. From Horbeit. 19th dynasty. Roemer and Pelizaeus Museum, Hildesheim.

Deceased and Divine

The intimate embrace of Ramesses III and the goddess Isis underscores the divine nature of the deceased Egyptian monarch. 20th dynasty. Tomb of Amenherkhepshef, Valley of the Queens, western Thebes.

While what we might call full deification occurred for some monarchs within their lifetimes, it was usually in death that this state was reached and a good deal of evidence seems to show that the deceased Egyptian king was venerated as a 'full' god. A number of Egyptian queens were also deified in death – including the illustrious Ahmose-Nefertari of the 18th dynasty and later queens such as Arsinoe II, Berenike II, and Cleopatra III, V, and VII of the Ptolemaic Period. Although the situation is somewhat different for deceased queens and cannot be examined in detail here, a number of similarities certainly existed between the deification of kings and queens.

Dead kings as living gods

The close relationship between the deceased king and the gods may be seen in the textual and representational evidence associated with the royal mortuary cults from early times. The Pyramid Texts clearly attempt to place the deceased king on the same level as the gods – both by directly asserting that he is a god, and by stating that he 'is' Osiris, Re, or some other deity. In some cases the texts not only show the deceased king's parity with the divine cohort, but they also stress his ascendance over the other gods, showing that he is certainly

not viewed as a minor deity in the afterlife. We do not know if these assertions of the deceased king's deity were originally statements of formally held belief or whether they represented a desired situation which was attempted through the use of the magical texts. The idea of the king's deified afterlife was certainly established by Old Kingdom times, however, and the same types of textual evidence are found in royal mortuary contexts throughout subsequent periods of Egyptian history. Representations of the deceased king in the presence of deities likewise indicate equality between the two from early times.

The very purpose of the royal mortuary cults seems to have been the affirmation of the deceased monarch's divinity, yet the specific nature of that divinity must not be overlooked. A number of years ago William Murnane showed, in a study of the texts and representations of the great mortuary temple of Ramesses III at Medinet Habu, that much of the focus of the royal mortuary cult was an ongoing reaffirmation of the king's divine kingship rather than eternal life *per se*. This conclusion was expanded in later studies of other mortuary temples dating back to the Old Kingdom, and it now seems clear that in many if not all cases the stress of all these royal mortuary establishments is on the

continuation of the king's reign on a divine level in the afterlife. It must not be forgotten that even from a relatively early date – perhaps by the end of the Old Kingdom – funerary spells for the afterlife transformation to the divine became available to other classes of society. Nobles, and later others, could also aspire to become gods in the afterlife. It is unthinkable that these individuals regarded their afterlife state to be equivalent to that of the king or the great gods. It seems far more likely that what was envisaged for both commoner and king alike was an afterlife which represented a kind of divinized state of their own social stations in life. In the case of the deceased king, there were specific associations which might be seen as elevating his position above that of his earthly reign. This is seen particularly in the concepts of the royal ancestors, and of the king as Osiris and Re.

The royal ancestors

Although in reality Egyptian civilization was ruled by kings of many houses and families, Egyptian kingship ideology made use of a particular fiction in the form of the 'royal ancestors'. This represented a kind of monarchical family line reaching back through the ages and linking the living king with his deceased 'forebears'. This does not mean that

direct lineage was implied – in fact the official genealogies omit unorthodox or aberrant rulers such as Hatshepsut or Akhenaten. However there was a kind of continuum between the living king, his 'forebears' and, ultimately, the gods who ruled as kings at the beginning of the world.

Some kings of the past were particularly venerated. Senwosret III of the 12th dynasty, for example, was remembered for his subjugation of the region to the south of Egypt and was honoured by a small temple built by Tuthmosis III some 400 years later at el-Lessiya in Nubia. Yet less illustrious rulers were also absorbed into the ancestral tradition upon their deaths, and most were chronicled in the king-lists inscribed in temples such as that of Sethos I at Abydos, where the cartouches of past rulers received veneration and offerings. Representations at a number of sites show that the ancestors also played an important role in various royal and religious rituals. Scenes carved under Ramesses II and Ramesses III showing the harvest festival of the god Min, for example, show statues of the royal ancestors being carried before the king. The statues, which are named in these New Kingdom scenes, include Menes, the legendary first king of the united Egypt. The oldest evidence for the royal ancestors preserve no names and shows simply

Peristyle court of the mortuary temple of Ramesses III with remnants of Osiride statues of the king. The royal mortuary temple aligned the deceased king with the gods Osiris and Re and also celebrated the divinity of the king in his own right. 20th dynasty. Medinet Habu, western Thebes.

61

(Above) Ka figure of King Ay. The royal ka seems to have incorporated the royal ancestors, as well as the ka of the living king, and as such represented one aspect of the divinity of the deceased king 18th dynasty. Tomb of Ay, western Valley of the Kings, western Thebes.

(Above right) Engaged pillar statues of Hatshepsut as Osiris. 18th dynasty. Temple of Hatshepsut, Deir el-Bahri, western Thebes.

the idea of a collective group of undifferentiated but deified ancestors. The royal ancestors were depicted as divine beings of a high order, and the deceased king was elevated in joining their ranks.

A particular aspect of the royal ancestors may be seen in the *ka* of the king. While the Egyptian word *ka* is usually translated as 'soul' or 'spirit' in general usage, the royal *ka* was more than just an individual spiritual 'double'. Lanny Bell, who has made detailed studies of the nature of the royal *ka*, has shown that it embraced the royal ancestors as well as the living king and was central to the Egyptians' concept of kingly accession. As Bell has written, the aspect of divinity attained by the living Egyptian king occurred only when he became one with the royal *ka* at the climax of the coronation ceremony. The royal *ka* was, in this sense, the symbolic and spiritual point of interface between the king and his deified ancestors.

The king as Osiris

Although the Egyptian sources equate the deceased king with several deities, there is a clear and constant emphasis throughout most of Egyptian history on the association of the king with the netherworld god Osiris. This was doubtless because the role of kingship fitted the Osiride mythology particularly well. Every pharaoh ceased to function as the earthly Horus – and son of Osiris – upon death and was identified by virtue of death with the deceased Osiris. He thus stood as predecessor in relation to the next living king as the mythical Osiris did to Horus. According to this symbolic metaphor, by becoming one with Osiris the dead king also became ruler of the afterlife region – switching realms, as it were, from rule over the living to rule over the dead.

As time progressed royal mortuary iconography was increasingly adapted to this equation of the dead king with Osiris. We find this manifested in dozens of ways. Osiride insignia such as the crook and flail were placed on New Kingdom royal coffins, showing continued afterlife rulership with Osiris despite the absence of an earthly crown in the king's afterlife representations. Also, the figures of Isis and Nephthys were placed at either end of the royal

coffin or sarcophagus to fulfil the role of mourning for the deceased Osiris. The decoration of the royal tombs of the New Kingdom also stresses the fusion of the deceased king and Osiris, though to a large extent this is overshadowed by the symbolic association of the king with the sun god Re. However, some scenes, such as those found on the side walls and tympana of the 19th-dynasty royal burial chambers, focus on the fusion of Osiris (who came to be viewed as the mummy or corpse of Re at this time), the sun god, and the king.

The king as Re

Although the Egyptian king became one with Osiris upon death, he was also fused with the sun god Re. This idea is at least as old as the Osiride association and is strongly attested from the Pyramid Texts onward. The situation actually parallels that described between the king and the netherworld god. Just as the living monarch was held to be the son of Osiris but fused with the deity upon death, so the living king known as the 'Son of Re' could fuse with his father Re upon his entry into the afterlife. Deified queens were also frequently associated with the goddess Hathor (or later Isis-Hathor) who was seen as the daughter of Re.

While the iconography associated with the body of the deceased king – i.e., the mummy, coffin, and sarcophagus – was associated primarily with Osiris, the imagery of royal tomb decoration as seen throughout New Kingdom monuments is primarily linked with the king's assimilation with the sun god. This assimilation or fusion involves the king's cyclic travel with Re into, through, and out of the netherworld regions in continuing renewal and rebirth. The imagery of solar assimilation may be varied, however. On the one hand the god-king is said to ride alongside Re in the celestial boat of the sun god and to act as a judge in the realm of Re, while on the other hand he is clearly said to be one with the solar god. Both are depicted iconographically, the latter when the name of Ramesses III is written within a solar image in that king's tomb. In either case, however, the deceased king's divinity is clear.

Scene of Re-Horakhty (at right) greeted by Merenptah symbolizing the afterlife joining of the king and the solar god. Tomb of Merenptah, 19th dynasty. Valley of the Kings, western Thebes.

Kingship Among the Gods

It is perhaps not surprising that the Egyptian king should aspire to retain his kingly role and office in the afterlife, but there is another aspect to the phenomenon of kingship among the gods. Textual and representational evidence clearly shows that the Egyptians envisioned their deities to be organized in a manner similar to human society, with the institution of kingship providing the governmental model among the gods themselves. Deities took kingly attributes and roles like those of their earthly counterparts, and the interaction between the two led to the concept of the 'king of the gods' which may have been of great importance in Egyptian theological development.

Gods as kings

Egyptian mythology is dogmatic that the institution of kingship was coeval with the rule of the gods. Thus, the king list preserved in the Royal Canon of Turin, which dates to the 19th dynasty, begins with a dynasty of 11 deities who ruled for over 7,700 years. Through creation Re became the king of gods and men and although he eventually tired and withdrew from the world he had made, he continued to hold sovereign power as god of the heavens. On earth, the rule of Re led to a royal succession among the gods themselves, and in the Canon the length of the reign of each god is given before the reigns of human kings. The texts state

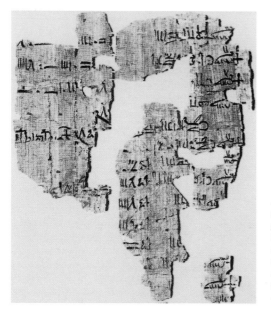

Part of the Royal Canon of Turin, a fragmentary papyrus, written in hieratic, which preserves a list of gods, demi-gods, spirits, mythical and human kings who ruled Egypt from the time of creation. 19th dynasty. Egyptian Museum, Turin.

that eventually Osiris became king of Egypt, and as the heir of Osiris, Horus next took over his father's kingship. However, his own rulership took on even wider, cosmic, proportions as it was fused with the rule of Re and with that of the ancient falcon god Horus, himself originally a cosmic deity. This level of kingship is made clear in the Coffin Texts:

'Horus…has become lord of the [solar] barque and has inherited the sky…
It is this Horus, the son of Isis, who rules over all the heavens and the gods therein.'

Coffin Texts VI 390

Horus, in turn, became the link with the living human king. Although, according to its primary

expression in the Heliopolitan theology, this story may be understood as much as an affirmation of the king's descent from the gods as a genealogy of divine kings, we must not lose sight of the fact that from an Egyptian perspective the myth links kingship to the gods just as much as it establishes it by means of the gods.

Hymns to the gods often name them as 'kings' – especially hymns of the later New Kingdom which also give deities many of the epithets used of kings such as 'royal ruler' and 'ruler of the Two Lands'.

Royal prerogatives of the gods

We find the idea of kingship among the gods depicted in a concrete fashion in the iconography employed in the representations of the gods in formal and informal contexts alike. This is particularly clear in the frequent use of royal insignias by deities. Egyptian gods were often depicted seated on thrones – especially Amun, revered as king of the gods in New Kingdom times, Re who ruled the heavens, Osiris who ruled the netherworld, and Horus. But many other deities were also depicted in this manner, and the image of the enthroned god or goddess is probably more commonly found in Egyptian art than examples of enthroned human kings – showing the motif's importance for the portrayal of deities.

Crowns are also of great importance as elements in the representation of kings and gods.

The enthroned Osiris, attended by Isis, Nephthys, Horus and Thoth. As king of the netherworld, Osiris personified one aspect of kingship in Egyptian mythology. Scene from the cult chapel of Amenophis at Saqqara. 19th dynasty. Egyptian Museum, Berlin.

Just as the personal birth and throne names of kings were usually placed within oval cartouches, the concept of gods as kings extended into this practice also and we find, for example, the name of Osiris written within the cartouche in Middle Kingdom times. It is an interesting aspect of Akhenaten's religion of the Aten that because the solar disk deity was interpreted as the true ruler of the universe, it was given a royal titulary (see p. 239) with his names being inscribed in cartouches. The Aten also celebrated his own royal jubilees so that the distinction between god and king was almost completely blurred in this period. While

Horus, shown crowned with the Double Crown of all Egypt, was mythological heir to Osiris and often personified the role of the living monarch. 18th dynasty. Tomb of Horemheb, Valley of the Kings, western Thebes.

Horus, Atum and Mut, for example, were commonly depicted wearing the Double Crown of Upper and Lower Egypt, while from the Third Intermediate Period youthful deities such as Ihy or Harpokrates may be shown wearing almost any of the various types of royal crowns. Likewise, royalty and deities both wore the uraeus emblem on these symbols of office and stature. Other typically royal insignias such as sceptres, staves and standards were also utilized in depictions of the gods. Although it could be argued that some of these objects were perhaps originally divine attributes utilized by the king (as for example the crook and flail of the god Andjety and later Osiris), the duality of their use still shows the interrelation of kingship and the divine roles of the gods.

The parallels between divine and kingly prerogatives do not end with physical items of insignia.

Akhenaten may have had his own agenda for this fusion, it must be remembered that the idea of the god as king was not without precedent and that Akhenaten's innovation in this area was essentially one of degree rather than one of type.

Kings of the gods

Although the attributes and roles of kingship are ascribed to many Egyptian deities, the portrayal of the highest god in a given period as king is naturally most common. In almost all eras of Egyptian history we find that one god or another rose to a pre-eminent position; this elevated role was attributed in turn to the ancient sky god Horus, the solar god Re, the hidden god Amun or the fused Amun-Re, and briefly but nonetheless actually to Akhenaten's favoured solar disk, the Aten. In the final age of ancient Egyptian history the pre-eminent position was occupied by Isis, the queen of heaven – and also, implicitly, monarch of the gods. In any period, the role of the king of the gods was a superlative one indeed, for while polytheistic religions are often viewed as lessening the importance of individual deities, the deity who ruled over the vast pantheon of ancient Egypt can only have been envisioned as transcendently great.

Amun-Re, often styled 'lord of the Two Lands' and 'king of the gods', crowns Hatshepsut on the pyramidion of one of her obelisks. 18th dynasty. Temple of Amun, Karnak.

(Left) The sun god Re, here in the form of Re-Horakhty, was also closely connected with the concept of kingship in Egyptian mythology. 19th dynasty. Tomb of Siptah, Valley of the Kings, western Thebes.

'Who does not know, Volusius, what monsters are worshipped by
demented Egyptians?
One lot reveres the crocodile, another goes in awe of the ibis…'

Juvenal, Fifteenth Satire

Although Juvenal's diatribe against the Egyptian gods was not
based on any depth of understanding of Egyptian religion, it
nevertheless portrays the seemingly unintelligible array of gods
and goddesses which characterized the pantheon of the Nile. But not
even satire could exaggerate the vastness of this pantheon, which
embraced hundreds upon hundreds of gods often as amazing in their
forms as they were astonishing in their numbers. This range of form
was particularly true of minor deities, 'demons' and the composite
deities of later Egyptian religion, which often stretched the limits of
the imagination in the variety of their hybrid natures. Yet for all their
often bizarre appearances, these deities are never without a certain
logic which appealed to the Egyptian mind and which personified its
ideas of the divine with utmost clarity.

   Despite their often alien outward appearances, the many gods of
Egypt included deities whose characters, myths and even forms
provide fascinating insights into the world views, concerns and
ethics of a society which was great long before Juvenal's Rome was
born and which would affect the world long after the gods of Rome
were lost in time.

*The craftsman Sennedjem, alone and with his wife, worshipping some of the many
forms of deities in the Egyptian pantheon. 19th dynasty. Ceiling of the tomb of
Sennedjem, Deir el-Medina, western Thebes.*

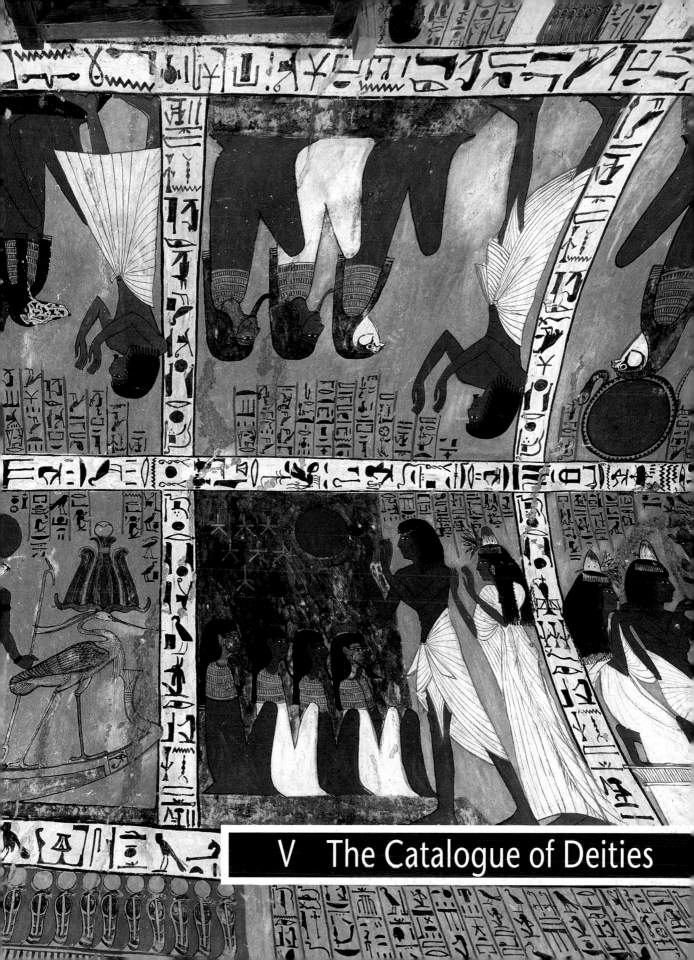

V The Catalogue of Deities

Many Faces of the Divine

While excellent short surveys of Egyptian deities have been produced in the past which simply list the various gods and goddesses by name according to alphabetical order, such an arrangement is problematic for many readers. This is due to the large number of diverse spellings of Egyptian deities' names (such as Shed/Pashed, Mehit/Hatmehyt, etc.), often making it difficult to locate them and impossible when a deity is known only from its representation. More fundamentally, such listings may be limited because alphabetic arrangement obscures to some degree the very nature of the Egyptian pantheon. The various deities existed not in isolation but in dynamic relationship to one another by reason of their particular forms,

List of Deities

The deities discussed in the book and their page numbers are listed below.

characters, and roles and by means of the mythological groups which they formed. On the other hand, while many attempts have been made to organize the Egyptian pantheon by means of mythologically-based classificatory systems, no such scheme can be completely successful because of the fluid nature of the deities themselves. A god or goddess who might well be described as a 'cosmic' or 'ancestral' or 'underworld' deity could at the same time also be a deity associated closely with creation or kingship or any number of other aspects of existence.

In this book, rather than simply utilizing an alphabetic listing, or attempting an arrangement of deities by their mythological roles, the many gods and goddesses included have been grouped by their appearance. This is to aid identification for the general reader and also to facilitate comparison and contrast of deities of similar types, such as leonine, bovine or serpentine gods. Even here it is impossible to create a classificatory scheme without some overlapping or ambiguity, but the system used minimizes redundancy and maximizes the reader's ability to view deities in useful contexts.

(Right) New Kingdom jar representing the god Bes by means of his characteristic facial features. 18th dynasty. Egyptian Museum, Berlin.

(Below) Generic star gods depicted in the seated pose of the 'deity' hieroglyph. 19th dynasty. Tomb of Irynefer, western Thebes.

The categories follow (with some modifications) those of the list of hieroglyphic signs printed in Sir Alan Gardiner's *Middle Egyptian Grammar*, which will be familiar to some readers and which allows the location of deities without frequent recourse to the Index. The categories utilized in the catalogue are: Groups of Deities; Male Anthropomorphic Deities; Female Anthropomorphic Deities; Mammalian Deities (which are divided into several sub-categories to aid identification); Avian Deities (divided into falcon deities and those represented by other avian species); Reptile, Amphibian and Fish Deities; Invertebrate and Insect Deities; and Inanimate Object Deities.

While many Egyptian deities could appear under several guises, almost all may be found more

frequently in one particular (usually the oldest) form, and that has been the category to which the deity has been assigned. To avoid repetition and to allow full study of all aspects of a given deity, the various forms of any god or goddess are discussed under the single heading of the most characteristic form. Usually, the head of a given deity represents its characteristic nature and reflects its most frequently depicted form. Thus, if a deity appears as an animal it can be found in the catalogue under its relevant category. If it appears as a human with the head of an animal (such as the falcon-headed Horus or Re) it will, again, appear under that animal's category. Where a deity appears as a fully human male or female it will be listed in its respective anthropomorphic section unless the fully human form is a variant of a more common zoomorphic deity. Later Egyptian representations sometimes show all deities in purely human form; but in any event, deities are cross-referenced within the catalogue where any confusion of form might occur, and an alphabetic listing is provided for use where that is preferred.

While it would be practically impossible to provide a description of all known Egyptian deities within a single volume, the following catalogue provides a reference to all of ancient Egypt's major gods and goddesses and most of the minor ones. The catalogue is complete not in the sense of listing 'every deity' (because many gods are known to have existed which are unknown other than by oblique references in the ancient texts, such as 'the god who is there', and others are known by single mention of their name alone but with no clue as to their identity or nature). Rather, the comprehensiveness of the following catalogue is a functional one in that coverage is provided of the whole range of types of deities found in Egyptian mythology.

(Right) The gods Osiris, Anubis and Horus in the Tomb of Horemheb, Valley of the Kings, western Thebes.

Groups of Deities

Egyptian mythology contains many groups of deities but these are of two distinct types, although they overlap occasionally. On the one hand, there exist what might be called 'numerical groups' formed from the uniting of independent deities usually related in some symbolic manner. On the other hand, many other deities – which may or may not have individual names and identities – exist only as members of generalized 'regional groups'.

NUMERICAL GROUPINGS

Numerical groups are almost always composed of deities with distinct individual identities organized to make groups of a symbolically significant size. Some of these groups, such as triads, follow the pattern of family and kinship units while others, such as enneads, are more abstract, but all are evidently symbolic in terms of the number of deities involved. In some cases the process of grouping can be seen historically as certain deities were aligned for religious or even political reasons, though in other cases deities were evidently grouped together from very early times for reasons which are not always understood.

Dyads

Deities were often grouped in pairs as the phenomenon of duality pervades Egyptian culture and is at the heart of the Egyptian concept of the universe itself – though rather than focusing on the essential differences between the two parts of a given pair, Egyptian thought usually stresses their complementary nature as a way of expressing the essential unity of existence. The endless duality found throughout the cosmic, geographic and temporal aspects of the Egyptian universe (heaven-earth, existence-nonexistence, stasis-change, north-south, desert-fertile, day-night, etc.) is found in pairs of gods and goddesses which represented these and many other binary aspects of the world. Deities were also 'created' as counterparts to established gods and goddesses in order to form balanced, sexually paired couples, as may well have occurred in the following instances:

Male Deity	Led to	Female Deity
Sokar	⟶	Sokaret
Inpu (Anubis)	⟶	Input
Tefen	⟵	**Tefnut**
Sesha	⟵	**Seshat**

Almost invariably, dyads are composed of male and female elements such as these, though there are a

Divine figures were frequently depicted in pairs, either for the sake of artistic symmetry or in the symbolic juxtaposition of beings related in some way. Detail of 21st-dynasty coffin of Padiamen, Luxor Museum of Mummification.

few examples of sibling dyads of the same sex such as the brothers Horus and Seth and the sisters Isis and Nephthys. Sometimes too, deities may be mentioned together in pairs when their roles or areas of influence are clearly related. Thus, the lunar deities Thoth and Khonsu, the solar deities Re and Atum, the two deified brothers Peteese and Pihor, and many others may be paired in this manner. Another way in which Egyptian religion formed groups of two deities is when two gods are utilized to represent a larger group. This may be seen in examples of Thoth and Horus who are sometimes depicted together to represent the four gods of ritual lustration, Horus, Seth, Thoth, and Nemty.

Triads

Groups of three deities are often aligned as members of a divine family of father (god), mother (goddess) and child (almost invariably a young male deity), with the triad of Osiris, Isis and Horus

(Left) The tutelary goddesses of Upper and Lower Egypt, Nekhbet and Wadjet, crown the king. Dyads such as these often represent otherwise unrelated deities linked by their specific roles. Temple of Horus at Edfu, Ptolemaic Period.

being the most prominent example. The Egyptian king sometimes functioned as the divine son or represented him in such familial triads. While not all combinations of three deities represent family groupings, this is the most common form. We find evidence of deities such as Amun and Osiris going from individual and independent gods to members of fully formed triads (in these instances, Amun-Mut-Khonsu and Osiris-Isis-Horus, respectively) without any evidence of groups of two – as Amun-Mut or Osiris-Isis – existing between the singular deities and their triadic groupings. On the other hand some deities which coexisted in pairs did eventually form triads which were only superficially regarded as families. This was evidently the case with Ptah and Sekhmet who were worshipped

Divine pairs were often depicted with the Egyptian king as their 'son', forming a family-based triad which strengthened the religious position of both its human and divine members. Tutankhamun (centre) with Mut and Amun. 18th dynasty. Egyptian Museum, Cairo.

(Right) The very loosely related deities Ptah and Sekhmet were united by their 'child' Ramesses II (centre, mythologically the god Nefertem) into a formal family triad. 19th dynasty. Egyptian Museum, Cairo.

(Below) Hathor, Mycerinus and the goddess of the Jackal Nome. Such non-family triads may link deities through their support of the king. 4th dynasty. Egyptian Museum, Cairo.

(Below right) The four sons of Horus in their protective role on the coffin of Psusennes, Egyptian Museum, Cairo.

together at Memphis long before the god Nefertem was brought into their local grouping and the triad Ptah-Sekhmet-Nefertem was formed.

Other groups of three deities may have been formed for purely symbolic reasons. The number three was an important one signifying plurality – or unity expressed in plurality – for the Egyptians, and this is probably the underlying significance of many groups such as the important New Kingdom triad of Amun, Re and Ptah. Beginning in the time of Tutankhamun, and very commonly in Ramessid times, we find these three deities grouped by virtue of their status or importance in the pantheon. Sometimes triads are grouped together by role alone. On the coffin of the 21st-dynasty king Pinedjem II, three deities with the heads of a ram, a lion, and a jackal stand in the coils of a serpent. The deities are named as Re, Isis, and Anubis respectively, though a number of variants of this same motif occur in which the gods may be depicted with the heads of other animals or given other names. This would seem to show that the groups are simply representative of important afterlife deities – the number three representing plurality rather than any specific group.

Tetrads

In Egyptian symbolism the number four frequently signified the four cardinal directions and hence a kind of spatial or geographic totality. This significance is seen in the four 'races' of mankind: Egyptians (north), Near Easterners (east), Nubians (south) and Libyans (west) depicted in some New Kingdom tombs. It is also apparent in a number of groupings of four deities, such as the four supports of the sky which may be personified as four individual deities or groups of deities (see p. 78) aligned with the four points or quarters of the heavens. The connection is strong enough, in fact, that even when groups of four deities do not seem to originally have this symbolic significance it may become attached to them. Thus the mortuary deities known as the four sons of Horus may sometimes be aligned geographically in representational contexts although this is not always the case. While the concept of completeness associated with the number four may have sprung entirely from the totality encompassed by the concept of the four cardinal points, the symbolic use of the number is frequently one of completion without any specific directional overtones at all. In the underworld books four forms of a given god or groups of four deities are frequently found and thus depicted in vignettes in the papyri and decorations of the royal tombs. An interesting example of this kind of tetrad is found in Ramessid times when the god Seth was elevated to the extent that he was

sometimes named along with the three great deities Amun, Re and Ptah. The four divisions of the Egyptian army were named after Seth and the other three deities in a group which clearly could be conceived as holding the symbolism of tactical or strategic completeness. While the members of dyads and triads are usually distinguished from one another in representational works, the deities found in groups of four are often undifferentiated – showing their apparently more 'generic' nature.

Pentads

Although not a common numerical grouping of deities, pentads are occasionally found in Egyptian mythology. The five 'epagomenal' days added at the end of the Egyptian year to raise the total of days from 360 (12 x 30-day months) to 365 were assigned as the 'birthdays' of the deities Osiris, Isis, Horus, Seth and Nephthys, making a distinct group of these related deities. In the Hermopolitan tradition the title 'Great of Five' was also applied to the god Thoth.

Hebdomads

While the number six does not seem to have held great symbolic significance for the Egyptians, the number seven is frequently found and, as the sum of three and four, may have been believed to embody the combined significance of these two numbers – plurality and totality. The number seven is therefore, not surprisingly, associated with deities in different ways. The sun god Re was said to have seven *bau* or souls, and several other deities were considered to be 'sevenfold' or to have seven forms. The many different manifestations of Hathor were frequently consolidated into a more manageable and comprehensible group of seven, but the fact that different groups of Hathors existed – comprised of different goddesses – shows that the sevenfold grouping was symbolically more important than the specific deities included. The number also appears in groups of different deities which were brought together. The company of gods revered at Abydos comprised seven gods, for example, and it is also probably not coincidental that the number of the 42 judges who sat in the tribunal of the afterlife to judge the deceased was a multiple of seven. The seven cows found in Chapter 148 of the Book of the Dead also provide a good example of this kind of group. While these bovines were sometimes identified as aspects of the goddess Hathor as the so-called 'seven Hathors' and individually named as 'Mansion of *ka*s', 'Silent One', 'She of Chemmis', 'Much Beloved', 'She who protects', 'She whose name has power', and 'Storm in the sky', they usually bear no clear association

beyond that of their own grouping and the fact that they fulfilled a cosmic role as goddesses of fate.

Ogdoads

As four (symbolic totality) doubled, and hence intensified, the number eight is found in several groups of gods, as when the god Shu created eight Heh deities to help support the legs of the goddess Nut in her guise as the great heavenly cow. Although the names of the gods or goddesses in such groups may vary in the Egyptian texts, the fact that they always add up to eight deities shows that the concept of the group of eight was of greater importance than the specific deities which comprised the group. Ogdoads of eight deities often represent two sets of four or four sets of two gods and goddesses with the latter being more common. The greatest ogdoad – that of Hermopolis (see below) – provides a good example as it was composed of four pairs of primeval deities which

(Top) Hebdomad of the Seven Divine Cows, differentiated and named with their bull, vignette to Chapter 148, Book of the Dead of Maiherpri. 18th dynasty. Egyptian Museum, Cairo.

(Above) The seven cows uniformly depicted and with the solar disk and plumes of Hathor with whom they were frequently associated. Third Intermediate Period. Papyrus of Nestanebettawy, Egyptian Museum, Cairo.

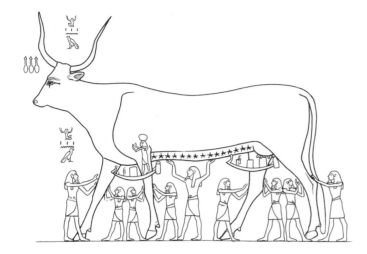

The eight Heh deities who, along with the god Shu, supported the divine cow who represented the heavens in one version of Egyptian cosmogony. Two of these deities supported each leg or 'pillar of heaven'. Outermost shrine of Tutankhamun, 18th dynasty. Egyptian Museum, Cairo.

represented the sum of existence before creation. The Hermopolitan Ogdoad was visualized in the form of four frog-headed deities – and their four respective consorts or female equivalents who were snake-headed goddesses. The nature of these deities was based on the symbolic idea of these animals as chthonic beings and as creatures associated with water and hence the primeval flood from which the created world emerged. The individual deities comprising this ogdoad were:

God	Goddess	Identity
Nun	Naunet	Water
Heh	Hauhet	Infinity
Kek	Kauket	Darkness
Amun	Amaunet	Hiddenness or Wind

Although the four goddesses are clearly only linguistically feminine forms of the names of the four gods, they are nevertheless seen as necessary complements of the male deities. It is also interesting that the four aspects of the primordial cosmos personified by these deities also seem to appear later in the creation account of the Hebrew Bible. According to the various forms of the Egyptian myths, the eight beings or deities together formed the original mound which rose from the primordial waters, or the lotus flower, or the cosmic egg, which preceded the birth of the sun god. The main cult centre of this ogdoad was the ancient Khemnu or Khmun meaning 'eight town' (the modern el-Ashmunein which is also derived from the Coptic *shmun* 'eight') in Middle Egypt with which the god Thoth was also associated, so that it was later known by the Greek name Hermopolis. The Hermopolitan concept of the ogdoad was accepted throughout Egypt, however, and Medinet Habu in western Thebes was regarded as the 'burial place' of the eight primordial deities, a location to which the kings of Egypt came every ten years in the Graeco-Roman Period to honour their primeval ancestors.

Enneads

The Greek term *enneas*, equivalent to the Egyptian *pesedjet* ('nine'), may refer to any group of nine gods. In the Pyramid Texts, for example, we find the Great Ennead (PT 1655, etc.); Lesser Ennead (PT 178); Dual Ennead (PT 121, etc.); plural enneads (PT 278, etc.) and even the seven enneads

(Above) Ennead of Heliopolis with the king as Horus, the son of Osiris and Isis. Second shrine of Tutankhamun, 18th dynasty. Egyptian Museum, Cairo.

(Right) Nine geese probably representing the members of the Theban Ennead headed by Amun. Votive offering, 19th dynasty, Roemer and Pelizaeus Museum, Hildesheim.

(PT 511). As three (plurality) multiplied by itself, the number nine seems to have represented the concept of a great number and was used of many groups. Most commonly, the number appears in conjunction with the Great Ennead of Heliopolis which bound together nine 'related' deities. The group consisted of Atum, the so-called 'father' of the Ennead, his 'children' Shu and Tefnut, 'grandchildren' Geb and Nut, and 'great-grandchildren' Osiris, Isis, Seth and Nephthys. A variant of this ennead included Horus the Elder as second-born after Osiris. Although this group may have been constructed by the priests of Heliopolis in order to incorporate Osiris and his related deities into their own theological system in a manner which placed the netherworld god at a lower position than their own sun god, together the various gods of the Heliopolitan Ennead nevertheless formed a group of great significance. The deities represented were not only those of creation but also of afterlife and, through Osiris and his eventual son Horus, of the ideology and mythology of kingship. Thus, the three areas which are arguably the most important concepts in ancient Egyptian religion were contained within the Heliopolitan Ennead.

Other cult centres constructed enneads of otherwise unrelated deities to which they awarded special veneration – as in the temple of Wadi Mia in the eastern desert where Amun, Re, Osiris, Ptah, Isis and Horus were grouped into an ennead through the addition of three forms of the deified Sethos I. The number of deities in these groups did not always equal nine, however, as the Egyptian term *pesedjet* can have a generalized meaning. Although the members of enneads are often specified, the number most often represents a general, all-encompassing group. The nine gods who stand before Osiris in the sixth hour of the underworld thus represent the rule of that deity over all the netherworld gods, just as the 'nine bows' symbolize all Egypt's traditional enemies.

Dodecads

While twelve may have basic temporal significance relating to the hours of the day and night (and hence, for example, the 12 goddesses of the night hours), as a multiple of both three and four the number may also connote the combined significance of those smaller numbers. Relatively few groups of twelve occur in Egyptian mythology, however, one example being the four groups of three gods with the heads of ibises, jackals, falcons and phoenixes which represented the 'royal ancestors' of the cities Hermopolis, Nekhen, Pe, and Heliopolis respectively. These deities are sometimes found in vignettes accompanying Chapters 107 and 111–16 of the Book of the Dead, though often not all twelve of the deities are depicted.

Regional groups of deities – meaning those of specific areas of Egypt, or of a given area of the cosmos such as star gods or netherworld deities – may or may not have individual names and identities. These groups could consist of any number of deities, and are often, in fact, of varying or indeterminate size. The category includes the deities of the hours of the day and night as these 'hour' gods and goddesses represented not only units of time but also parts of the cosmos as imagined by the Egyptians.

(Left) Turtle, bull and ram-headed deities guard a 'gate' of the underworld. Late Period sarcophagus of Djhutirdis, Egyptian Museum, Cairo.

(Below) Netherworld deities associated with specific regions of the Beyond. Scene from the Amduat, tomb of Tuthmosis III. 18th dynasty, Valley of the Kings, western Thebes.

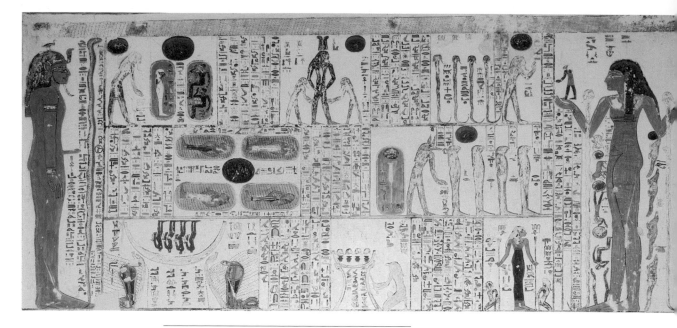

Scene from the fifth section of
the Book of Caverns in the
Tomb of Ramesses VI, Valley
of the Kings, western Thebes.
According to this funerary
work the netherworld
contained a number of caves
or caverns in which various
deities dispensed punishment
or assistance to the deceased.
20th dynasty.

Cavern Deities

According to the ancient Egyptian conception of
the underworld, there existed a number of caves
or caverns in the nether regions which contained
various deities who were involved in the punishment of the wicked. These cavern deities were
systematically enumerated in the so-called 'Spell
of the Twelve Caves', a composition known from a
papyrus of the time of Amenophis II (Cairo 24742),
and from the walls of the southern chamber of the
Osireion at Abydos. Part of this text (caves 8–12)
was also included in the Book of the Dead since
the 18th dynasty and is found as Chapter 168 in
that work. The caverns are places of punishment
and execution – usually by beheading – of the
enemies of Re, but the deities in these texts also aid
the justified dead. The first seven caverns contain
alternating groups of three mummiform and three
anthropomorphic deities, two being male and one
female in each group. The eighth to twelfth caverns
contain varying numbers of deities with the eighth
cavern having seven individuals and groups, for
example, and the ninth having as many as twenty.
Beneath the representations of these cavern
deities, their names and numbers are listed along
with the offerings prescribed for them and in some
cases the beneficent deeds the deities were reputed
to perform on behalf of the deceased, such as the
ability to move freely in the underworld, or to have
light, food and protection. Understandably, offerings were sometimes made by living Egyptians to
these gods.

The deities of the tenth cavern are representative
of the types of individual and group deities found
in these texts:

*Deities of the tenth cavern –
Action performed for the deceased*

Those who belong to the sunshine – give light.
Those who take hold – grant that the deceased be
acclaimed.
The nine gods who guard those in the cavern – give the
breath of life.
The nine gods whose arms are hidden – grant that the
deceased be a worthy spirit.
The hidden goddess – grants that the deceased's soul be
strong and his corpse intact.
The souls of the gods who became members of Osiris –
grant that the deceased have peace.
Those who worship Re – grant the deceased not be
turned back from any gate of the underworld.
Those whose faces are warlike – grant that the deceased
be cool in the place of heat.

*Cavern Deities
(from the royal tombs of the Valley of the Kings)**

Cavern	Representative Deities	Enemies of Re
1	Serpent guardians of the Silent Region, Osiris	Beheaded, bound
2	Flame-breathing serpent, Osiris, deities in sarcophagi	Bound, decapitated, upside down
3	Aker, catfish-headed gods, forms of Osiris	Upside-down, females
4	Serpent Great One on his belly, forms of Osiris	Upside-down, bound, without *bau*
5	Nut, Osiris, Tatenen	Punished in cauldrons
6	Anubis, Horus, Osiris	Beheaded males, bound females, *bau* and shadows punished

* Note: Other versions of the cavern myths present 12
caverns, but with many variant deities.

Demons

There is no Egyptian word which corresponds to the English word 'demon', but Egyptological literature often uses this term to describe what are also called 'minor divinities'. From the ancient Egyptian perspective, as Dimitri Meeks has shown, such minor deities were subordinate to the major gods and goddesses and performed specified tasks upon demand; and while the major gods tended to be more universal in nature, 'demons' were often defined by specific actions, behaviour and location. These beings were often associated with caves, pits and tombs and also with bodies of water – all of which were considered entrances into the underworld – and the greatest number of demons were, in fact, denizens of the beyond. These netherworld demigods constituted different categories. While some were clearly portrayed as frightening instruments of punishment for the damned, many were not inimical and may often better be classed as minor guardian deities such as the keepers of the various gates of the underworld. Some were creatures specifically tasked with the protection of the king or the deceased in the journey through the netherworld. These latter demons were also capable, of course, of aggressive behaviour in order to fulfill their protective roles. Such demons may be depicted zoomorphically but usually take human form or are portrayed semi-anthropomorphically with human bodies and the heads of creatures such as turtles, which were considered malevolent but whose power could be used for protection. A number of images of such demons appear in vignettes of the afterlife books and in some of the tombs in the Valley of the Kings and Valley of the Queens.

Demons were often represented with the heads of fierce or fabulous creatures and many were depicted with weapons such as knives. The character of these minor deities could be protective or vengeful, however, as shown by the various funerary texts in which they appear. Tomb of Amenherkhepshef, Valley of the Queens, western Thebes.

Demons could also be associated with the world of the living, however, and once again we find benevolent and malevolent types. The latter type included demons associated with Sekhmet and other great deities in their aggressive aspects, while more benevolent demons were often called upon to give protection from these. Interestingly, Egyptian texts show that it was possible for a demon to be freed from its subordinate role and responsibilities and to become a 'greater god' through a process of promotion, showing once again the difference between 'demons' and 'gods' was primarily one of degree rather than type.

Gate Deities

The Egyptian conception of the underworld included many gates, portals or pylons that the sun god must pass on his nightly journey, by the deceased king as part of the sun god's entourage (or fused with the god), and by the deceased who must pass these barriers in order to reach the place of afterlife existence. Different accounts of the netherworld gates were preserved in the various funerary texts with over 1,000 deities depicted, but in all cases the barriers were guarded by minor gods who would allow only those who knew their secret names – and thereby had power over them – to pass.

The demon called Sahekek was depicted in the pose of a naked child with a bad headache. Demons such as this were believed to be responsible for many ailments and illnesses. From a New Kingdom ostracon.

81

(Above and above right) Knife-wielding demons seated before 'gates' of the underworld. According to the New Kingdom Book of Gates, the Book of the Dead, and other texts, each underworld portal was guarded by at least one such demon. Tomb of Sennedjem, Deir el-Medina, western Thebes.

On the walls of the royal tombs of the Valley of the Kings twelve pylons or gates were commonly incorporated into the funerary texts – such as versions of the Book of Gates – inscribed during the New Kingdom. Although each gate was depicted as an architectural feature, it was named as a goddess and protected by a fire-spitting serpent and by its own guardian deity. The fifth gate, for example, is termed 'she of duration', its serpent is called 'flame-eyed' and its resident deity is 'true of heart'. In the funerary papyri composed for nobles and others there is more variation. In Chapter 144 of the Book of the Dead, for example, seven gates are mentioned, each with its own god, a doorkeeper and a herald. Thus the seventh gate is watched by the god 'sharpest of them all', the doorkeeper 'strident of voice' and the herald 'rejector of rebels'. In other texts there are 21 gates known as the 'secret portals of the mansion of Osiris in the field of reeds', each of which is given a number of names or epithets and guarded by a zoo-anthropomorphic deity usually depicted seated and holding a large knife. The names of the gates are mixed in nature, being sometimes fearsome and sometimes innocuous as with Gate 14 'mistress of anger, dancing on blood' or Gate 3 'mistress of the altar'. The guardian deities are usually given terrifying or repulsive names such as 'swallower of sinners' or 'existing on maggots' in order to heighten their threatening effect – although in some cases they are unnamed in the texts, adding to the number of Egyptian deities known to have existed but impossible to catalogue.

The following shows the 12 gates as depicted in the royal tombs of the Valley of the Kings:

Gate	Representative Deities	Features of the areas
1	The gods in the entrance, the 4 weary ones	4 cardinal points
2	Apophis, 2 enneads	Lake of fire
3	Goddesses of the hours, Osiris, Horus	Lake of life, lake of uraei
4	Gods of space and time, Osiris	Throne of Osiris
5	Osiris, Apophis, 12 restraining gods	Circular lake of fire
6	Osiris, the blessed and punished dead	Stakes of Geb
7	Lords of provision in the West	Fields of provisions
8	Fire-breathing serpent, sons of Horus, ba souls	Waters of the drowned
9	Deities with nets, Apophis	Area leading to 'emergence'
10	Apophis, face of Re, goddesses of the hours	Area of restraint of Apophis
11	Gods who carry the blazing light, baboons of sunrise	Area directly before dawn
12	Isis, Nephthys, Nun, Nut, the reborn sun	The primeval waters from which the sun emerges

Hours of the Day Deities

Each hour of the day was personified in Egyptian religious thought by a deity – all of which were associated with the sun in some way and many of whom were often depicted along with the solar god in representations of his day barque, the *mandet*. Although these gods and goddesses were clearly linked with units of time, they are grouped here – as are the hours of the night – as 'regional' deities, as each hour of the day and night was also a place – a physical part of the sun's transit across the sky or through the netherworld and the liminal areas of the two horizons. The first of these deities was Maat, the daughter of Re, and the others were descendants of the sun god or his servants or helpers:

Hour	Deity
1	Maat
2	Hu (annunciation)
3	Sia (perception)
4	Asbet
5	Igaret
6	Seth
7	Horus
8	Khonsu
9	Isis
10	Heka (magic)
11	The one who is given the tow-rope of the solar barque
12	The one who gives protection in the twilight

Hours of the Night Deities

Each hour of the night (corresponding to a region of the netherworld) was represented by a goddess who was protective or assistive in nature, with a particular role according to her position in the topography of the underworld. All of the goddesses strengthened the sun god in some manner until the final hour when the twelfth goddess, 'beholder of the beauty of Re', witnessed the glorious rebirth of the rejuvenated sun at the night's end. Accordingly, the hour goddesses were given power by Re to control the life spans of all living things. George Hart has suggested that the ithyphallic figure called 'he who conceals the hours' that is depicted in the burial chamber of the tomb of Ramesses VI could symbolize the power desired by the monarch to negate the power of time that these goddesses might wield over the deceased king. The epithets of the goddesses are as follows:

Hour	Epithet
1	Splitter of the heads of Re's enemies
2	The wise, guardian of her lord
3	Slicer of souls
4	Great of power
5	She on her boat
6	Proficient leader
7	Repeller of the snake (Apophis)
8	Mistress of the night
9	Adorer
10	Beheader of rebels
11	The star, repulser of rebels
12	Beholder of the beauty of Re

The hour goddesses were not frequently depicted, but they appear in characteristically anthropomorphic form in some representations of the New Kingdom funerary texts known as the Book of Gates and the Amduat. In the burial chamber of the tomb of Ramesses I in the Valley of the Kings, for example, the twelve goddesses are represented in an illustration of the third division of the Book of Gates. The goddesses stand in two files, six on either side of a summary depiction of the netherworld, in the centre of which is a huge coiled serpent 'he who should be removed'. The goddesses each wear a five-pointed star on their heads but are undifferentiated except for their names and the alternating colours of their individual costumes.

The twelve hours of the night were personified as goddesses in the Book of Gates where they were depicted in vignettes showing the twelve deities grouped around a twisting serpent which represented the endlessness of time.

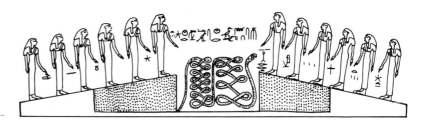

Judgment Deities (Great Tribunal, Deities of the Hall of Justice)

References to an afterlife judgment by a tribunal of gods may appear as early as the Pyramid Texts (PT 317, 386, etc.). Such references are clear in the Middle Kingdom Coffin Texts, and by the time the Book of the Dead became the chief funerary text, this judgment was seen as the crucial event in the deceased's entrance to the afterlife. Spell 125 of the Book of the Dead gives the so-called 'negative confession' or 'declaration of innocence' of the deceased before a tribunal of 42 gods who were the assessors who judged the dead in the netherworld Hall of Justice or 'Hall of the Two Truths'. The declaration takes the form of an address by the deceased to each judge – who is named along with the protestation of innocence regarding the specific crime judged by that god. The gods were listed

according to their individual names and usually either a geographical area or some other identifying characteristic. Together, the 42 deities 'who hear cases' were apparently believed to represent all possible types of evil. The names of some of these deities are reminiscent of more well-known gods (such as Nosey of Hermopolis = Thoth; White of Teeth = Sobek) whom they may represent.

The council of assessor gods is frequently depicted in vignettes illustrating Chapter 125 of the Book of the Dead, though only occasionally are all 42 of the gods shown. More frequently a representative selection of the deities is made. The gods may be shown squatting in the position of the 'seated god' hieroglyph, or standing, and may hold knives or *maat* feathers as symbols of their judicial power.

(Below) The 42 deities of the afterlife tribunal which judged the dead in the netherworld 'Hall of Justice'. Each deity was responsible for a particular crime which ranged from murder and rapaciousness to religious transgressions such as blasphemy or damaging the image of a god.

	Name of God	Identification	Crime judged
1	Far-strider	Heliopolis	falsehood
2	Fire-embracer	Kheraha	robbery
3	Nosey	Hermopolis	rapaciousness
4	Swallower of shades	the cavern	stealing
5	Dangerous One	Rosetau	murder
6	Double lion	the sky	destruction of food
7	Fiery eyes	Letopolis	crookedness
8	Flame	Came forth backwards	stealing offerings
9	Bone Breaker	Herakleopolis	lying
10	Green of flame	Memphis	taking food
11	You of the cavern	the West	sullenness
12	White of teeth	Fayum	transgression
13	Blood-eater	the shambles	killing a sacred bull
14	Eater of entrails	House of Thirty	perjury
15	Lord of truth	Maaty	stealing bread
16	Wanderer	Bubastis	eavesdropping
17	Pale One	Heliopolis	babbling
18	Doubly evil	Andjet	disputing
19	*Wamemty*-snake	place of execution	adultery
20	See whom you bring	House of Min	misbehaviour
21	Over the Old One	Imau	terrorizing
22	Demolisher	Xois	transgressing
23	Disturber	Weryt	being hot-tempered
24	Youth	Heliopolitan nome	unhearing of truth
25	Foreteller	Wenes	making disturbance
26	You of the altar	the secret place	hoodwinking
27	Face behind him	cavern of wrong	copulating with a boy
28	Hot-foot	the dusk	neglect
29	You of the darkness	the darkness	quarrelling
30	Bringer of your offering	Sais	unduly active
31	Owner of faces	Nedjefet	impatience
32	Accuser	Wetjenet	damaging a god's image
33	Owner of horns	Asyut	volubility of speech
34	Nefertem	Memphis	wrongdoing, beholding evil
35	Temsep	Busiris	conjuration against the king
36	You who acted willfully	Tjebu	wading in water
37	Water-smiter	the abyss	being loud voiced
38	Commander of mankind	your house	reviling God
39	Bestower of good	the harpoon nome	doing ...?
40	Bestower of powers	the city	making distinctions for self
41	Serpent with raised head	the cavern	dishonest wealth
42	Serpent who brings and gives	the silent land	blasphemy

Nome Deities

Egypt was traditionally divided into administrative districts which the Egyptians called *sepaut* and the Greeks *nomoi*, from which the word nome comes. For most of the dynastic era there were 22 Upper Egyptian provinces or nomes and in the later periods Lower Egypt was also divided into 20 nomes. Each of these nomes had its own emblem – usually that of its titulary deity/deities or some other distinguishing element – which was displayed

upon a pole or standard so that the nomes were recognized and named after their symbols, with names such as ibis, fish, or crocodile nome.

In the representations carved on the walls of Egypt's temples, the nomes were depicted as either female or androgynous figures, usually bearing the emblems of their districts on their heads.

Their depictions show them processionally carrying offerings into the temple to signify the gifts of their areas to the upkeep and welfare of the god's houses. Usually the 22 nomes of Upper Egypt were depicted on the southern walls of temples and the 20 nomes of Lower Egypt were depicted on the northern walls.

(Above) The judgment of the deceased in the Hall of Justice from the 19th-dynasty Book of the Dead of Hunefer, British Museum. Hunefer is shown undergoing the weighing of the heart, before the throne of Osiris, and also kneeling before a variant of the Heliopolitan Ennead with certain additional deities. Other vignettes of the Book of the Dead show some or all of the 42 deities who were believed to oversee this judgment.

Fecundity figures personifying nomes, cities and estates – and sometimes identified with the king – are frequently depicted in Egyptian temples in the symbolic presentation of produce and offerings. 19th dynasty. Temple of Ramesses II, Abydos.

Nome		Name	Location (modern)	Major Deities
1		Ta-Seti	First cataract to north of Gebel el-Silsila	Khnum, Satis, Anukis, Isis, Horus the Elder, Sobek
2		Throne of Horus	Region of Edfu	Horus
3		Shrine	Kom el-Ahmar to north of Esna	Horus, Nekhbet, Khnum, Neith
4		Sceptre	Region of Armant and Luxor	Amun, Mut, Khonsu, Montu, Buchis, Sobek
5		Two Falcons	Region of Qift	Min, Seth
6		Crocodile	Region of Dendera	Hathor
7		Sistrum	Region of Hiw	Bat
8		Great Land	Region of Abydos and Ghirga	Khentamentiu, Osiris, Onuris
9		Min	Region of Akhmim	Min
10		Cobra	Region of Qaw el-Kebir	Seth, Mihos, Nemtywy
11		Seth	Region of Deir Rifa	Seth
12		Viper Mount	Region of Deir el-Gebrawi opposite Asyut	Nemty
13		Southern Sycamore and Viper	Region of Asyut	Wepwawet, Anubis
14		Northern Sycamore and Viper	Region of Meir and el-Qusiya	Hathor
15		Hare	Region of el-Amarna, el-Ashmunein and el-Bersha	Thoth, Ogdoad, Aten
16		Oryx	From Beni Hasan to north of el-Minya	Pakhet, Khnum
17		Jackal	Region of Samalut	Anubis
18		Nemty	Region of el-Hiba to opposite el-Lahun	Nemty
19		Two Sceptres	From el-Bahnasa to Biba	Seth, Mormyrus fish
20		Southern Sycamore	Region of Beni Suef	Heryshef
21		Northern Sycamore	Region of el-Wasta and Meidum	Khnum, Seneferu
22		Knife	From Atfih to region of Dahshur	Hathor

Nome	Name	Location (modern)	Major Deities
1	White Wall	Region of el-Lisht and Memphis	Ptah, Sokar, Apis
2	Foreleg	SW Delta around Ausim	Horus, Kherty
3	West	NW Delta region west of Rosetta branch of Nile	Hathor
4	Southern Shield	SW Delta N. and S. of Samadun	Neith
5	Northern Shield	Region of Sa el-Hagar to coast	Neith
6	Mountain Bull	Central Delta to coast	Re
7	Western Harpoon	NW Delta region east of Rosetta branch of Nile	Ha
8	Eastern Harpoon	E. Delta along Wadi Tummilat	Atum
9	Andjety	Central Delta S. of Samannud	Osiris, Andjety
10	Black Ox	SE Delta below Benha	Horus
11	Ox count	East Delta around Tell el-Muqdam	Shu, Tefnut, Mihos
12	Calf and Cow	NE Delta from Samannud to coast	Onuris
13	Prospering Sceptre	SE Delta apex	Atum, Iusaas, Mnevis
14	Foremost of the East	Eastern Delta S. of Port Said	Seth
15	Ibis	NE Delta region of Damietta branch of Nile	Thoth
16	Fish	NE Delta from Tell el-Rub'a to coast	Banebdjedet, Hatmehyt
17	Behdet	NE Delta region around el-Balamun to coast	Horus
18	Prince of the South	SE Delta around Tell Basta	Bastet
19	Prince of the North	NE Delta E. of San el-Hagar	Wadjet
20	Plumed Falcon	E Delta above Wadi Tummilat	Sopdu

The four sons of Horus, tomb of Ay, western Valley of the Kings, Thebes. This unique representation depicts the sons of Horus as seated mummiform figures wearing the White Crown of Upper Egypt (at left, on the southern side) and the Red Crown of Lower Egypt (at right, on the northern side). 18th dynasty.

(Right) Limestone canopic jars with the heads of Duamutef, Qebehsenuef, Imsety and Hapy. Originally, jars depicting the sons of Horus were made with human-headed stoppers but near the end of the 18th dynasty they were given the characteristic forms seen here. Egyptian Museum, Cairo

Sons of Horus

The earliest reference to these four gods is found in the Pyramid Texts where they are said to be the children and also the 'souls' of Horus. They are also called the 'friends of the king' and assist the deceased monarch in ascending into the sky (PT 2078–79). The same gods were also known as the sons of Osiris and were later said to be members of the group called 'the seven blessed ones' whose job was to protect the netherworld god's coffin. Their afterlife mythology led to important roles in the funerary assemblage, particularly in association with the containers now traditionally called canopic jars in which the internal organs of the deceased were preserved. At first the stoppers of these jars were often carved into the shape of human heads representing the head of the deceased, but from the 18th dynasty they were carved in the form of the four sons of Horus who had become the patron deities of their contents. Each deity was in turn said to be guarded by one of the funerary goddesses, though there was some variation in this linkage. The group may have been based on the symbolic completeness of the number four alone, but they are often given geographic associations and hence became a kind of 'regional' group.

The four gods were the human-headed Imsety who guarded the liver (and who was himself guarded by Isis); the baboon-headed Hapy who guarded the lungs (protected by Nephthys); the jackal-headed Duamutef who guarded the stomach (often protected by Neith); and the falcon-headed Qebehsenuef, guardian of the intestines (who was often protected by Serket). The four gods were sometimes depicted on the sides of the canopic chest and had specific symbolic orientations, with Imsety usually being aligned with the south, Hapy with the north, Duamutef with the east and Qebehsenuef with the west. They were also depicted on the long sides of coffins and sarcophagi with Hapy and Qebehsenuef being placed on the west side while Imsety and Duamutef were placed on the east. During the Third Intermediate Period embalming practices changed and the preserved organs were returned to the body cavity, each with an amulet of its respective son of Horus attached. Later similar figures of the four

Name	Appearance	Organ	Orientation	Tutelary Deity
Imsety	Human	Liver	South	Isis
Duamutef	Jackal	Stomach	East	Neith
Hapy	Baboon	Lungs	North	Nephthys
Qebehsenuef	Falcon	Intestines	West	Serket

gods were also often stitched onto the outside of the wrapped mummy.

In the vignettes of the various funerary texts the four sons of Horus could be represented in differing ways. In the Book of the Dead they may be shown as diminutive figures standing on a lotus blossom before the throne of Osiris, and on the third funerary shrine of Tutankhamun they appear as heads fused with the body of a protective serpent. In late New Kingdom times the sons of Horus were also represented as star gods (see p. 91) in the northern sky.

The four sons of Horus depicted as mummiform figures and as deities on a stylized mound. The four deities became increasingly important in the Egyptian mortuary sphere. Papyrus of Ani, British Museum.

Souls of Nekhen and Pe

The sacred ancestral *bau* 'souls' of the Lower Egyptian city of Pe (Buto) and the Upper Egyptian city of Nekhen (Hierakonpolis) symbolized the predynastic rulers of the two regions and were regarded as powerful spirits or deities who served the deceased king and who also assisted the living king. In the Pyramid Texts the souls of Pe mourn the death of Osiris – the symbolic father of the king – and urge the vengeance of Horus – the living king – against Osiris' murderer (PT 1004–07); and

Ramesses I depicted between a falcon-headed 'soul' of Pe and a jackal-headed 'soul' of Nekhen. The bau *or souls celebrate the regeneration of the king who has also become a* ba. *Tomb of Ramesses I, Valley of the Kings, western Thebes.*

the souls of both areas are likened to stars (PT 904) who provide a gilded 'ladder' for the deceased king to climb into the sky (PT 478–79, 1253).

The souls of Pe are represented as falcon-headed and those of Nekhen as jackal-headed gods. They are both often depicted in the kneeling *henu* or 'jubilation' position as they salute the rising sun or participate in other celebratory rituals. In the tomb of Ramesses I in the Valley of the Kings they are shown flanking the king in this position, celebrating the rejuvenation of the king's *ba* or soul, as they themselves are *bau* or souls. In this particular representation, the written *henu* hieroglyph is visible in the inscription above the figures of the gods which are, in fact, simply hieroglyphs made large. In a similar representation from the 18th-dynasty temple at Buhen in Nubia, the falcon-headed gods of Pe are accompanied by an inscription which states 'May they give all life and power…[and] all stability which they have…' showing that the gesturing figures could also be symbolic of divine gifts. In temple scenes the souls of Nekhen and Pe (or masked priests) may carry the barque shrine of the god on poles placed upon their shoulders, or, as in the temple of Horus at Edfu, they may carry the enthroned god himself by means of carrying poles beneath his chair.

Star Deities

Egyptian astronomical texts and representations mention many gods and goddesses of the night sky – some representing planets as well as astral bodies – which are conveniently called star deities. Most important of these were the 'Imperishable Ones' representing the northern circumpolar stars which were visible each night, as opposed to the great majority of stars which appeared and disappeared from view according to the earth's orbital movements. These constant stars symbolized the idea of eternal survival for the Egyptians and it seems to have been the goal of early kings to join their number in the afterlife. Evidence for this early astral cult is clearly found in the Pyramid Texts alongside the solar theology which had achieved dominance before the 5th dynasty. The two approaches are not always successfully syncretized, so that the deceased king is said to be the morning star on the one hand, while he is also said to cross the sky in

(Right) Part of the elaborate ceiling decoration of the burial chamber of Ramesses VI showing the overarching body of the goddess Nut, the newly born sun, and a number of netherworld deities and gods of the various hours of the day. The scene illustrates the New Kingdom composition known as the Book of the Day and shows the stars travelling along the inside of the sky goddess's body during the diurnal period. 20th dynasty. Valley of the Kings, western Thebes.

the boat of the sun god. The growth of the cult of Osiris also led to the stars being called the 'followers' of that god, so that it is clear that the major theological systems attempted to incorporate the star deities into their own schemes.

The brightest object in the night sky after the moon, the planet Venus (the 'morning star'), was viewed even from early times as an important deity; and from at least the Middle Kingdom the Egyptians recognized five of the planets, which they called 'stars that know no tiredness' and which were represented as gods who sailed across the heavens in their own barques. These were Mercury (Sebegu, perhaps a form of Seth), Venus ('the one who crosses' or 'god of the morning'), Mars ('Horus of the horizon' or 'Horus the red'), Jupiter ('Horus who limits the Two Lands'), and Saturn ('Horus bull of the heavens').

As time progressed, many of the brighter stars were mapped into constellations, though these have proved extremely difficult to identify in some cases. At the least, equivalents of the modern constellations of Orion, the Great Bear, and perhaps Leo and Draco are recognizable, however; and these and other groupings represented either standard deities within the Egyptian pantheon or unique astral deities with their own identities. Already by the Middle Kingdom complex 'star-clocks' or calendars had been constructed which divided the night sky into 36 decans or groups of stars which were visualized as 'star gods' who rose and moved across the sky in the course of ten days, the most important being Sirius (Sothis – see p. 167), whose rising

approximated the beginning of the Nile's inundation. In several of the royal tombs of the Valley of the Kings – such as those of Sethos I and Ramesses VI – the night sky is depicted on the ceiling of the burial chamber and many of the important star deities are represented and named. At this time many familiar deities – such as the four sons of Horus – also appeared as star gods.

(Above) Personified constellations, ceiling of the burial chamber of Sethos I, Valley of the Kings, Thebes.

(Below) Three star deities including Imsety (centre – as a goddess), and Hapy (right). Tomb of Pedamenope, Thebes.

Male Anthropomorphic Deities

Amenophis Son of Hapu

Mythology

Amenophis Son of Hapu was born in the Delta town of Athribis *c*. 1430 BC and rose to distinction as a royal scribe and overseer of all the king's works under Amenophis III. He appears to have moved to the royal court at Thebes in about 1390 BC and lived there until a man of venerable age, having directed the construction of some of the greatest architectural wonders produced in ancient Egypt. Amenophis' works included not only the planning and construction of great monuments in the area of Thebes – such as the mortuary temple of Amenophis III and its great Colossi of Memnon – but also the temple of Soleb in Nubia and temples in other areas of the realm. Accorded great honour during his lifetime, after his death Amenophis was deified for his wisdom and in later periods for his healing powers. In these roles he was paired during Ptolemaic times, in Thebes at least, with Imhotep, the legendary 3rd-dynasty architect of Djoser.

Iconography

As a deified person Amenophis Son of Hapu was depicted only in human form. During his lifetime several granite statues were set up showing him as a scribe in the temple of Amun at Karnak (fine examples are now in the Egyptian Museum in Cairo and the Luxor Museum) and he appears in a beautifully carved scene in the tomb of his relative, the vizier Ramose, at Thebes. The Son of Hapu lived to be 80 years old, and a statue of him as an elderly official survives.

Worship

Unlike the more widely spread veneration of Imhotep, the worship of Amenophis Son of Hapu was limited mainly to the Theban area and can be seen to have grown in two stages. Even in his lifetime his importance led to the erection of a funerary cult temple next to that of Amenophis III on the west bank of Thebes. While small compared to the temple of the king, Amenophis' own monument was still of considerable size and larger than the

Honoured during his lifetime with statues such as this one, and with his own mortuary temple, **Amenophis Son of Hapu,** *the master architect of Amenophis III, was deified after his life and venerated both for his wisdom and healing powers. Black granite statue, from Karnak. Egyptian Museum, Cairo.*

temples of some kings in the same area. It was also the only private cult temple situated among the royal monuments in this location. A 21st-dynasty copy of a royal decree pertaining to the Son of Hapu's temple indicates that his cult continued to be celebrated for at least three centuries after his death. The veneration of the deified Amenophis as a god of wisdom and healing also saw a resurgence in the Ptolemaic Period. Together with Imhotep, chapels were dedicated to him in the temple of Hathor at Deir el-Medina and in Hatshepsut's temple at Deir el-Bahri. The statues erected for him in the temple of Amun at Karnak were also utilized as intermediaries with Amun, and prayers were offered to them.

Amun, Amun-Re

Mythology

One of the most important gods of ancient Egypt, Amun is first mentioned, along with his consort Amaunet, in the Pyramid Texts (PT 446). He appears as a local god of the Theban region from at least the 12th dynasty when four rulers took the name Amenemhet or 'Amun is pre-eminent'. Within a century and a half Amun gradually displaced the old god of that region, Montu, and the ascendancy of the Theban kings in Middle and New Kingdom times eventually propelled him (as the combined Amun-Re) to the position of supreme god of the Egyptian pantheon. He was associated with two other deities who together made up the local divine triad of Thebes: his consort, the goddess Mut – who largely replaced Amaunet in this role – and the lunar god Khonsu who was worshipped as their son (see illus. pp. 31, 47). His character developed over the millennia into that of a rich and varied personality. The Egyptians themselves called him *Amun asha renu* or 'Amun rich in names', and the god can only be fully understood in terms of the many aspects which were combined in him.

Concealed god: The Greek writer Plutarch quotes the Egyptian chronicler Manetho as stating that Amun meant 'that which is concealed' or 'invisible', and the god was also commonly given epithets such as 'mysterious of form' – suggesting an essentially imperceptible nature – and it is possible that his name originally referred to Amun as the invisible power of the wind. While it is true that his name was written without a defining determinative, this was also true of some other creator gods, but the aspect of Amun as a mysterious, hidden god was primary to his nature.

Creator god: In addition to being a member of the Ogdoad, the group of eight primeval deities worshipped in Hermopolis (see p. 77), Amun was worshipped as *Amun kematef* or 'Amun who has completed his moment', a creator god in the form

of a snake that renewed itself. In this form Amun was said to predate the other members of the Ogdoad, and it was probably this form of Amun that Plutarch refers to as 'Kneph' – an eternal, self-engendering god worshipped by the inhabitants of Thebes. By the 18th dynasty Karnak Temple was said to occupy the 'mound of the beginning' where Amun brought the world into being; and a number of New Kingdom hymns extol Amun for creating the cosmos through his thoughts, an important step in the theological development of cosmogonic ideas.

Solar god: In the Book of the Dead Amun is called 'eldest of the gods of the eastern sky', an epithet reflecting both his primeval character and solar-associated nature, and an 18th-dynasty hymn to Amun preserved on a stela in the British Museum refers to Amun when he rises as Horakhty (see p. 201), directly fusing the hidden one with the visible sun. When he

was syncretized with the god Re, as the composite Amun-Re, Amun took on a number of aspects of the solar deity, though these were clearly secondary to his hidden nature and the god was regarded as antithetical to the sun during the Amarna Period.

Fertility god: From the 12th dynasty *Amun kamutef* – literally, 'bull of his mother' – was the ithyphallic form of Amun depicted in ritual scenes in the temples of Thebes and especially Luxor Temple. The epithet suggests both that the god was self-engendered – meaning that he begot himself on his mother, the cow who personified the goddess of the sky and of creation – and also conveys the sexual energy of the bull which, for the Egyptians, was a symbol of strength and fertility *par excellence*. In this ithyphallic aspect Amun was related to the fertility god Min (see p. 115) and is sometimes called Amun-Min.

The great god Amun-Re – depicted in both his normal anthropomorphic form (second from right) and as the ithyphallic Amun-Min (at left). **Amun** *was venerated in a number of roles but his identity as king of the gods and as a powerful fertility god were of primary importance in New Kingdom times. 19th dynasty. Temple of Sethos I, Abydos.*

Warrior god: It seems likely that some of the character of the old Theban war god Montu (see p. 203), whom Amun largely displaced, was absorbed by the ascendant deity. The Theban rulers of the 13th dynasty had made their city a rallying point against the invading Hyksos and, when the Hyksos were finally driven from Egypt (*c.* 1550 BC), it was Amun who received credit for the military victories of the time. Likewise, in the succeeding period of New Kingdom Empire Amun was not only said to instigate Egyptian expansion and to protect the Egyptian king in battle, but the 'lord of victory' and 'lover of strength' was specifically given credit for successful military strategy.

King of the gods: Pyramid Text 1540 states 'you have come, O king, as the son of Geb upon the throne of Amun', and from the Middle Kingdom the god was styled 'Lord of the thrones of the Two Lands' of Upper and Lower Egypt. The first known example of Amun's title 'king of the gods' appears on the 12th-dynasty 'White Chapel' of Senwosret I at Karnak and is used frequently thereafter. He was also called 'chief of the gods' in

this same role of divine king. By Ptolemaic times Amun was directly equated with Zeus, and his Greek name Amonrasonther may be based on the Egyptian title *Amun-Re nesu netcheru*, 'Amun-Re king of the gods'.

Universal god: Unlike deities who were thought to personify the sky, earth or some other limited region or phenomenon, Amun was held to be a universal god who, at least in his developed theology, permeated the cosmos and all it contained. While a few other gods could be said to be 'universal' in nature, it is with Amun that we find a developed rationale for this claim. As the god 'who exists in all things' and the one in whom all gods were subsumed, Amun came particularly close to being a kind of monotheistic deity (see p. 38) and was sometimes revered as the *ba* or soul of all natural phenomena.

Iconography

Usually Amun was represented in human form wearing a short kilt (to which is often attached a bull's tail), a feather pattern tunic and a double-plumed crown. It has been suggested that these tall

Ram-headed sphinxes, symbolizing the procreative energy and power of **Amun***, line the western entrance to the god's great temple at Karnak. Erected by Ramesses II, each criosphinx originally held an image of the king protectively between its paws. 19th dynasty. Thebes.*

feathers were a way of representing Amun as a god of the wind – either as it could be seen ruffling the feathers or as it might be generated by feather fans – though this is purely speculative. The twin feathers would seem to reflect some aspect of the basic dualism which pervades Egyptian symbolism, and each feather was itself also frequently divided into the significant number of seven sections. Anthropomorphic images of Amun are found in two forms – with red and blue skin. The god's original colour was red, like that of most other gods, but after the Amarna Period (and apparently in some instances before), the god was also shown with a blue complexion, possibly in order to symbolize his aspects as a deity of the air and of primeval creativity. In depictions of the god standing, Amun is usually shown in a striding pose, though in his form of Amun-Min he stands with legs together, and as befitting his position as king of the gods, Amun is frequently also depicted seated on a throne.

Probably because of its procreative vigour, the ram (*ovis platyra aegyptiaca* – recognized by its curved horns) could symbolize Amun. The processional routes which led to Amun's chief temple

Amun-Re in ram-headed form (at right) with the god Khnum. The two deities are differentiated by the curved horns of Amun and the straight or undulating horns of Khnum (reflecting different species of ram), as well as by the characteristic tall plumes of Amun.

at Karnak were flanked with prone rams or ram-headed lions symbolizing the god, and the great festival barque of Amun 'lord of the two horns' was decorated with rams' heads at its prow and stern. Occasionally, Amun is depicted as a man with the head of a ram, a form easily confused with that of the evening form of the sun god. The Nile goose (*Alopochen aegyptiaca*) was also a symbol of Amun, probably because of its association with the creation of the primeval world (see Gengen-Wer); and for the same reason Amun also could be depicted as a serpent, though the iconographic use of this form is rare. Finally, in his solar-related form, combined with Re, Amun could also be associated with the lion, and the criosphinxes which represented him as ram-headed lions must be understood in this way.

Worship

Although of great importance at Thebes during the Middle Kingdom, relatively little is known of the worship of Amun before the New Kingdom when the god rose to the position of supreme state god. The monuments which were built to him at that time were little short of astounding and Amun was worshipped in many temples throughout Egypt, though in Thebes itself, on the east bank of the Nile, two temples in particular were greatly enlarged in his honour. The main temple of Amun at Karnak – called by the Egyptians *Ipet-sut* ('most select of places') – remains the largest religious structure ever created and consisted of a vast enclosure containing Amun's own temple as well as several subsidiary temples of other gods. This complex was connected via a processional way with *Ipet-resyt*, the 'southern sanctuary' of Luxor Temple,

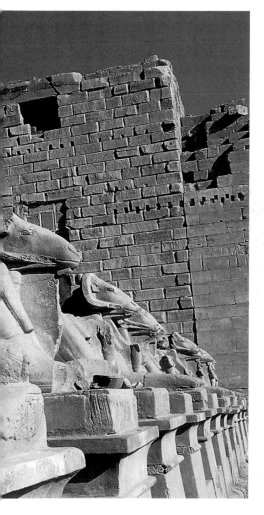

*The god **Amun** (at right),
in his role as supreme state
god and named as 'Lord of
the thrones of the Two Lands
[of Upper and Lower Egypt]',
grants the gift of life to
Ramesses III. 20th dynasty.
Mortuary temple of
Ramesses III, Medinet Habu,
western Thebes.*

which the god visited annually in the 'Beautiful Festival of Opet'. In this most important of Amun's festivals, the god's cult statue was taken to his southern temple to celebrate union with his divine consort Mut in the form of the ithyphallic Amun of Luxor who appeared in the guise of the fertility god Min. On the western bank of Thebes Amun also had smaller but theologically important cult areas in the temples of Deir el-Bahri, Medinet Habu and elsewhere that were also visited by the god in festival processions which crossed the Nile and travelled from one shrine to the next. In the New Kingdom and later Amun was incorporated into many Lower Egyptian centres, notably at Perunefer (the river port of Memphis) in the 18th dynasty, at Per-Ramesses in the 19th, and on a vast scale at Tanis in the eastern Delta where Karnak was almost virtually recreated during the 21st dynasty.

As a result of royal gifts following successful military campaigns during the New Kingdom and other sources of income, tremendous wealth flowed into the Theban cult centre of Amun, so that by the time of Akhenaten (*c.* 1353 BC) it is clear that the priesthood of Amun held a vast share of the wealth – and doubtless power – in Egypt. Whether this fact affected the religious revolution attempted by Akhenaten to any degree is unclear, but Amun certainly suffered the brunt of Akhenaten's religious 'reform', the names and images of the god being zealously erased from temples throughout Egypt. In the period of restoration which followed the Amarna interlude the prestige and power of Amun were rapidly regained. By the time of Ramesses III Amun's holdings extended to a full one-third of the cultivable land in Egypt; and by the close of the New Kingdom the first priest of Amun was powerful enough to rival the contemporary pharaohs who ruled from the north. During the 21st dynasty a practice had been established in which the daughter of the reigning king was consecrated to Amun as the 'divine wife of Amun', a custom which helped maintain the balance between Egypt's earthly rulers and her divine king. The Kushite kings of the 25th dynasty continued this practice, and their rule actually led to a resurgence in the worship of Amun as the Nubians had accepted the god as their own. Even after the invading Assyrians sacked Thebes in 663 BC, Amun still held great sway in the religion of Egypt; the god was sought out and honoured by Alexander the Great and, under the name of Zeus-Ammon, continued to be worshipped throughout the Greek and Roman Periods.

The worship of Amun also extended to the non-formal veneration of popular religion. The god was regarded as an advocate of the common man, being called 'the vizier of the humble' and 'he who comes at the voice of the poor' (see p. 51), and as 'Amun of the Road' he was also regarded as the protector of travellers. Most amulets of the god do not seem to predate the Third Intermediate Period but are often made of expensive materials and seem to have been worn in life, perhaps by the priests in his service. The god was well represented in the spells and charms of Egyptian magic and seems to have been especially regarded as a god who cured eye ailments. His power was also invoked in spells against scorpions, crocodiles and other dangerous creatures.

Andjety

Mythology

The god Andjety (Egyptian 'he of Andjet') was the local god of the 9th Lower Egyptian nome (see Nome Deities) centred at Busiris, the ancient Andjet or Djedu in the Delta. The deity seems to have been one of the precursors of Osiris in the sense that he was eventually absorbed by that god who took over his attributes and characteristics (see Osiris). In the Pyramid Texts he is one of the gods with whom the deceased king is identified, and juxtaposed with Anubis, ruler of the west as 'Andjety who presides over the eastern nomes' (PT 220, 1833). Judging by his insignia (see below) and the earliest textual evidence, it is possible that Andjety may have originally been a locally deified dead king of Busiris or somehow personified the concept of rulership. Andjety also had clear fertility aspects. Even in the Pyramid Texts we find the substitution of a stylized uterus for the two feathers in the writing of the name of Andjety which probably reflects these aspects in some way, and in the Coffin Texts of the Middle Kingdom Andjety is also given the epithet 'bull of vultures', doubtless based on a mythological role as the consort of several early goddesses.

Iconography

Andjety was worshipped in anthropomorphic form, apparently as a deified ruler, and his iconography clearly demonstrates his influence on Osiris. From the beginning of the 4th dynasty he was depicted wearing a high conical crown decorated with two feathers very similar to the Atef Crown later worn by Osiris. Andjety also held two sceptres – a crook and flail – which likewise became Osirian insignia (see illus. p. 121).

Worship

The assimilation of Andjety by Osiris at an early date precludes a clear picture of the worship of the former god, but Andjety's position in the Pyramid Texts indicates a wide-ranging influence and worship of the deity in Lower Egypt in early times. He did continue as an independent deity after the rise of Osiris, but the two gods are seldom far removed in later times and from New Kingdom times may be combined, as in the funerary temple of Sethos I at Abydos where the king is depicted presenting incense to Osiris-Andjety – a clear fusion of Osiris with the deity who was perhaps his most important forerunner.

Arensnuphis

Mythology

An anthropomorphic deity of Meroitic Nubia, Arensnuphis' origins are unclear, but the god seems to have been indigenous to the area to the south of Egypt. Unfortunately, the Egyptian interpretation of his name as *Iry-hemes-nefer* – 'the good companion' – suggests only a benign deity, and provides no real indication of his origins or essential nature. In the temple of Arensnuphis at Philae the god is called the 'companion' of Isis, but this title does not seem to be based in any mythological background. It is more important that he was equated with the Egyptian gods Onuris and Shu, sometimes being merged with the latter as the syncretic deity Shu-Arensnuphis.

Iconography

Arensnuphis was usually depicted in the form of a man wearing a feathered crown, sometimes holding a spear. His association with Shu (see p. 129) and Onuris (see p. 118) probably led to similarities of iconography shared by these gods. Arensnuphis could also be depicted in the form of a lion, though in this form he may not be distinguishable from other lion gods.

Worship

The cult of Arensnuphis is first attested in Nubia at Musawwarat el-Sufra east of the Nile's sixth cataract in the 3rd century BC. The god's worship spread into Egyptian Nubia during the Graeco-Roman Period, and a small kiosk was jointly built and decorated for him on the island of Philae by Ptolemy IV (*c.* 221–205 BC) and the Meroitic king Arqamani (*c.* 218–200 BC). Arensnuphis was also depicted in the temple of Dendur near the first cataract of the Nile where he is shown worshipped by the Roman emperor Augustus.

Ash

Mythology

The name Ash cannot be analyzed as Egyptian and the god is often thought to be of foreign origin. Nevertheless, Ash appears to have been an ancient god and is first attested on seals and inscriptions of the Early Dynastic Period. He was venerated as the god of Egypt's western desert region, including the outlying oases and the area of Libya or 'Tehenu', and this gave the god a somewhat dual nature as he was associated both with the barren desert regions and, at the same time, with the fertile oases. Because he was venerated as god of the desert, a close association between Ash and the god Seth occurred from quite early times. This connection was enhanced by the fact that Ash appears to have been the original deity of Ombos (with the epithet 'nebuty' or 'he of Nebut' [Ombos]), the Upper Egyptian town which also became a cult centre of Seth.

Iconography

Ash is normally depicted in fully anthropomorphic form, but the god may also be depicted with the head of a hawk, or because of his association with Seth (see p. 197), the appearance of that god. It is possible that he is represented as a lion, vulture and serpent-headed being on a late coffin, though this is uncertain and the god is seldom depicted in the later dynastic periods.

Worship

The god was without an established cult but he was depicted in certain temple scenes, as in the 5th-dynasty pyramid temple of Sahure at Abusir.

Atum

Mythology

Atum was the great primeval deity of Heliopolis. His cult was a very ancient one and by the Old Kingdom he had risen to a very high level of importance in Heliopolitan theology. Atum is one of the

*The god **Atum**, his name written before him, seated within a solar disk on a divine barque. The image thus particularly reflects the important solar aspect of this deity. New Kingdom papyrus.*

eight or nine most frequently mentioned gods in the Pyramid Texts and we thus have a good deal of early information regarding the god's mythological roles and characteristics. His most essential nature is that of the 'self-engendered one' who arose at the beginning of time and who created the first gods through his semen – or, according to another story, through his saliva (see p. 17). Atum had many other facets, however. The word *tem* on which the name of the god is founded means 'complete' or 'finish' in both constructive and destructive senses, and this range of meanings fits well with a number of aspects of the god's nature.

Lord of totality: Atum was the monad – the one from whom all else originally came. One of the ways in which his name might be translated carries the idea of 'totality', and in the Coffin Texts and elsewhere he is specifically called the 'lord of totality' (CT III 27). From this perspective, everything which existed was a part of the 'flesh' of Atum, and every individual thing was said to be one of the millions of the god's *ka*s, a concept which not only stressed the god's primacy in coming before all else but also his importance as a universal god. By means of the magical formulae contained in the Pyramid Texts, the deceased king hoped to unite with Atum and thus become one with the supreme deity (PT 147).

Creator: According to the Heliopolitan cosmogony (see p. 17), Atum was god of the creative principle whereby the world was created from primeval chaos. In the Pyramid Texts the god was 'he who came into being' of himself (PT 1248), and this independence of prior causality was what allowed him to exist as creator. Atum's creative nature has two sides to it, however, because Atum can be seen as the one who completes everything and finishes everything. In this sense he is the uncreator as well as the creator. Thus, in the Book of the Dead, Atum states that at the end of the world he will destroy everything he has made and return to the form of the primeval serpent (BD 175).

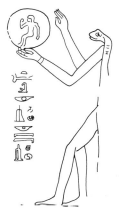

Atum in serpent form and as – or with – the young sun. The god's primal aspect gave him associations both with creatures such as the snake and the image of the newly born sun. Papyrus, Brooklyn Museum of Art.

*The god **Atum** (at right), invested with his distinctive Double Crown by Sethos I. 19th dynasty. Limestone relief, temple of Sethos I, Abydos.*

Father of the gods and the king: As the creator god Atum was the father of Shu and Tefnut, the first divine couple, and hence 'father of the gods' (PT 1521, 1546). According to the viewpoint of Egyptian mythology Atum copulated with himself to produce the first divine pair (PT 1248–49), with the hand utilized by the god in this act representing a personification of the female principle inherent within himself. Because the 'family tree' envisaged by the Heliopolitan theologians led from the god through Shu and Tefnut eventually to Osiris and his son Horus (see p. 18), Atum was also the genealogical father of the Egyptian king, and the Pyramid Texts make clear the father-son relationship was held to be a close one even from early times: 'O Atum, raise this king up to you, enclose him within your embrace, for he is your son of your body for ever' (PT 213).

Primal mound: Atum was not only viewed as the creator but also the original creation itself. He was thus the primeval mound which rose from the waters of creation and was represented in this aspect by the sacred *ben-ben* stone, which was worshipped at Heliopolis from the earliest dynasties and which may have originally been a meteorite or some other sacred stone.

The sun: Because the sun was regarded as a primary factor in the process of creation Atum was also linked to solar religion as the 'self-developing scarab' (PT 1587) who represented the newly created sun. In fact, in the Pyramid Texts and Coffin Texts Atum is often fused with the sun god as Re-Atum. When Re and Atum are viewed separately, Re is usually the rising sun of the day and Atum is the setting sun of the evening, but this is not always the case. In the Coffin Texts he is specifically said both to 'emerge from the eastern horizon' and to 'rest in the western horizon', so that he is in this way the complete sun. In funerary contexts, however, Atum was certainly more commonly the aged form of the sun which set each evening and travelled through the underworld before being reborn the following day. As such he plays an important role in many of the later mortuary books.

Chthonic god: As a primeval god and as the evening sun Atum had strong chthonic and underworld connections. His power is thus invoked in many netherworld scenarios. In the funerary books inscribed on the walls of the New Kingdom royal tombs in the Valley of the Kings, Atum is shown as an aged, ram-headed figure who supervises the punishment of evildoers and enemies of the sun god, and also subdues hostile netherworld forces such as the serpents Apophis and Nehebu-Kau. In non-royal funerary texts Atum also provides protection for the deceased from netherworld dangers.

Iconography

Atum is most frequently represented in anthropomorphic form and is usually depicted in this manner wearing the dual crown of Upper and Lower Egypt. He may also be represented with the head of a ram, though this is more usual in depictions showing his solar or underworld aspects. The god is often depicted seated on a throne and when standing he may be shown standing erect or, to stress his aged aspect, leaning on a staff.

*The god **Atum**, seated on a royal throne and crowned with the Double Crown of Egypt. 18th dynasty. Luxor Museum.*

*The 'body' or 'flesh' of **Atum** upon a serpent from the seventh hour of the Amduat. Like the sun god Re, with whom he was associated, Atum was constrained to pass through the netherworld regions in the cycle of death and regeneration.*

Zoomorphically, Atum could be represented or symbolized as a serpent in reference to his chthonic and primeval nature, and also, in other aspects, as a mongoose, lion, bull, or lizard, and as an ape – sometimes in this latter guise armed with a bow with which he shoots his enemies. In terms of his solar connections he may be depicted as a scarab, and the famous giant scarab statue which now stands by the sacred lake at Karnak was dedicated to Atum. Yet again, in terms of his primeval nature, Atum could also be represented by the image of the primeval hill, and in the First Intermediate Period 'Atum and his hand' appear as a divine couple.

Worship

Atum was perhaps the most important god originally worshipped at Heliopolis, although his cult was eventually eclipsed by that of Re (see p. 205). Atum retained a good deal of his importance, however. The god is often called 'Lord of Heliopolis', and even after the rise of Re his influence continued to be exerted in the solar cult centre. Atum's importance was by no means limited to the north, or to the Old Kingdom, however. It is Atum, along with the Theban god Montu, who escorts the king in New Kingdom representations in the temple of Amun at Karnak. Atum's close relationship with the Egyptian king is seen in many cultic rituals, and a papyrus dating to the Late Period in the Brooklyn Museum shows the god's importance in the New Year's festival in which the king's role was reconfirmed. Atum is relatively rarely encountered in the popular religion of ancient Egypt, but amulets and small reliquaries of lizards – which were one of his symbols – were worn in honour of the god in the Late Period.

Baal

Mythology

Baal was the West Semitic storm god, the equivalent of the Amorite deity Adad or Hadad, and the centrally important deity of the Canaanites. The Hebrew Bible records the ancient Israelites apostasizing interaction with this god, and Late Bronze Age texts found at Ras Shamra (the ancient Ugarit) on the Levantine coast show that by c. 1400 BC Baal had displaced the god El to become the most prominent deity in the local pantheon. Believed to be active in storms, he was known as 'rider of the clouds' and 'lord of heaven and earth'; he also controlled the earth's fertility. According to the surviving ancient Near Eastern myths, Baal vanquished Yam, the tyrannical god of the sea, but was eventually himself overcome by Mot, a personification of death, and descended into the underworld. Baal returned to life with the help of his sister-consort Anat in a manner similar to the death and resurrection of Osiris; and although

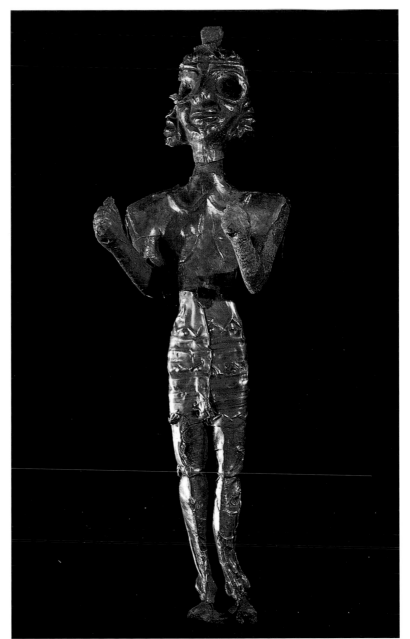

the two gods do not seem to have been directly connected in Egypt, the similar background may well have aided Baal's acceptance there. His bellicose nature as god of storms meant that he was naturally equated with the Egyptian god Seth, and Ramesses II himself was said to appear at the Battle of Kadesh like Seth and 'Baal himself'.

Iconography

Usually represented in anthropomorphic form, Baal was depicted as a powerful warrior, with long hair and a full, slightly curved Syrian-style beard. He wore a conical, funnel-like helmet with two horns attached at its base and often carried

*Gold and silver foil-covered image of the Canaanite god **Baal**. The god's name means 'lord' or 'master' and could apply to several deities with similar characteristics. Canaanite, c. 1900 BC.*

a straight-bladed sword at the belt of a short kilt. The god was also often depicted grasping a cedar tree club or spear in his left hand and a weapon or thunderbolt in his upraised right hand. This imagery is common to many Near Eastern storm gods and may have been the origin of the later iconography of the Greek god Zeus. Baal's cult animal was the bull – symbolizing his power and fertility – and in Near Eastern art he is frequently depicted standing on the back of a bull.

Worship

By the 18th dynasty Baal worship had penetrated Egypt, and the god was formally served at several sites, an important cult centre being located at Baal Saphon near Peluseum in the northern Delta. He was also popular at Memphis and in several other areas, his popularity being attested in Egyptian theophoric names during New Kingdom and later times.

Ba-Pef

God of uncertain nature, though probably a deity of pain or woe, Ba-Pef means simply 'that soul', but the use of the non-specific name implies fear or taboo of mentioning the god's real name. In the Pyramid Texts the netherworld house of Ba-Pef 'wherein is woe' is mentioned, but no other details are given. There is some evidence of a priesthood of Ba-Pef in Old Kingdom times (in the tomb of Meresankh III at Giza), though the god does not seem to have been of great importance in any period.

Bes

Mythology

The name Bes (perhaps from the word *besa*, 'to protect') is a relatively late term used to describe what are really a number of deities and demons of Egypt, perhaps not all originally related, though all of similar form. Perhaps ten separate gods – Aha, Amam, Bes, Hayet, Ihty, Mefdjet, Menew, Segeb, Sopdu and Tetetenu – share similar, if not identical, characteristics making 'Bes' a complex and not always clearly understood figure. Although the developed deity came to be one of the most popular and widespread of Egyptian gods, little can be said with certainty of his beginnings. In the past different scholars have assigned him both African and Near Eastern roots, but this is unnecessary and the god is attested in Egypt – if somewhat indirectly – since Old Kingdom times. He (or related deities such as Aha: 'fighter') appears on scores of artifacts of Middle Kingdom date, but it is not until the New Kingdom and later that Bes figures and images become truly widespread and reflect popular acceptance of the developed deity.

Despite his appearance, which changed in many details over time, Bes was deemed beneficent to humans and he was accepted by all classes of Egyptians as a powerful apotropaic deity. He was especially associated with the protection of children and of pregnant women and those giving birth and often depicted alongside Taweret in this role. Just as the Bes figure subsumed various minor gods and demons, in later times he was himself syncretized with other protective deities, forming the 'core' of a composite deity whose elements included Amun, Min, Horus, Sopdu, Reshef and other gods. Mythologically, Bes could also be associated with Re, Hathor and Horus – sometimes as the combined Horbes – and a female form of the god, Beset, sometimes appears as the mother of Horus.

Iconography

While the appearance of the god has been compared with models as diverse as African pygmies and with prehistoric Libyan images, James Romano demonstrated a number of years ago that the origin of the Bes iconography is most likely to be found in the image of a male lion rearing up on its hind paws. Later aspects of the deity – from New Kingdom times – also display characteristics of achondroplastic dwarfism so that in his developed form the god is usually portrayed as dwarf-like with shortened legs and an enlarged head which is usually depicted from the front in two-dimensional representations. His mask-like and invariably bearded features frame large staring eyes and a protruding tongue, and he is often depicted with the mane of a lion and a lion's tail, which preserve his leonine origins. Some Egyptologists believe that these are remnants of an original iconography in

(Left) **Bes** figures – typically brandishing knives or playing musical instruments – were often associated with the hippopotamus goddess Taweret, as on this arm panel from the chair of Princess Sitamun from the Valley of the Kings. Egyptian Museum, Cairo.

(Right) The leonine figure of this unguent jar from the tomb of Tutankhamun exhibits several aspects and attributes of the god **Bes** and may have been chosen because of the lion's connection with Bes. 18th dynasty. Egyptian Museum, Cairo.

which the god wore a lionskin cape rather than physically possessing these characteristics. After the New Kingdom Bes is sometimes depicted wearing the leopard skin worn in certain ritual contexts. For much of his history Bes is also frequently depicted wearing a plumed headdress and he is often given a large belly and sometimes protruding breasts – probably tying him to his role as a patron and protector of pregnant women.

Because Bes was believed to provide protection from snakes, he is frequently depicted holding or biting serpents, and in this form he assimilated, or was himself an avatar of, the demon Aha who strangled serpents in his bare hands. Representations of Bes also commonly carry musical instruments, knives, or the hieroglyphic *sa* sign signifying protection, as these attributes all reinforced the god's protective nature. Unlike other representations of the god, those showing him dancing with musical instruments or with snakes frequently show him in profile view as was necessary for indicating movement.

From the Third Intermediate Period on, images of just the head or mask of Bes occur both as independent amulets and as parts of other compositions – the power of the mask alone being clearly considered to be sufficient for protective purposes. Conversely, in his later composite form Bes is depicted as the head and sometimes body of a four-armed, winged and many-headed god with the tail of a falcon and the attributes of many of the deities with whom he was combined. In the Graeco-Roman Period images of the god sometimes carry a sword and circular shield to heighten his protective qualities or perhaps because he was adopted as a military deity. The effect is heightened in Roman times when he is sometimes shown wearing the full costume of a legionary.

Worship

Although not worshipped in any formal temple cult, Bes was widely venerated as a protective deity in the later dynastic periods of Egyptian history. The image of the god protected the mammisi or

Faience image of **Bes** holding an infant in his role as protector of childbirth. The tall plumed crown of the god is common in his iconography from the 18th dynasty. Harer Collection, San Bernardino.

he protected the sleeper, as well as on mirrors, unguent jars and other cosmetic items, as unguents and cosmetics were used for protection from inimical influences as well as for adornment. In the same way, and in addition to the Bes-like figures of the so-called magical 'knives' or 'wands' of the Middle Kingdom, the image of Bes surmounted that of the infant Horus on many of the much later protective and healing-related plaques known as *cippi* of Horus. Individuals may have dressed in Bes masks or costumes to perform dances aimed at protection, and an example of a lion/Bes mask found by Petrie in a Middle Kingdom house at Kahun showed signs of frequent wear and repair, possibly indicating a professional role for the wearer. Another aspect of the god is prominent in Ptolemaic times from which we find 'incubation' or 'Bes chambers' with images of Bes and a naked goddess that seem to have been used in healing rituals.

The popularity of Bes spread well beyond Egypt, and images of the god have been found on ivory work from Cyprus, from Syria, and from Nimrud in Assyria.

Celestial Ferryman

The 'Celestial Ferryman' of Egyptological literature represents a deity of numerous names. Frequently attested in the Pyramid Texts, the god ferries the deceased king across the 'Shifting Waterway' (which may perhaps be identified with the ecliptic – the apparent path of the sun and planets through the heavens), to the abode of Re, or to the afterlife 'field of offerings' (PT 999, etc.). The divine ferryman is known as Her-ef-ha-ef 'He whose face is behind him' or by any of a dozen other names – many of which have similar meaning such as Ma-ha-ef 'He whose sight is behind him' – and which seem to be linked to his role. Less frequently attested in later periods, the god is sometimes depicted in the vignettes of the New Kingdom funerary texts seated or standing in his barque and being hailed by the deceased. In the Papyrus of Ani he is shown, according to many of his descriptive names, with his head facing backwards.

*Protective images of **Bes** such as this surmounted the columns of the Roman mammisi or birth house at Dendera.*

birth houses of temples in the Graeco-Roman Period and perhaps earlier, and the figure of Bes has also been found painted in rooms ranging from the palace of Amenophis III at Malqata to the workmen's houses at Deir el-Medina – perhaps all being rooms associated with childbirth or children. The vast range of objects upon which Bes was depicted and the large number of his images and amulets demonstrate his great popularity as a household deity. His image was incorporated into jewelry and his amulets were worn in life, and the god is frequently depicted on headrests and beds, where

Mythology

Originally a Nubian deity, Dedwen was known in Egypt from at least Old Kingdom times when the king is identified with 'Dedwen, who presides over Nubia' in the Pyramid Texts (PT 994, 1476). At a very early date Dedwen had come to represent not only Nubia but also its resources, and especially incense – which was imported into Egypt from the south. The god was thus identified as the supplier of incense for the gods and was also said to burn incense at royal births (PT 803, 1017).

Iconography

Depicted anthropomorphically, Dedwen was portrayed as a male deity, usually with no special characteristics and sometimes differentiated only by name. In the Old Kingdom his name was sometimes written with the hieroglyphic sign for a certain type of bird, but the god himself was not depicted in avian form or with the head of a bird. At Kalabsha Dedwen is depicted with the head of a lion, and the god could also be assimilated to Amun or Khnum in the form of a ram.

Worship

Apart from his association (through incense) with the cults of Egyptian gods and kings, the worship of Dedwen seems to have remained largely limited to Nubia itself. However, the god was honoured in many pharaonic temples built in Nubia. Dedwen was included, for example, with other deities in a small temple built by Tuthmosis III at el-Lessiya; and on the island of Uronarti near Semna, a temple (perhaps of Middle Kingdom origin) was dedicated to Dedwen and Senwosret III by Tuthmosis. A Late Ptolemaic granite chapel at Kalabsha, re-erected in the 1960s on the new site just south of Aswan, was also dedicated to Dedwen.

Mythology

A third-generation deity, the son of Shu and Tefnut, Geb was the god who personified the earth and was one of the most important of Egypt's primeval gods. His stature since early times is seen in the fact that he is one of the most frequently mentioned deities found in the Pyramid Texts, where he is often juxtaposed with Re or other gods who were of great importance in Egyptian afterlife beliefs. The god's power was sometimes inimical. Earthquakes came of his laughter and he could withhold his blessings in dry times or in barren areas. More importantly, as god of the earth *par excellence*, Geb could also represent the grave and it is stated in the Pyramid Texts, for example, that the deceased king 'will not enter into Geb' or 'sleep within his house' (PT 308). Geb usually had a more beneficent aspect, however. As god of the earth, grain was said to sprout from his ribs and vegetation from his back. He was also the source of fresh waters and ultimately all that the earth produced so that Geb was directly associated with the fertility of both the earth and livestock; and Hapy, bountiful god of the Nile inundation, was said to be the 'friend of Geb'.

As the son of Atum and Shu, Geb was the 'heir of the gods', and as father of Osiris, the mythical king, Geb also maintained a strong association with kingship. The Egyptian king himself was called the 'heir of Geb' and was said to sit upon 'the seat of Geb'. The god was thus involved in the transmission of kingship, and in the mythical story known as the 'Contendings of Horus and Seth' (preserved in the 20th-dynasty Papyrus Chester Beatty I), it is Geb who acts as the presiding judge in determining the rightful heir to the throne. This role of support for the king is present even as early as the Pyramid Texts where Geb champions the king as Horus over Seth.

*(Left) 'He whose face is behind him' is one of the many names of the god often called the '**Celestial Ferryman**'. Papyrus of Ani, British Museum.*

*(Right) The enthroned **Geb** is represented in both the Red and White Crowns on this gold and lapis lazuli bracelet of 17th-dynasty Queen Ahhotep from western Thebes. Egyptian Museum, Cairo.*

The late tradition, unattested before the 30th dynasty, that Geb lusted after his own mother and violated her upon his father's death, appears to have been based on the Greek myth of the usurpation of the place of Ouranos by his son Chronos whom the Greeks identified directly with Geb.

Iconography

As with other cosmic deities Geb was usually represented anthropomorphically. He may be depicted as a man wearing the crown of Lower Egypt, or in terms of his mythological role, reclining on his side supporting himself with one arm beneath the personified sky. In such scenes his phallus may be shown stretching upwards toward the goddess Nut, signifying their relationship. Geb's mythological associations meant that he could, however, also be represented as a white-fronted goose (a creature associated with creation) or as a man with a goose on his head, and in the tomb of Ramesses VI the figure of Geb is represented with the head of a hare. In any of his forms Geb may be depicted with green skin in order to symbolize his fertile nature and the vegetation which springs from him, and in some cases his body is decorated with plants.

Worship

Although not honoured with a major cult of his own, Geb was represented in many temple scenes and was also important in some aspects of popular religion. The god was associated with healing and was particularly invoked in spells combating scorpion stings. His healing powers were wide-ranging, and one magical text describes how Osiris

commanded Geb to restrain the malicious spirits which caused colds and fevers.

Ha

Ha was a desert deity, of fairly limited importance outside the arid regions, but of some significance in the western deserts and their oases where he was thought to provide protection from enemies such as desert nomads and invading Libyan tribesmen. The god is attested as early as the 3rd dynasty and his association with the western regions increased as time progressed. Depicted anthropomorphically, Ha is recognized by the three hills of the hieroglyphic symbol for 'desert' or 'foreign lands' which he wore on his head. Sometimes he is depicted with a knife or bow as a symbol of his protective role. The titles of priests of Ha have survived, but little more is known of any cult of the god.

Hapy

Mythology

The god Hapy (to be distinguished from the son of Horus with the same name – see p. 88) was primarily identified by the Egyptians as the inundation of the Nile – its yearly flooding which brought fertility to the land through widespread watering and the new silt spread over the fields by the swollen river. While it is often stated that Hapy was purely this inundation rather than simply the Nile itself, there are some indications of overlap, so that it is sometimes possible to characterize the god as representing the divine power of the Nile in general. More usually, however, Hapy is clearly the Nile Flood and the inundation was called by the Egyptians 'the arrival of Hapy'. The Nile was both the primary source of life in ancient Egypt and, by virtue of its cyclic rhythm, a manifestation of cosmic order so that Hapy is thus called creator god and even 'father of the gods' due to his life-giving and creative ability. He was also appealed to as a caring father and a god who maintained balance in the cosmos. Although the Nile was usually predictable, occasional weather disruptions in sub-Saharan Africa meant that severe famine could result from occasional excessively low or high levels of flooding, and thus it was Hapy who held the key to this proper balance of flooding and fertility. As a result of his nature Hapy was called 'lord of the fishes and birds', and numerous crocodile gods and frog goddesses were in his retinue. The power of Hapy was also expressed as both chthonic and sexual. The Late Period Famine Stela expresses these ideas in stating 'It [the cavern which is the god's dwelling] is the house of sleep of Hapy,…he brings the flood: Leaping up he copulates as man copulates with woman…' – imagery which was applied

Geb, god of the earth, reclines beneath his spouse Nut from whom he is separated by the air god, Shu. The body of Geb is covered with hieroglyphs for 'reed' suggesting his fertile nature. Detail from the Papyrus of Tentamun, 21st dynasty. Bibliothéque Nationale, Paris.

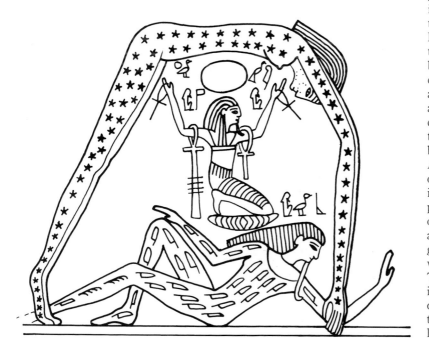

to many of the gods who represented aspects of fertility and primeval creation.

Iconography

Representations of Hapy usually show the god as a swollen-bellied man wearing an abbreviated belt or loincloth and with long hair and pendulous, female breasts. Often, the god was depicted with a clump of papyrus upon his head, and he is frequently shown carrying papyrus and lotus stems and bearing a tray laden with offerings. Most often he was shown with blue skin, though other colours are occasionally found. All of these attributes represented the fertility Hapy supplied and as such were interchangeable with those of other so-called fecundity figures (see p. 131). Beginning in the 5th dynasty (in the mortuary temple of Sahure), the lower registers of temple walls were often decorated with depictions of Hapy and other fecundity figures bearing offerings into the temple as gifts and sustaining supplies for the temple's divine owners. Statues showing Hapy bearing loaded offering trays were also made – sometimes with the features of the reigning king, thus linking the monarch with the fecundity deity.

Beginning in the 19th dynasty, reliefs portraying two figures of Hapy, one wearing the papyrus of Lower Egypt and the other the heraldic plant of Upper Egypt, and binding together the two halves of Egypt (symbolized by the respective plants being used as ropes around the *sema* or 'union' hieroglyph) were often carved on temple walls and on the bases of colossal seated statues of kings. An instance of Hapy depicted with the double head of a goose appears in the temple of Sethos I at Abydos.

Dual depictions of **Hapy** *– representing Upper and Lower Egypt – tie the symbolic plants of the two lands together in the sema-tawy motif. The corpulent bodies of the gods and the plants atop their heads suggest the bounty of the Nile's inundation which they represent. Throne decoration, colossal statue of Ramesses II, Luxor Temple. 19th dynasty.*

107

*The god **Hapy**, 'father of the gods', clasping symbols of life, receives the worship of Ramesses III in a scene of harvest and fertility. 20th dynasty. Mortuary temple of Ramesses III, Medinet Habu, western Thebes.*

Worship

Hapy was especially worshipped in areas where the Nile was particularly turbulent such as Gebel el-Silsila and near the supposed source of the Nile where the god was believed to dwell in a cavern in the vicinity of Aswan. Although it was said of Hapy that 'he has no shrines, nor portions, no service of his choice' (The Hymn to Hapy), he was widely venerated outside his cult centres and frequently depicted in the temples of other deities. One text, relating how 1,089 goats were sacrificed to Hapy, shows something of his importance. Many Egyptians celebrated the god's annual festival and composed hymns and paeans of praise to him.

Hauron

Mythology

The Canaanite god Hauron was a somewhat obscure deity of the desert and the earth, perhaps, according to Canaanite mythology, a son of Astarte. Hauron may have been a god associated with herdsmen and those who wandered the desert areas; in Egypt he was known as 'the victorious herdsman'. He is attested in Egyptian texts from Middle Kingdom times in the form of a Canaanite theophoric name, but the appearance of Hauron as an adopted Egyptian deity seems to date to around the time of Amenophis II at the earliest. The god was associated with the Great Sphinx at Giza, but the reason for the equation is not clear. Perhaps it was as a result of the presence of Canaanite or Syrian workers who were located in the area of the Sphinx, or it may have been as a result of some mythological connection which is no longer evident.

Iconography

Hauron was usually depicted in anthropomorphic form as an armed man, but he could also appear in other ways. In a famous statue in the Egyptian Museum in Cairo the god is represented in the form

of a falcon standing behind and protecting the crouching figure of Ramesses II who is shown as a child.

Worship

A temple or chapel of this god, the 'house of Hauron', was constructed in front of the Great Sphinx at Giza in New Kingdom times. Hauron also obviously entered Egyptian popular religion in his capacity of divine herdsman, as a spell to be cast over a field is known which invokes a number of deities – including Hauron – to protect cattle from attacks by wild animals.

Heh

Mythology

Heh was the personification of infinity – usually in the temporal sense of eternity. In hieroglyphic writing the figure of Heh was used to denote a million. The god was thus associated with the idea of millions of years and is sometimes paired with the female deity Hauhet representing the alternative Egyptian word for eternity, *djet*. Mythologically, however, Heh – along with his consort Hauhet – was a member of the ogdoad of eight primeval deities worshipped at Hermopolis Magna. The god was also associated with the myth of the 'celestial cow' who was supported by Shu and eight Heh deities – two at each leg – and with the solar barque which Heh (or Nun) lifted back into the sky at the end of its nocturnal journey through the netherworld.

Iconography

Heh is depicted in male anthropomorphic form, with divine wig and beard, usually kneeling and

*(Below left) The god **Hauron** in falcon form. Statue of Ramesses II from Tanis, Egyptian Museum, Cairo. The statue base is inscribed 'Ramesses, beloved of Hauron'. 19th dynasty.*

*(Below) **Heh**, the personification of infinity, holds the notched palm branches which were the ancient method of recording time and thus the hieroglyphic signs for 'years'. Detail of decorated chair of Tutankhamun. 18th dynasty. Egyptian Museum, Cairo.*

grasping in each hand a notched palm branch which was used for ceremonial time/record-keeping in the temples and was thus used as the hieroglyphic symbol for 'years'. Sometimes a palm branch is also placed on the god's head. In detailed representations the palm branches are given additional elements such as the tadpole glyph for '100,000' or the *shen* ring of 'eternity'. The god often kneels on a basket signifying 'all' or universality, and may have *ankh* signs suspended from his hands or arms. Heh deities may also be depicted in the mythological settings described above – supporting the celestial cow or the solar barque of Re.

Worship

These iconographic characteristics reinforced the use of the figure of Heh to express the wish of millions of years of life or rule, so that the god is frequently depicted in amulets from as early as late Old Kingdom times, and in royal iconography – especially on household or personal items associated with the king. A number of objects from the tomb of Tutankhamun, for example, were decorated with the figure of Heh, and these would indicate that the god's presence was an important addition to the New Kingdom royal funerary assemblage.

Heka

Mythology

For the Egyptians, *heka* or 'magic' was a divine force which existed in the universe like 'power' or 'strength' and which could be personified in the form of the god Heka. Mythologically, *heka* was believed to have existed from the time of creation and to have empowered the creation event so that the god Heka could likewise be seen as a creator god. At Esna, although doubtless based on a late popular etymology, his name is thus explained as 'the first work'. Magic empowered all the gods, and Heka was also a god of power whose name was tied to this meaning from the 20th dynasty onward by being written emblematically with the hieroglyph for 'power', although originally the god's name may have meant 'he who consecrates the *ka*', and he is called 'Lord of the *ka*s' in the Coffin Texts (CT 261). Because of his great power the Pyramid Texts make it clear that Heka was feared by the gods themselves (PT 472), and he was said to accompany the sun god in his barque as well as to protect the god Osiris in the underworld.

Iconography

Invariably portrayed in anthropomorphic form, Heka was usually represented as a man, with the usual garb and curved beard of the gods. In the Late Period, however, Heka was venerated in the form of a child – as were several other male deities – and was thus shown accompanying various divine couples as their 'son' in a number of representations.

Worship

Like most deities representing areas or aspects of the cosmos, Heka was not served by a regular cult, though his role in religion was of considerable importance. He was naturally invoked in many magico-religious contexts and at Esna in Roman times, for example, a statue of the god was taken in procession from the temple through the surrounding fields to ensure their productivity. Heka also played a role in afterlife beliefs. Because he was viewed as a god of inestimable power, the Pyramid Texts directly claim his authority (PT 539) and the Coffin Texts contain a spell 'to become the god Heka' (CT 261).

Horus

see p. 200, *Avian Deities* section

Hu

Hu personified the concept of 'authoritative utterance' and was thus closely connected to ideas of power and control. He was said to have come into being from a drop of blood from the phallus of the sun god and therefore was tied to the power of the pre-eminent deity Re. However, he is also closely linked – at least conceptually – with the Memphite idea of creation, in which the god Ptah created the universe through his own authoritative utterance (see p. 123). Hu is often found in connection with Sia, the personification of perception, understanding or knowledge, especially in contexts such as creation or the sun god's journey through the underworld. Hu's association with the netherworld

and afterlife is an early one. In the Pyramid Texts the god appears as the companion of the deceased king in the heavens (PT 251), and these texts repeatedly assert that the king assumes authority – in one instance explicitly saying 'authority [Hu] has bowed his head to me' (PT 697) – showing that the king maintains his monarchical authority and has power over the forces of the afterlife. Hu was rarely represented pictorially, but is sometimes depicted as an anthropomorphic deity and appears as such in scenes showing the boat of Re and his attendant deities in the underworld.

Iah

Iah was a lunar god whose name means 'Moon' and who is known from relatively early times. Originally an independent deity, he was later largely absorbed by Khonsu and is thus viewed sometimes as an adult form of that god and sometimes independently. Iah appears in the Pyramid Texts where the deceased king announces that the moon (Iah) is his brother (PT 1001) and father (PT 1104), but by New Kingdom times Khonsu and Thoth play more dominant roles as lunar deities. Nevertheless, Iah is found as an amulet and in other representations in later dynasties he is depicted as a standing man, often wrapped in the same manner as Khonsu, and wearing the same full and crescent moon symbols, though often these are surmounted by an Atef Crown with yet another disk above it. In addition to the divine beard, the god usually wears a long tripartite wig rather than the sidelock of Khonsu, and may also carry a tall staff. To a lesser degree Iah was also fused with Thoth and may be depicted as ibis-headed like that god. One of Tutankhamun's pectorals has a winged scarab holding up the boat of the lunar eye above which is a crescent moon and disc – imagery that could refer to Iah.

Imhotep

Mythology

A high official of the 3rd dynasty, Imhotep is best known as the vizier and 'overseer of works' of King Djoser, for whom he constructed the great Step Pyramid complex at Saqqara – the first Egyptian pyramid and the world's first known monumental stone structure. Although apparently a commoner by birth, he served as a priest of Ptah and his connection with the god led eventually to the myth that he was the son of Ptah by a human mother named Khreduankh. During his lifetime Imhotep rose through the ranks of temple and government offices to become a high priest and courtier of great importance. In addition to his work as architect, he seems to have been a man of considerable learning associated with many other intellectual achievements and he became a patron of medicine, of writing and of knowledge in general. Although his medical achievements are not contemporaneously documented, the fact that Imhotep became known

Step pyramid of Djoser, Saqqara. The greatest accomplishment of the 'overseer of works' **Imhotep***, the step pyramid became the basis of the architect's lasting fame and eventual veneration.*

(Left) The god **Hu***, directly in front of the deceased, stands with Khepri, Thoth and Isis in this afterlife scene. 20th dynasty. Tomb of Inherkha, western Thebes.*

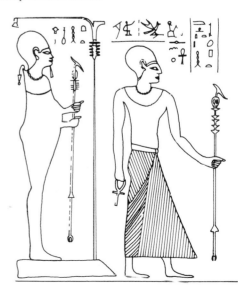

(Right) The deified **Imhotep** *(at right) shown before the craftsman god Ptah with whom he was often associated. Private stela, Saqqara. Late/Ptolemaic Period.*

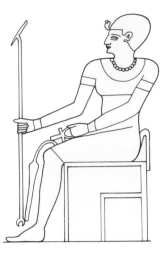

*(Right) The scholar and architect **Imhotep** is often shown enthroned and accorded full attributes of divinity in images from the Late Period and Graeco-Roman era.*

*(Below) In the Ptolemaic Period inner sanctuary of the temple of Hatshepsut at Deir el-Bahri, **Imhotep** was venerated along with the deified Amenophis Son of Hapu (not shown).*

Iconography

Surviving statue fragments from Saqqara demonstrate that Imhotep was granted the unique privilege of being named alongside his king, Djoser, in formal statuary, but representations of the priestly architect are not known till much later. Nevertheless, from the Late Period onwards votive bronzes and other small sculptures as well as amulets of Imhotep were common. Usually he is depicted in scribal fashion, seated and wearing a long kilt and skull-cap or shaven head with a papyrus roll unscrolled across his lap to symbolize his scholarly nature and scribal patronage.

Worship

The veneration of Imhotep grew to deification in the Late Period and the Graeco-Roman era when his cult reached its zenith, and a number of shrines and temples were dedicated to the deified scholar. His main areas of worship appear to have been in the area of Saqqara, on the island of Philae, and at Thebes where he was also worshipped along with the deified 18th-dynasty sage Amenophis Son of Hapu at Deir el-Bahri and in the Ptolemaic temple at Deir el-Medina. An important inscription regarding him was placed in the temple of Ptah at Karnak in

as a virtual medical demigod within a century or so of his death seems to indicate that he may well have been a highly skilled physician. As a result of his reputation for learning, Imhotep was also linked to the cult of the god Thoth. The tomb of Imhotep has never been found, though it is possible that the large uninscribed mastaba numbered 3,518 at Saqqara is in fact that structure.

the reign of Tiberius. His cult centres were places of pilgrimage for sufferers who prayed and slept there in the hope that the god would heal them or reveal remedies to them through inspired dreams. As the patron of medicine he was identified by the Greeks with their god of medicine, Asklepius, and his cult centre at Saqqara is called the 'Asklepion'. Mummified ibises were left by worshippers as votive offerings for Imhotep in the underground catacombs in this area, and pilgrims also left models of injured limbs or diseased organs there in the hope of being healed by the god. While Imhotep's position as a deified commoner was not unique in ancient Egypt, he was unrivalled in the high degree and widespread level of veneration he received.

Khonsu

Mythology

The god Khonsu was a moon god whose earliest attested character is considerably different from his later manifestation in New Kingdom Thebes where he appears as the benign son of Amun and Mut. In the Pyramid Texts he appears in the famous 'Cannibal Hymn' as a bloodthirsty deity who assists the deceased king in catching and slaying those gods that the king 'feeds upon' in order to absorb their strength (PT 402). Later the god appears to have been associated with childbirth, but it is in his role as an integral member of the all-powerful Theban triad (Amun, Mut, Khonsu) that Khonsu is best known. There Khonsu was primarily viewed as a lunar god, but he exhibited several different aspects, appearing among other forms as Khonsu *pa-khered* ('Khonsu the Child'); Khonsu *pa-ir-sekher* 'Khonsu the provider' (the Chespisichis of the Greeks); Khonsu *heseb-ahau* 'Khonsu, decider of the life span'; and Khonsu *em-waset nefer-hetep* 'Khonsu in Thebes Neferhotep' – apparently the most important Theban manifestation of the god. The various forms of the god interacted with one another as can be seen from the inscription known as the Bentresh Stela – inscribed in Thebes in the 4th century BC but purporting to record a pronouncement of Ramesses II some 800 years earlier. The stela tells how the Egyptian king loaned a statue of Khonsu *pa-ir-sekher* to the king of Bakhtan to aid in the healing of his daughter, Bentresh, and includes discourse between this form of Khonsu and the more senior Khonsu in Thebes. Although firmly associated with Amun and Mut at Thebes, at Kom Ombo Khonsu was regarded as the son of Sobek and Hathor, and at Edfu Temple Khonsu was linked to Osiris as 'the son of the leg', referring to the relic of the netherworld god said to be preserved at that site. As a moon god Khonsu was also sometimes associated with Shu, god of the air, and with Horus. Like Thoth, he participated in the reckoning of time and was believed to influence the gestation of both humans and animals. In the past the name of Khonsu was thought to be derived from the elements *kh* 'placenta' and *nesu* 'king' as a personification of the royal placenta, but it is now generally believed to be based on the verb *khenes* 'to cross over' or 'to traverse', meaning 'he who traverses [the sky]'.

Iconography

Khonsu is usually depicted in anthropomorphic form – most often as a young man enveloped in mummy bandages or a tightly fitting garment, though his arms may be partially or completely unrestrained. He frequently wears his lunar symbol consisting of the full lunar disk resting in a crescent new moon upon his head; in his role as divine child of Amun and Mut he commonly wears the sidelock of youth, though he may also wear the curved beard of the gods. The god was often depicted holding the crook and flail associated with Osiris and Horus, and a *was* or *djed*-headed staff (see illustration below),

*Black and red granite statue of **Khonsu** with the features of Tutankhamun. The sidelock of youth and the curved divine beard are both characteristic of the god's iconography. Egyptian Museum, Cairo.*

but his most distinctive attribute is usually the necklace he wears with its crescent-shaped pectoral element resting on his chest and its heavy counterpoise on his back. This counterpoise is usually depicted in an inverted 'keyhole' shape and can be used to differentiate the god from representations of the god Ptah whose necklace counterpoise is of a different shape. As a sky deity Khonsu can also be depicted with the head of a falcon – usually differentiated from Horus and Re by the lunar disk and crescent. As a lunar deity one of his symbols was the *Cynocephalus* baboon, though Khonsu himself does not appear in this form as frequently as does the god Thoth. Small amulets representing Khonsu in human form are known from the later dynasties, as are plaques depicting the god in fully human or falcon-headed form, sometimes with his divine parents Amun and Mut, or like Horus, standing on the back of a crocodile on the healing plaques known as *cippi* (see p. 132).

Worship

Khonsu had many sanctuaries throughout Egypt, but his main cult centre was Thebes. Begun in the 20th dynasty by Ramesses III and completed by a number of later rulers, the temple of Khonsu was erected within the precincts of the great Amun temple at Karnak. In certain of his festivals – such as the New Year's festival at the temple of Luxor where the god participated in the celebrations with his parents, Amun and Mut – the cult statue of Khonsu was transported from his precinct at Karnak on a sacred barque which was identified by a falcon's head at its prow and stern. The god processed along his own statue-lined avenue running from his temple to Luxor indicating his importance in this and other festivals. Khonsu's fame as a god of healing was also widespread and enhanced in later times by the fact that he was believed to have personally healed one of Egypt's kings, Ptolemy IV, who called himself 'beloved of Khonsu who protects the king and drives away evil spirits'.

Khonsu in his falcon-headed form with the characteristic attributes of disk and crescent moon. 20th dynasty. Tomb of Montuherkhepeshef, Valley of the Kings, western Thebes.

Mandulis

Mythology

A local solar god of the Lower Nubian region, whose actual Egyptian name was Merwel, this god is usually called Mandulis – the Greek version of his name. Little is known of the god's origins or early history but his nature was undoubtedly solar, and a late text known as the 'Vision of Mandulis' equates him quite naturally with Horus and with the Greek god Apollo. He was also equated with the Greek Helios and at Philae he was called the 'companion' of Isis.

Iconography

Mandulis was depicted in anthropomorphic form wearing a crown of ram-horns, sun disks and cobras surmounted by tall plumes. He could also be represented in the form of a human-headed bird, not unlike the Egyptian *ba* bird, but wearing the god's complex characteristic crown.

Worship

Although he was worshipped throughout Lower Nubia, the best evidence for the cult of Mandulis is found at New Kalabsha where the god is represented along with various Egyptian deities on the walls of the re-sited Roman Period temple. The remains

showing that his cult was already established. He is also found in the Coffin Texts where the deceased associates himself with the 'woman-hunting' Min in order to possess the god's sexual powers. During the Middle Kingdom Min became associated with the god Horus as Min-Hor and as a result he was sometimes described as the son of Isis, though the association also led to Min being worshipped as the consort of Isis and father of Horus. As god of the eastern regions and because of his associations with sexuality and fertility, it was natural that Min gained as consort the Syrian goddess Qadesh whom he shared with the Syrian storm god Reshep. Of greatest importance to the mythological history of Min is the fact that during the 18th dynasty the god became increasingly associated with Amun of Thebes and became in essence the manifestation of Amun as primeval creator god, somewhat analogous to Atum's relationship with Re at Heliopolis. The Amun-Min association had direct political overtones, however, and from Middle Kingdom times the coronations and jubilee festivals of the pharaoh seem to have incorporated rituals of Min aimed at promoting the potency of the king. This form of Min revered in the Theban area was known as Min-Amun-*ka-mutef* or simply Amun *ka-mutef* 'Amun, bull of his mother'. The Greeks associated Min with their god Pan.

Iconography

Min was usually depicted in fully anthropomorphic form as a wrapped or mummified ithyphallic man standing upright and wearing a cap or crown to which long streamers are attached and surmounted by two tall plumes. His legs are always held tightly together – either as a result of his swathed body or in continuity of the form of the earliest sculptural representations of the god – and only his erect penis, held in his left hand, and right arm project from the wrappings enveloping his body. The god's right arm is raised with his hand extended upwards and appears to be held behind him in two-dimensional representations, though sculptural works make it clear that this is a result of artistic convention and the arm is in reality held upward at the god's right side. The gesture is not really understood, but may well be protective or smiting in nature, as this appears to be its meaning among several other Near Eastern raised-arm deities. Usually a flail is placed on or above the god's raised arm. Representations of Min may depict him with various other items such as a collar or pectoral and braces, but none of these items is a fixed attribute. In coloured representations the god's skin is always black, perhaps symbolic of the black soil which was the basis of all fertility in Egypt. Min was depicted as a falcon in the 5th Upper Egyptian nome, but this was not a standard aspect of the god's iconography, while in his cult centres of Gebtu and Khent-Min, the god was

(Left) The Nubian god **Mandulis** *in the form of a human ba but with his characteristic plumed crown. Ptolemaic Period. Temple of Kalabsha, Nubia.*

(Below) Bronze figurine of the god **Min**. *While the ithyphallic nature of the god clearly relates to his fertility role, the significance of his raised arm is not fully understood. Late Period. Egyptian Museum, Cairo.*

of a chapel dedicated to the god may also be seen adjacent to the eastern colonnade of the Great Temple of Isis at Philae.

Min

Mythology

Min was one of Egypt's most ancient and enduring deities, acting as the supreme god of male sexual procreativity and as a deity of the eastern desert regions throughout dynastic history. The origin of his name, Menu, is unknown and gives us no clue to his nature, though the Greek writer Plutarch claimed that it meant 'that which is seen', doubtless based on a similarity with a form of the verb to see. That he was already worshipped in predynastic times is seen in the early presence of his emblem and in the three apparently predynastic colossal statues of the god discovered by Petrie at Coptos in 1893 and now in Oxford's Ashmolean Museum. Although not mentioned by name in the Pyramid Texts, Min may be the god referred to as the deity 'who raises his arm in the east', and a reference to the 'procession of Min' occurs in a 5th-dynasty tomb at Giza,

worshipped in the form of a white bull, which clearly represented Min's sexual potency. The cos lettuce (*Lactuca sativa*) which was often depicted in pots or on offering tables with the god from the 6th dynasty through Roman times was also a sexual reference, as the milky white sap of the lettuce seems to have been viewed as symbolic of semen and the plant may have been considered an aphrodisiac. The strange emblem of Min may also be an iconographic clue to the god's original character, but it remains enigmatic, having been interpreted as everything from a fossil belemnite and a lightning bolt to the sliding bolt of the god's shrine.

Worship

Although Min was venerated throughout Egypt, two cities were particularly associated with the god. The oldest site is that called by the Greeks Coptos and the Egyptians Gebtu (the modern Qift, between Qena and Luxor) at the western end of the Wadi Hammamat which led to the mining regions of the eastern desert – and hence represented Min's role as a tutelary deity of that area. The original

god of Gebtu may have been the ithyphallic Rahes who is called 'Foremost of Upper Egypt' in the Pyramid Texts, and it was this god that was represented with Min in falcon form on the 5th Upper Egyptian nome sign, though the creatures were later identified as Horus and Min. Archaeological evidence of the worship of Min dating to the Old Kingdom has been found at Coptos as well as in the foundation deposits of a New Kingdom temple, though the surviving ruins are of Graeco-Roman date. The other major site associated with Min was Khent-Min or 'Shrine of Min' which the Greeks called Panopolis (the modern Akhmim, near Sohag), and the emblem of the nome standard in this area was the Min emblem itself. Khent-Min was the home of the high priest of Min Yuya, who was the father-in-law of Amenophis III and father of Tutankhamun's successor Ay, who built a rock-cut chapel to the god in that area. Min's role as a god of fertility was of understandable importance in an agriculturally dependent area such as ancient Egypt, so we find scenes such as a relief of Ramesses III at Medinet Habu where the king is shown cutting wheat before Min; and the god's major festival, 'the coming forth of Min', which was celebrated at the beginning of the harvest season, was among the most important religious-agricultural festivals in Egypt. Amulets of Min occur from an unusually early date with one in gold being known from a 12th-dynasty burial at Abydos. Most amulets of the god date to the Late Period, however, and may have been utilized by men for the sake of the god's procreative powers.

Neper

The god Neper was a grain deity whose agricultural origin was an early one and who may well have predated that aspect of Osiris whom he resembled in several ways. The Coffin Texts mention Neper as a god 'living after he has died' (CT II 95), and the god was largely assimilated with Osiris as time progressed. The hieroglyphic writing of Neper's name includes the symbol for grain; and in a procession of deities carved in the reign of the 5th-dynasty king Sahure the body of the god is dotted to symbolize the grain which Neper represented. Because the harvest was so dependent upon the yearly flooding of the Nile, the inundation deity Hapy was said to be 'lord of Neper', but the god was honoured in his own right as an important deity of the harvest and prosperity. Neper was often associated with the cobra goddess Renenutet who also was a patron of the harvest. A cult centre of the god is known to have been constructed in the southern Fayum by Amenemhet III and IV.

Nun

Mythology

Nun personified the primeval waters which existed at the time of creation and from which the creator sun god arose. He was thus called the 'father' of the gods, but this was mainly a temporal distinction as he bore no genealogical relationship to them. Like other members of the Ogdoad (see p. 77), he was essentially an element of the unformed cosmos and thus persisted as a feature of Egyptian religion but without any developed mythology. Nun, however, was considered to continue to exist outside the bounds of the created universe even after the world ceased to be. In this sense Nun was the hidden abyss and is referred to in this manner throughout the Pyramid Texts and in later literature more as a location than as a deity. The only relationship between this world and the outlying waters of Nun is found in the fact that beings such as still-born babies and condemned souls who had no part in the afterlife were consigned to this area beyond existence. On the other hand, any terrestrial body of water could also be called Nun and we find the

Nile River, sacred temple lakes, artificial pools and ponds, and even underlying ground water all called by the god's name or said to be his. The consort of Nun was Naunet who was really only a linguistic and logical complement to the god without any true individual identity.

Iconography

When Nun was depicted in scenes representing the creation or recreation of the sun god he was shown in anthropomorphic form as a large figure with the tripartite wig and curved beard of the gods whose upraised arms lift the sun (usually held in a boat) into the horizon from which it was reborn into a new day. This image appears both in the vignettes of funerary papyri and also on the walls of New Kingdom royal tombs such as that of Ramesses VI in the Valley of the Kings. The deep 'well' shafts and some steeply descending passages in some of

*The god **Nun** lifts the solar barque with the new-born sun from the waters of creation. The original creation was also mirrored in the cycle of the daily sunrise. Papyrus of Anhai, British Museum.*

these New Kingdom royal tombs appear to symbolically descend toward the underlying waters of Nun in order to tie them to the underlying basis of creation and thus recreation and rebirth. Nun was also represented in another symbolic manner in the undulating mudbrick enclosure walls constructed around many temples. The convex and concave courses of these walls are believed to have represented the waters of Nun, symbolically depicting the outlying parameters of the universe which was modelled in the architectural programme of Egyptian temple design.

Worship

As an aspect of the precreated world Nun had no personal cult and had no temples, priests or certain rituals, though the ritual purification of the priests in the sacred lakes constructed within the precincts of temples came closest to this, as the pious ablutions not only physically cleansed the sacred officiants but also allowed them to rise, renewed by the waters of Nun.

Onuris

Mythology

The Egyptian god Anhur, more commonly known by his Greek name Onuris, was a god of war and hunting originating in the Thinite region around Abydos. His name means 'he who leads back the distant one' and appears to be based on the mythical manner in which Onuris is said to have journeyed to Nubia in order to bring back the leonine 'Eye of Re' who became his consort as the lioness-goddess Mekhit. In this legend Onuris parallels the Heliopolitan god Shu who was also considered to have brought back the fearsome 'eye' as his own consort, Tefnut, though the meaning of the name Anhur suggests the story may have been original with him. In any event, Onuris was often equated with Shu and was also linked to the sun god under the epithet 'son of Re' who hunted and slew the enemies of his solar-deity father. Onuris was also associated with Horus. In the Ptolemaic Period Onuris was identified by the Greeks with their own war god, Ares, and the Romans also maintained this martial identity of Onuris as may be seen in a representation of the Emperor Tiberius on a column shaft in the temple of Kom Ombo which shows the Roman wearing the characteristic crown of the god.

Iconography

Onuris was depicted as a standing god, bearded and with a short wig surmounted by a uraeus and either two or four tall plumes. As 'lord of the lance' the god stands with his right hand raised as if to thrust a lance or spear, while in his left hand he often holds a length of rope perhaps symbolic of his role in capturing his lioness consort. In some

cases the rope is not shown and the god may be represented grasping his raised spear in both hands, while in other cases neither spear nor rope are shown and the god is simply depicted with his arms raised as if he were holding these attributes. The iconography of the god clearly shows that he is intended to be seen as preparing to thrust his spear downward into a subdued enemy rather than in the act of throwing the spear. Onuris thus controls rather than simply attacks his enemies. The god is most frequently depicted wearing a long kilt which is often decorated in a feather-like pattern.

Worship

Although the original cult centre of Onuris was at This near Abydos in Upper Egypt, his main area of worship in later times was in the Delta town of Sebennytos (the modern Samannud) where he was venerated alongside or as a form of the god Shu. A temple of Onuris-Shu at this site has been dated to the reign of Nectanebo II of the 30th dynasty though worship of Onuris here would seem to have predated this structure. Silver and bronze amulets of the god occasionally occur in Late Period burials in different areas.

Osiris

'Hail to you Osiris,
Lord of eternity, king of gods,
Of many names, of holy forms,
Of secret rites in temples!'

'The Great Hymn to Osiris'

Mythology

Osiris was unquestionably one of the most important deities of ancient Egypt, figuring prominently in both monarchical ideology and popular religion as a god of death, resurrection and fertility. Both the meaning of the god's name and his exact origins are enigmatic. The etymology of the name Osiris (Egyptian Usir) is made confusing by its abbreviated hieroglyphic spelling, but a recent study concluded that it is most plausibly 'mighty one' (Egyptian *useru*). His birthplace was said to be Rosetau in the necropolis of the western desert near Memphis, but this is doubtless a mythical placement related to the god's funerary role.

The developing character of Osiris: It seems likely that Osiris was originally a fertility god with chthonic connections based in his identification with the earth, and that he was also associated at some point with the Nile's inundation, perhaps through its resultant alluvium and fertility. Yet the direct association of Osiris with agriculture seems to have occurred later. As time progressed and the cult of Osiris spread throughout Egypt, the god assimilated many other deities and rapidly took

The warrior-hunter god **Onuris** *in the pose of a spear-holding deity. Detail of a Late Period bronze dyad, Musée des Beaux-Arts, Budapest.*

on their attributes and characteristics. It seems probable, for example, that the god took over the story of an earthly ruler who was resurrected after his death from the ancient god Andjety of Busiris whose insignia were also the same as those used by Osiris. Many of the epithets accorded Osiris may also be seen to have been taken over from other deities. From the ancient jackal god Khenty-imentiu of Abydos Osiris took the title 'foremost of the westerners', and from Anubis he took the title 'he who is in the god's tent', relating to the temporary booth of embalming, etc. Many of the titles and epithets applied to him also reflect the god's nature as a funerary deity, which if not original to Osiris certainly became central in his identity. Chief among these, the title *wenenefer,* from which the Greek name Onnophris was taken, probably means something like 'he who is in everlastingly good condition', showing the god's victory over the decay of death. His seemingly anomalous title 'Lord of the living' is also a purposeful denial of death and refers to those 'living' in the netherworld. An important development of Osiris, however, which went beyond his basic identity as a resurrected god and ruler of the underworld, was the role he played as judge of the dead.

The mythic cycle of Osiris: In the Pyramid Texts Osiris is of primary importance as one of the three most frequently mentioned deities along with Horus and Re. It seems clear that once Osiris began to rise to widespread importance the priests of Heliopolis incorporated him along with certain other deities into their own theological framework. The Osiride legends thus incorporate Osiris' 'siblings' Isis, Nephthys, and Seth as well as his son Horus, and represent the most extensive mythic cycle in ancient Egyptian culture. In their developed form the core myths were preserved by the Greek writer Plutarch in his work *De Iside et Osiride,* where essentially it is claimed that the god once ruled Egypt as a king until he was murdered and cruelly dismembered and scattered by his jealous brother Seth. Due to the loyalty and dedication of his wife Isis and with the help of their sister Nephthys, Osiris was found and revivified and became the god of the netherworld. Horus, the posthumously conceived son of Osiris and Isis, avenged his father's death by defeating Seth and in time became the king of all Egypt as the rightful heir of Osiris. This story had great appeal both as a theological rationale for the Egyptian monarchial system in which the deceased king was equated with Osiris and was followed to the throne by his 'Horus' successor, and also as a story which proffered the hope of immortality through resurrection – which had a universal appeal and was claimed at first by kings and eventually by nobles and commoners also. On the other hand, it is equally true that as a chthonic god Osiris retained a measure of fearsomeness and could be regarded with awe. The Pyramid Texts preserve this darker aspect of the god in spells which imply the king's protection from Osiris by Re, as do the Coffin Texts, which speak of Osiris as a threatening power in some cases, and the Book of the Dead – which along with the god's positive titles also lists epithets such as 'the terrible'. Overall, however, the human origin, vulnerability, and resurrection of the god and the emphasis on family devotion and loyalty which runs through

Enigmatic depiction of **Osiris** *as a reclining ithyphallic figure associated with the sun god Re. The scene cannot be ascribed to a known funerary 'book' but appears in the tomb of Ramesses IX and in certain funerary papyri. Papyrus, Egyptian Museum, Cairo.*

the Osiride myths meant that Osiris was viewed as a benign deity, who represented the clearest idea of physical salvation available to the ancient Egyptian.

The relationship of Osiris with other gods: Outside of the Osiride myths themselves Osiris was associated with several other deities. For example, the *ba* or soul of the god was thought to reside in the sacred ram Ba-neb-djedet which was worshipped in the Delta town of Mendes; and the Apis bull of Memphis, normally associated with Ptah, was seen as a manifestation of Osiris. A complex and particularly important relationship existed between Osiris and the sun god Re. Although Osiris was incorporated into the Heliopolitan theological system at a relatively early date, the god continued to grow in importance and by New Kingdom times his stature as an independent god was considerable, as is seen in titles which were applied to him such as 'lord of the universe', 'ruler of eternity' and 'king of the gods'. Osiris' position became, in fact, comparable to that of the sun god himself. He came to be regarded not only as the counterpart of Re in the netherworld, but also in some cases as the sun god's own body – so that Osiris and Re came to be considered as representing the body and soul, respectively, of a single great god. The solar cycle was thus imagined as the *ba* of Re descending into the underworld to unite with Osiris as his own corpse. Nevertheless, Osiris and Re maintained independent characteristics, identities, and realms. The fusion of the two gods was mainly a product of New Kingdom theological expression in specific contexts and Egyptian theology never totally overcame the dichotomy implicit in the idea

of Re as lord of the heavens and Osiris as lord of the underworld. Osiris was also mythologically connected with the moon, however, though this was a relatively minor association. The ultimate fusion of Osiris with other deities occurred in the reign of Ptolemy I who introduced the hybrid Serapis as a fusion of Osiris, Apis and various Greek gods – an artificial creation which nevertheless become one of the most important deities of Egypt at the end of the dynastic age. The Greeks themselves associated Osiris with their own god Dionysus.

Iconography

Osiris is usually represented in anthropomorphic form, as a human mummy whose skin may be white – perhaps to symbolize the mummy wrappings – or more usually black as the colour of chthonic deities and of the dark Nile alluvium, or green as representative of vegetation and fertility. The god is invariably depicted standing or sitting stiffly erect with both legs together and with his hands projecting from his wrappings to grasp the crook and flail which are his chief attributes. These items of regalia have been thought to represent pastoral implements, but the origin of the flail is not clear and it may have had other meanings. In any event, it seems more likely that both items were taken over together from royal regalia as they are present in representations of kings from the time of Narmer on. Sometimes the god holds a *was* sceptre, but this is clearly a later usage taken over from the iconography of other gods. Regional variation has been shown to affect the manner in which the regalia are held. In Middle Egyptian Osiride figures the arms are usually held at the same level, whereas in Upper Egypt they are frequently crossed at the wrists.

*Nefertari before the throne of **Osiris** 'Wennefer…ruler of eternity'. Diminutive figures of the four 'sons of Horus (or Osiris)' stand before the seated god. 19th dynasty. Tomb of Nefertari, Valley of the Queens, western Thebes.*

(Left) The crook, flail and feathered Atef Crown, although taken over by Osiris, became unmistakable attributes of the netherworld god. Basalt statue of **Osiris**, from the tomb of Psamtik, Saqqara, 26th dynasty. Egyptian Museum, Cairo.

(Right) Horemheb before **Osiris**. The pose (except that he is standing) and dress of the god are virtually identical to those in the statue opposite but are viewed according to the canons of Egyptian two-dimensional representation. 18th dynasty. Tomb of Horemheb, Valley of the Kings, western Thebes.

The earliest known representation of Osiris, which dates to the 5th dynasty (a partial representation on a block from the reign of King Djedkare-Isesi), depicts the god wearing a divine wig; but from the Middle Kingdom he is frequently shown wearing the White Crown of Upper Egypt – possibly indicating his Upper Egyptian origin – and this crown is found in Osiride iconography throughout all later periods. Another crown closely associated with the god is the so-called Atef Crown – similar to the White Crown but with two side feathers and occasionally with horizontal horns and solar disks attached. This crown, either placed directly on the head or atop a royal wig, appears to have originated with the god Andjety, however, and to have a secondary association with Osiris. Osiris is sometimes shown wearing other crowns and, especially in later periods, these can be of complex, fused forms, but the White and Atef forms remain standard. From New Kingdom times the god is often shown wearing a broad collar and sometimes bracelets worn at the wrist. Later iconographic forms also often tend to incorporate an increasing amount of detail in their

depiction of the god's mummy wrappings – as in instances showing bands crossed over the chest, a sash tied at the waist, a counterpoise attached to the broad collar, etc. The association between Osiris and the symbol known to the Egyptians as the *djed* column or pillar meant that the god was often depicted in the form of the *djed*, sometimes as a partially-personified pillar with human arms or as an anthropoid mummy with a *djed*-pillar head. Although the death of Osiris was never depicted in Egyptian art, the god is frequently shown lying on the funerary bier, mourned by Isis and Nephthys.

Osiris' close connection with kingship and his role as king of the dead mean that he is probably more often depicted enthroned than any other deity. In funerary scenes the deceased is thus frequently shown before the enthroned god who is supported, at his rear, by Isis and Nephthys (less frequently by Hathor as mistress of the west). When depicted in this seated manner, the god is sometimes shown with the diminutive figures of the four sons of Horus before him or, in other cases, the so-called *imiut* fetish.

Due to the gradual unification of solar and Osirian ideas during the New Kingdom, Osiris is also sometimes depicted in the syncretized form of Osiris-Re or Re-Osiris. Usually this fusion takes the form of a mummiform body (Osiris) with the head of a falcon, ram, or beetle (Re) as seen in the tomb of Nefertari in the Valley of the Queens, which depicts a ram-headed mummy identified both as 'Re resting in Osiris' and 'Osiris resting in Re'. The relationship between Osiris and Re is also seen in many representational works which juxtapose the symbols of the respective gods in the same composition – such as mummy and falcon, *djed* and sun disk, etc. Because Osiris was also mythologically associated with the moon, the god may sometimes be represented by the lunar disk – especially in depictions where this is shown with Anubis.

Worship

The cult of Osiris lasted well over 2,000 years. It was already well established by the end of the 5th dynasty when the god's name appears in both the Pyramid Texts and inscriptions in private mastabas, and flourished till the end of the dynastic age. It was also universal in that the god had many cult centres and was venerated throughout Egypt. Due to the mythical scattering of the dismembered body of Osiris, a number of sites claimed pieces of the god and were thus at least locally important centres of his worship. Such, for example, were Athribis which claimed the god's heart; and Biga, Edfu, Herakleopolis and Sebennytos which all claimed one or more of his legs. The most prominent sites linked with Osiris were Abydos and Busiris, the two locales most closely associated with the god and his chief cult centres in Upper and Lower Egypt respectively. Abydos, the ancient town of Abdju, represents the oldest known sanctuary of Osiris and the remains of an Old Kingdom temple of the god are still extant there. The area also boasted the Osireion, a symbolic 'tomb of Osiris' adjoining the temple of Sethos I, and the 1st-dynasty tomb of Djer which was traditionally venerated as the tomb of Osiris from at least New Kingdom times. The symbol of the Abydene area was a beehive-like container surmounted by two tall plumes which was interpreted to represent a reliquary containing the god's head. Busiris in the middle Delta was the Lower Egyptian counterpart of Abydos. Its ancient name was Djedu, the hieroglyphic writing of which contained two *djed* columns, and the later Greek

name Busiris means 'house of Osiris'. The temple of the god at this site was also early: it is mentioned in Old Kingdom inscriptions and the cult centre was supposed to hold the burial of the god's backbone.

The worship of Osiris was as diverse in its manifestations as it was widespread in its extent. In the funerary sphere, the god was honoured in many different ways. Although the prayers for offerings in the tombs of courtiers of the Old Kingdom were at first addressed to Anubis, by the 5th dynasty Osiris had assumed an important role in private burials and the funerary texts came to reflect this with the standard opening 'An offering which the king gives to Osiris [on behalf of the deceased]...'. Of particular importance was the identification of the dead with Osiris so that deceased individuals of all classes came to be called 'the Osiris...' in which the person's name was added to that of the god. The god is found in many aspects of the funerary cult and is seen, for example, in the utilization of the so-called Osiris-bed in New Kingdom times. The corn- or grain-Osiris, corn-mummy or Osiris-bed, was a hollow frame constructed in the form of the god and filled with earth – usually Nile mud – in which seed grain was sprinkled. The frame was sometimes wrapped in linen winding sheets to complete the Osiride appearance of the effigy and the resulting germination of the seed corn was seen as a powerful symbol of the resurrective power of Osiris. In addition to its funerary usage the object was also used in religious festivals honouring Osiris such as the great Khoiak festival of the 4th month of the Egyptian year. Temple rituals and celebrations honouring Osiris were also diverse, though often opaque. We have evidence from as early as Old and Middle Kingdom times of some of these rituals, the most important of which was the annual festival of Osiris at Abydos. In this festival the cult statue of Osiris was carried from his temple to his traditional tomb in the area known today as Umm el-Qab or 'mother of pots' from the countless cups, jars, bowls and other pottery offering vessels left by ancient pilgrims. A stela of the Middle Kingdom official Ikhernofret now in Berlin describes aspects of this festival and is instructive in the clear stress placed on the 'mysteries' of the god which were extensive even by Egyptian theological standards. Osiris was certainly one of the most important of those deities honoured in the 'popular religion' of ancient Egypt, although surprisingly, amulets of Osiris are quite rare and only

*Plants sprout from a mummy in a visual image reminiscent of the seeded 'grain-**Osiris**' figures which were sometimes placed in Egyptian tombs. Coffin detail, Fitzwilliam Museum, Cambridge.*

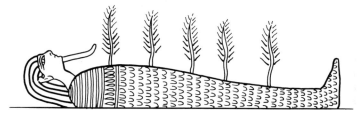

a few are known from the Third Intermediate and Late Periods. Small bronzes of the god are more common, many made as pendents, and Osiris was, of course, frequently represented in funerary decoration. He was also invoked in many spells and protective texts, some written in the form of royal decrees made by Osiris as king of Egypt.

Although the cult of Osiris grew by its own power and appeal throughout most of Egyptian history, it became especially widespread beyond the borders of Egypt in Graeco-Roman times due to its close link to the cult of Isis – who offered her followers a form of physical salvation based almost entirely on her role in the mythical drama of Osiris.

Panebtawy

Divine child of Haroeris (see Horus) and his consort Hathor-ta-senet-nefret at Kom Ombo, Panebtawy, whose name means 'the lord of the Two Lands', personified the pharaoh as the divine son of Horus the Elder and thus the rightful heir to the kingdom of Egypt. He was depicted as a young man with the side-lock of youth, his finger placed at his mouth.

Pataikos

Mythology

Pataikos represents a type of minor amuletic deity named from a passage in Herodotus which mentions dwarf-like protective images with which the Phoenicians adorned the prows of their triremes. Herodotus thought that these dwarfish figures represented pygmies and wrote that they were similar to the statue of Hephaistos (Ptah) in Memphis. The Egyptian images so named may well have originated with the craftsman god Ptah as the epithet 'Ptah the dwarf' is known and dwarfs seem to be always present in Old Kingdom scenes of metal workshops.

Iconography

The Egyptian pataikoi are similar to the god Bes in appearance but have some distinctive differences. Like Bes they usually represent a small, short (and usually bow-legged) male with hands resting on his hips. They may also brandish knives and hold or bite snakes, but their overly large heads are without facial hair, and they do not have the enlarged eyes and prominent tongue associated with Bes. The figures have bald or closely-cropped human heads or sometimes the head of a falcon or a ram upon which they may wear a sidelock, a scarab beetle or an Atef Crown. In some cases pataikoi are two-headed or may be represented back to back with other deities, notably Bes and Harpokrates (see Horus). The pataikoi themselves also often show affinities with Harpokrates, as when they are shown standing on crocodiles in the manner of that god.

Worship

Crudely produced amulets of Pataikos seem to appear in the late Old Kingdom, but it is not until New Kingdom times that clearly detailed examples are found and they then continue throughout the later dynastic periods.

Peteese and Pihor

Peteese and Pihor were deified brothers who were worshipped as minor gods in the region of Dendur a little to the south of Aswan in Lower Nubia. The two brothers seem to have lived during or around the 26th dynasty and apparently were elevated to divine status as a result of drowning in the Nile and subsequently becoming associated with Osiris. The Emperor Augustus built a small temple to honour the brothers on the west bank of the Nile at Dendur which was moved to avoid flooding by the rising waters of Lake Nasser and which is now in the Metropolitan Museum of Art in New York. Reliefs in the temple show Peteese and Pihor presenting offerings to the superior deity Isis.

Ptah

Mythology

Ptah appears to be one of the oldest of Egypt's gods and is attested representationally from the 1st dynasty onward. Nevertheless, the great god of Memphis was perhaps originally only a locally important deity whose influence developed and

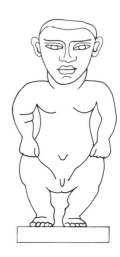

*The dwarf god called **Pataikos** was associated with Ptah of Memphis but also had an independent existence as an apotropaic deity. Glazed amulet, British Museum.*

*The god **Ptah** embraced by Senwosret I. Detail of a pillar from Senwosret's destroyed temple at Karnak. 12th dynasty. Egyptian Museum, Cairo.*

spread slowly over time. Even in the Pyramid Texts Ptah is mentioned only indirectly a very few times, though it is difficult to ascertain if this is due to an early relative lack of importance, a lack of function in the mortuary sphere, or the desire on the part of the Heliopolitan theologians to minimize the position of the Memphite deity. Mythologically, the consort of Ptah was the lioness-goddess Sekhmet, and her son Nefertem completed the major divine triad of the Memphite region. Eventually the god fulfilled several important roles.

Ptah, lord of Memphis: There is no doubt that the primary geographic association of Ptah was with the general region of Memphis. The founding of 'Ineb-hedj' or 'White Walls' – the city later called Memphis – as the administrative capital of Egypt at the time of the unification of the country around 3000 BC doubtless had a profound effect on the development of Ptah's importance, and the god soon became the chief deity of the area. By the Middle Kingdom Ptah was thus called 'Lord of Ankh-tawy', referring to the city of Memphis; and many scholars believe that the name Egypt itself is based on the Greek form of the Egyptian 'Hut-ka-Ptah', 'the temple of the *ka* of Ptah'. The Memphite locality was also the origin of several of Ptah's frequent titles such as Ptah *res-ineb-ef*, 'Ptah who is south of his wall', in reference to the position of the god's sanctuary beyond his temple's great temenos wall to the south of Memphis, and Ptah *khery-bak-ef*, 'Ptah who is under his moringa tree', referring to an ancient tree-god of Memphis who was absorbed by Ptah at an early date.

Ptah the craftsman: If Ptah was not originally a god of craftsmanship, this aspect of his identity was certainly an ancient one as it can be seen at an early date and then remains constant throughout the god's history. The artistic and cultural development of the Old Kingdom and the great increase in the number of craftsmen needed to serve the capital of Memphis and to produce the funerary goods needed for its necropoleis could well have been influential in the rise of the god. During the Old Kingdom the high priest of Ptah bore the title *wer-kherep-hemu* 'great leader of the craftsmen'; and while the god's name gives no firm clue to his origin, it is perhaps based on a root of later words meaning 'to sculpt' and thus related to his identity as a craftsman god. In this role Ptah was both the sculptor or smith of mankind and creator of the arts and crafts, and the Memphite deity of craftsmen became particularly associated with the dwarves who seem to have traditionally worked as jewellers and artisans in Old Kingdom workshops. Ptah was also clearly associated with other groups of craftsmen such as the workers of Deir el-Medina who constructed the royal tombs in the Valley of the Kings. Naturally enough the Greeks

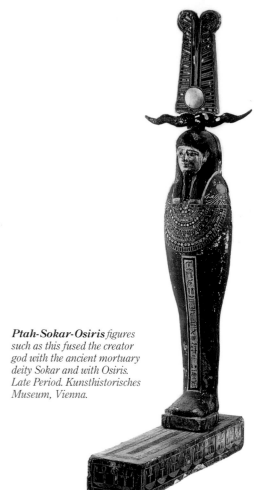

Ptah-Sokar-Osiris *figures
such as this fused the creator
god with the ancient mortuary
deity Sokar and with Osiris.
Late Period. Kunsthistorisches
Museum, Vienna.*

and Romans associated Ptah directly with their own smith gods Hephaistos and Vulcan.

Ptah the creator: As a result of his identification with craftsmanship, or concurrent with it, Ptah became a god of creation and was known as the 'sculptor of the earth' who, like the ram god Khnum was believed to form everything on his potter's wheel. More fundamentally, Ptah came to be known as the 'ancient one' who united in his person both the masculine primeval deity Nun and his feminine counterpart, Naunet, so that he was seen as the primordial deity whose creative power was manifest in every aspect of the cosmos. He was sometimes worshipped as Ptah-Nun or even Ptah-Naunet in this role, though the creative process was also attributed to the god alongside the old Memphite earth god Tatenen under the name Ptah-Tatenen. The story of creation as attributed to Ptah by the priests of Memphis – whereby the god was said to have created the world through his thought and creative word or command (see p. 18) – was one of the most intellectual creation myths to arise in Egypt and in the whole of the ancient world.

Ptah the chthonic and afterlife god: As a result of his proximity to the Memphite earth god Tatenen and the mortuary deity Sokar, Ptah took on some of the aspects of those deities. He was thus sometimes venerated in a creative, chthonic aspect as Ptah-Tatenen. Although Ptah himself was not frequently associated with the afterlife, as the composite deity Ptah-Sokar and later as Ptah-Sokar-Osiris, he gained considerable importance in this area also. The mummiform nature of Ptah in his painted and carved representations also must have served as a constant reminder of the funerary and afterlife associations of the god.

Ptah, hearer of prayers: As with most deities, the epithets accorded Ptah were wide-ranging and complimentary. Honourific titles such as *nefer-her* 'merciful of face' or *neb-maat* 'lord of truth' are often given to the god in inscriptions, but epithets extolling the god as a hearer of prayers seem to have had particular significance. Many votive stelae have been found in the area of Ptah's temple at Memphis and elsewhere in Egypt carved with representations of human ears and dedicated to the god as *mesedjer-sedjem,* 'the ear which hears', who would hear the petitions of his devotees. As both the god of craftsmen and hearer of prayers we find evidence of Ptah being beseeched by the workmen of Deir el-Medina such as one Neferabu who admits on a votive stela that he made a false oath in Ptah's name and subsequently lost his sight in some manner so that he begs 'the ear which hears' for forgiveness. On the perimeters of temples we also find shrines or chapels of the hearing ear which likewise served the purpose of transmitting the individual's prayers to the deity within the temple. The god Ptah often figures in these shrines, as in the one constructed at the entrance to the great mortuary temple of Ramesses III at Medinet Habu.

Iconography

The iconography of Ptah was particularly stable and persisted in essentially the same form throughout most of the dynastic age – beginning with the earliest known depiction of the god on a 1st-dynasty bowl from Tarkhan. Ptah was almost invariably represented anthropomorphically as a standing, mummiform figure with feet together and with his hands protruding from his tightly wrapped shroud to hold his characteristic sceptre (comprising a *was* sceptre surmounted by *ankh* and *djed* symbols). The god usually wears a close-fitting skull cap without any additional elements of headdress, though in his association with Osiris Ptah sometimes is depicted with a small disk atop his head flanked by the two tall plumes worn by that god.

From the Middle Kingdom onwards he wears a distinctive straight beard rather than the usual curved divine beard found on representations of

(Above) **Ptah** within his shrine. The straight beard and particular style of necklace counterpoise at the god's back are distinctive attributes rarely seen with other deities. Tomb of Amenherkhepeshef, Valley of the Queens, western Thebes.

(Left) Gilded statuette of **Ptah** the creator from the tomb of Tutankhamun. The pedestal upon which the god stands may represent the mound of creation or the craftsman's level and the hieroglyphic symbol for truth. 18th dynasty. Egyptian Museum, Cairo.

other Egyptian gods. Ptah is also usually depicted wearing either what appears to be a large tassel at the rear of his garment or a broad collar which is balanced by a counterpoise hanging behind his back. This counterpoise is rounded at the top and sometimes flared at the bottom like a narrow, tube-like bell and is distinctive enough to allow even partial images of Ptah to be differentiated from similar representations of the god Khonsu who wears a key-hole shaped counterpoise. Usually Ptah is represented standing on a narrow plinth like one of the hieroglyphs used to write the word *maat* or 'truth' and which also resembles the measuring rod used by Egyptian workmen, or upon a stepped dias suggestive of the primeval mound. Frequently he is depicted within an open shrine.

The god was perhaps also depicted as a dwarf, as Herodotus claimed to see statues in this form in the temple of Hephaistos (Ptah) at Memphis (see Pataikos), and though these statues could also have been votive representations of dwarf workmen rather than the god himself, the god also appears in the form of a dwarf on some of the magical *cippi* (healing plaques) of the Late Period.

Worship

Although little remains of Ptah's chief temple at Memphis, surviving historical and archaeological evidence indicates that it was a great complex befitting a god who ruled supreme in his own area for well over 2,000 years. The present remains date mainly to New Kingdom times, though it is evident that there were structures honouring Ptah at this site at far earlier dates. It was also at Memphis that the sacred Apis bull, which served as a manifestation and intermediary for Ptah, resided with an important cult of its own. Although he was perhaps originally associated only with the Memphite area, the veneration of Ptah soon spread throughout Egypt and the god is represented in almost all major Egyptian sites. He had his own sanctuary in the precinct of the great temple of Amun at Karnak since at least Middle Kingdom times and this temple continued to be expanded and embellished throughout the rest of the dynastic age, showing a clear continuity in the god's importance and worship in Upper Egypt. Ptah was also venerated in Egyptian Nubia where his presence is found in a number of temples including those of Ramesses II at Abu Simbel, el-Derr, and Gerf Hussein. The god's particular importance in New Kingdom times is also seen in his inclusion in the grouping of the major deities Re, Amun and Ptah (as seen in the statuary group in the shrine of the Great Temple of Abu Simbel) and in the names of a number of kings such as Merenptah (beloved of Ptah) and Siptah (son of Ptah), as well as high-ranking officials.

As the patron deity of craftsmen, Ptah was particularly venerated at sites such as Deir el-Medina where workmen and artisans lived; and as the god 'who hears prayers' he remained a favourite deity frequently addressed by the common people, although amulets of the god are surprisingly rare. Of those that do exist the plaqueform amulets depicting the god flanked by Sekhmet and Nefertem are mainly of 26th-dynasty date and may have been utilized primarily in life rather than in funerary contexts. Ptah also played at least an indirect role in the funerary aspect of Egyptian religion by way of the 'opening of the mouth' ceremony performed on funerary statues and on the mummy of the deceased by the *setem*-priest who utilized a ritual metal chisel suggestive of the craftsman deity.

Reshep

Mythology

Reshep was the West Semitic god of war and thunder who was assimilated into Egyptian religion, along with various other Near Eastern deities, in New Kingdom times. The god was identified with the Mesopotamian deity Nergal, god of pestilence and warfare, and is attested in the Hebrew Bible and at ancient sites ranging as far afield as Spain. He was probably introduced into Egypt by the Hyksos and is first attested in names of foreign origin, but by New Kingdom times he was connected with Egyptian deities with whom he shared pestilent or martial affinities, especially Seth and the Theban war god Montu, though he retained his alien character and identity. The consort of Reshep was the goddess Itum who is mentioned alongside

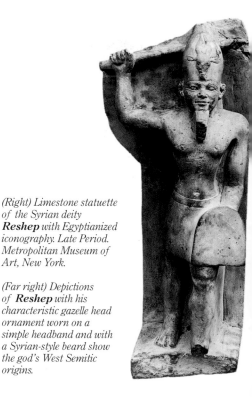

*(Right) Limestone statuette of the Syrian deity **Reshep** with Egyptianized iconography. Late Period. Metropolitan Museum of Art, New York.*

*(Far right) Depictions of **Reshep** with his characteristic gazelle head ornament worn on a simple headband and with a Syrian-style beard show the god's West Semitic origins.*

the god in Egyptian texts; however he was also associated with other Near Eastern deities, and was frequently venerated as part of a triad consisting of Min, Qadesh and Reshep.

Iconography

Always represented anthropomorphically, Reshep was depicted as a bearded god (usually with the full Near Eastern style beard), wearing a short kilt and the White Crown of Upper Egypt, which was often decorated with a long streamer and either the horns or complete head of a gazelle. This ornament may have reflected the god's desert origins or could have been a result of his identification with Seth, though in some instances Reshep may wear a uraeus in place of the gazelle emblem. Usually represented standing in striding stance, the god characteristically brandishes weapons of various kinds, most commonly a spear, mace, axe, or sickle sword in the right hand and in the left hand a shield or sometimes a *was* sceptre or *ankh* sign.

Worship

Reshep was worshipped in a temple at Memphis and perhaps in other locations where Asiatic peoples settled, though evidence of the god has been found throughout Egypt from Delta to Sudan. Well attested in New Kingdom times, he continues to appear well into the Ptolemaic Period both in temple lists and in artifacts of various types. Many bronze statuettes apparently depicting the god have been found, as well as a single clearly identified stone statue, and he appears on numerous stelae

– either alone or with other deities, particularly Min and the Syrian goddess Qadesh. The image or name of the god also occurs on many scarabs. The martial nature of Reshep made him an ideal royal deity, and his adoption in this way is seen in the famous stele set up by Amenophis II near the Great Sphinx at Giza and in other monuments of that king. His martial nature could turn to healing, and Reshep was sometimes named in spells to over-power inimical influences such as the demon Akhu who was believed to cause abdominal pain.

Sah

The god Sah personified the constellation of Orion – the most distinctive of all the constellations in the night sky. While not part of the 'imperishable' circumpolar stars, the constellation became important in Egyptian mythology especially as it rose directly before the adjacent star Sirius (the Egyptian Sothis) – the brightest fixed star which was utilized in the calculation of the Egyptian calendar. The constellation god was thus connected with the star Sothis from an early date and the two came to be viewed as manifestations of Osiris and Isis respectively.

Sah is mentioned quite frequently in the Pyramid Texts where he is called 'father of the gods' (PT 408), and the deceased king is said to enter the sky 'In the name of the Dweller in Orion, with a season in the sky and a season on earth' (PT 186). The association of Sah with Sothis is also clear in these early texts where the king is told, 'You shall reach the sky as Orion, your soul shall be as effective as Sothis' (PT 723). In the funerary texts of the New Kingdom Orion is said to row towards the stars in a boat and Sah is sometimes depicted in this manner in representations found in temples and tombs – as a god surrounded by stars who sails across the sky in a papyrus skiff.

Serapis

Mythology

The hybrid god Serapis was a composite of several Egyptian and Hellenistic deities introduced at the beginning of the Ptolemaic Period in the reign of Ptolemy I. The god thus answered the needs of a new age in which Greek and Egyptian religion were brought face to face and the new deity was created to form a bridge between the two cultures. Linguistically, the god's name is a fusion of Osiris and Apis, and a cult of Osirapis had in fact existed in Egypt before the rule of the Ptolemies, but to this Egyptian core were added a number of Hellenistic deities which predominated in the god's final form. Zeus, Helios, Dionysus, Hades and Asklepius all added aspects of their respective cults, so that Serapis emerged as a thoroughly Egypto-Hellenistic deity

127

(Right) The hybrid deity **Serapis** *wearing his characteristic modius or kalathos crown in the form of a grain measure. Panel from a triptych of Serapis, Isis and a private citizen. Roman Period, AD 180–200. J. Paul Getty Museum, Malibu.*

(Below) The enthroned **Serapis** *wearing the triple Atef Crown. Detail from a late relief at Meroe.*

who personified the aspects of divine majesty, the sun, fertility, the underworld and afterlife, as well as healing. The mythology of Serapis was, therefore, the mythology of his underlying deities, but the aspects of afterlife and fertility were always primary to his nature. The consort of Serapis was said to be Isis, the greatest Egyptian goddess in Hellenistic times.

Iconography

The Hellenistic elements of Serapis dominate the god's iconography and attributes. He was portrayed in anthropomorphic form as a man wearing a Greek-style robe with Greek hairstyle and full beard and usually bearing a tall corn modius or measure on his head. In some depictions Serapis is also given curving ram's horns. Sometimes, as a result of the chthonic and fertility aspects of the god and his consort Isis, the two deities were depicted as serpents – one, with a beard, representing Serapis.

Worship

The cult centre of Serapis was the great Serapeum Temple at Alexandria which was regarded as a wonder and a site of pilgrimage throughout the Mediterranean world until it was destroyed by order of the Emperor Theodosius in AD 389. Other, smaller temples and shrines were dedicated to the god in locations throughout Egypt and the god's cult was spread through much of the Graeco-Roman world by traders and converts. A Roman Period sculpted head of the god was found in London, and a temple of Serapis is even recorded in an inscription found at the Roman site of Eburacum (modern York) in England, showing that his importance was great enough to reach even the distant areas of the Roman Empire. In Egypt itself, however, the Egyptians never fully accepted the hybrid god and the evidence for his popular worship is considerably less than for other traditional Egyptian deities.

Shay

Mythology

Shay was the personification of the idea of destiny in Egyptian religion and as such was the god of lifespan, or more broadly of fate and fortune. In the Instructions of Amenemopet, for example, it is said that 'none can ignore Shay', though this is meant in the abstract sense of the inevitability of fate rather than the imminence of a predatory deity. Shay could thus be invoked as much as an idea as a personified god, as may be seen in inscriptions from the reign of Akhenaten where the solar Aten is sometimes said to be 'Shay who gives life'. As a personified god Shay is sometimes mentioned along with certain goddesses such as Meskhenet and Renenutet who shared an affinity with his role, and in the Ptolemaic Period he was identified with Agathodaimon, the Hellenistic serpent deity venerated for his fortune-telling ability.

Iconography

Shay was rarely represented in Egyptian art, but he sometimes appears in the form of an anthropomorphic god in vignettes depicting the weighing of the heart scene in New Kingdom funerary papyri. In these scenes he is shown as an undifferentiated divine figure with the curved beard of a god but identified primarily by name.

Worship

Textual references to Shay and the few representations of the god which have survived indicate that he was recognized more as an abstract personification or conceptualization of destiny than a personal deity to be venerated or served.

Shezmu

Mythology

The god Shezmu was a deity of wine and oil presses with a strongly bipolar personality who could equally bless or destroy. He is attested from Old Kingdom times on and in the famous 'Cannibal Hymn' of the Pyramid Texts (PT 403), Shezmu is the fearsome being who butchers and cooks the gods themselves that the king might absorb their strength. In the Coffin Texts of the Middle Kingdom the god lassoes the damned and corrals them for slaughter, squeezing their heads like grapes in a bloody image of destruction (CT VI, 6). In the later texts of the Book of the Dead Shezmu also appears in connection with the nets which captured beings in the afterlife (BOD 153). Yet despite the apparent cruelty of his nature Shezmu could also be beneficent, and as god of the presses he provided wine, oil and perfumes. By the New Kingdom there is more stress on these positive aspects, and Shezmu became known as the provider of perfumes for the gods. The Book of the Dead also contains the statement, 'Shezmu is with you, he gives you the best of the fowl' (BOD 170). This role of beneficent provision finally became primary in the Graeco-Roman Period.

Iconography

Shezmu is not frequently depicted in Egyptian art but was usually shown in anthropomorphic form as the master of a press. One mythological papyrus of the 21st dynasty depicts hawk deities working the presses of retribution which must surely represent Shezmu, and the god may also be depicted in leonine form or with the head of a lion – an iconography in keeping with the more ferocious aspect of his personality. Some late representations also show Shezmu in ram-headed form.

Worship

There is some evidence that Shezmu already had a priesthood during the Old Kingdom, and by the Middle Kingdom his cult was certainly well established in the Fayum and probably elsewhere. As the benign aspect of the god's nature was increasingly stressed, he probably became more widely accepted as an ancillary in the cults of the other gods until, in Ptolemaic times, in temples such as Edfu and Dendera, special rooms for the production and storage of oils and unguents and other products used in temple service were presided over by Shezmu 'master of the perfumery'.

Shu

Mythology

Shu, whose name may mean 'emptiness' or 'he who rises up', was the god of the air and also of sunlight. In the Ennead of primary deities organized by the priests of Heliopolis, he was created by the demiurge Atum, either from his semen or mucus. Shu was husband of Tefnut, the goddess usually said to represent moisture, and the pair

in turn produced Geb, god of the earth and Nut, goddess of the sky. According to Egyptian myth, Shu separated these two after Nut swallowed the constellations and Geb became angry with her for 'eating' their children. Shu is mentioned in the Pyramid Texts where the deceased king is purified in the 'lakes of Shu', which may represent mists, and is said to climb up to heaven upon the 'bones of Shu' which are probably the clouds. The god was also associated with light – perhaps perceived as an aspect of the air – from Old Kingdom times, and even the arch iconoclast Akhenaten honoured the god who was said to dwell in the sun's disk. For reasons which remain unclear Shu was associated with the lunar deities Thoth and Khonsu, perhaps in terms of the light of the lunar disk, or because his wife Tefnut was often associated with the moon. The god was also sometimes equated with the protective deity Bes; but on the other hand he had a darker aspect, for in the netherworld he was said to operate an executioner's block, although he also helped to protect the sun god from the serpent-fiend Apophis. According to one mythic story recorded on a Ptolomaic Period granite shrine, Shu ruled as king of Egypt for many years until he became weak and tired. Then he ascended to the heavens and took up residence along with the sun god Re.

Iconography

In his iconography Shu could be represented as a lion but is usually seen in human form as a god wearing a feather – the hieroglyphic symbol for his name – upon his head. He is often depicted with his arms raised supporting the sky goddess Nut and holding her apart from her consort Geb with the assistance of the magical Heh deities. The god also appears in certain other mythologically-based scenes such as that portrayed in the famous head-rest found in the tomb of Tutankhamun. In that

(Below) **Shu**, *god of the air and of sunlight, is commonly identified by the tall feather worn on his head.*

(Bottom) **Shu** *was frequently depicted in Egyptian art holding the body of his daughter, the sky goddess Nut, above his son, the earth god Geb.*

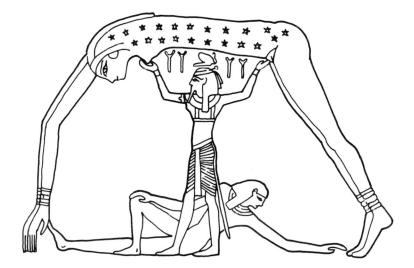

*Ivory head-rest from the tomb of Tutankhamun showing the god **Shu** who supported the head of the king – symbolically the sun – as it 'set' and 'rose' between the lions of yesterday and tomorrow. 18th dynasty. Egyptian Museum, Cairo.*

artifact the god kneels between two lions symbolizing Shu and Tefnut and the horizons of yesterday and tomorrow, to support the sleeper's head on his upraised arms, doubtless symbolic of his upholding the sun. Although not found frequently in three-dimensional representations, he does appear in amuletic form, usually kneeling with his arms raised – often supporting a sun disk.

Worship

Apart from early references in the Pyramid Texts and Coffin Texts, the cult of the air god is not actually attested until New Kingdom times when he is mentioned in many texts of differing kinds. His chief cult centre, which he shared with his consort Tefnut, was at the ancient Nay-ta-hut (modern Tell el-Muqdam) which the Greeks called Leontopolis or 'lion city' after the form in which the two deities were worshipped there. In the later Dynastic Period Shu was increasingly credited with powers that renewed the cosmos, as the god who filled the universe with the very air which was the breath of life. As a result Shu was incorporated into everyday religion in prayers and positive spells as well as certain magical texts where the 'poisons' of the god were conjured to defeat demonic threats.

Sia

Sia was the personification of perception and could be said to be the equivalent of the 'heart' or mind of the god Ptah which underlay creation in the Memphite theology. According to myth, Sia, like Hu – the god personifying spoken command or utterance – came into existence from drops of blood spilled from the cut phallus of the sun god Re. Hu also might be equated with the spoken creative word of Ptah, so that just as Ptah created everything through the two aspects of mind and word,

the two deities Sia and Hu form a dyad which would seem to represent the same aspects of the mind and word of Re. Usually depicted in anthropomorphic form, during the Old Kingdom Sia was visualized as a kind of divine functionary who stood at the right side of Re and held the god's sacred papyrus scroll. In the New Kingdom too, Sia was depicted along with Hu and other deities, accompanying the sun god in his underworld barque, as in a number of the tombs in the Valley of the Kings.

Tatenen

Mythology

Tatenen was a Memphite god who first clearly appears in the Middle Kingdom, although he may be identical to an earlier deity known as Khenty-Tjenenet attested in Old Kingdom times. The god's name means 'risen land' and, like the Heliopolitan ben-ben (see p. 212), he symbolized the emerging of the primeval mound from the waters of original creation, though in a secondary sense Tatenen could also symbolize the emergence of the fertile silt from the Nile's annual inundation, and by extension the resultant vegetation. From Ramessid times Tatenen was associated with the great Memphite god Ptah and was often viewed as a manifestation of that god and fused with him as Ptah-Tatenen. As an earth god Tatenen could also symbolize Egypt itself and could be associated with the earth god Geb. His primeval aspect meant that he could be viewed as a bisexual deity and in one text he is called the creator and 'mother' of all the gods. Tatenen also had a chthonic aspect in which he was viewed as a protector of the deceased king in the netherworld. In the New Kingdom Litany of Re he is cited as the personification of the phallus of the dead king, perhaps based on a linguistic play on the idea of rising or risen conveyed in his name.

Iconography

Usually Tatenen was represented anthropomorphically as a bearded man with a headdress consisting of a sun disk with ram's horns and two plumes. Because he was a chthonic deity and linked to the emergence of vegetation, his face and limbs may be painted a dark hue of green or some other colour.

Worship

The cult of Tatenen is known to have flourished at Memphis, and although the god may be found in temples in other areas of Egypt, his own sanctuaries remained primarily in the Memphite area.

Wadj-Wer

A Hapy-like fecundity figure whose name means 'the great green', Wadj-Wer was long believed to

have personified the Mediterranean Sea, or the sea in general, but actually may have represented the large lakes and lagoons of the north Delta region. This conclusion is based on the fact that certain texts seem to describe the crossing of the 'great green' by foot – which could refer to travelling between nearly contiguous lakes – and some texts use the determinative sign for dry land rather than that for water in writing the term. In any event, the deity is attested as early as the Old Kingdom in the mortuary temple of the Pyramid of Sahure at Abusir, where he is depicted with water lines across his body along with other 'fecundity figures', and it is clear that he represents the rich yield of the area he represents. The god's protective underworld role also meant that he appears in the New Kingdom royal tombs, and he is clearly depicted in the monument Ramesses III made in the Valley of the Queens

for his son Amenherkhepeshef. The god seems to have been represented in amulets, but these may also represent the combined Ptah-Tatenen.

Weneg

A little known god who appears in the Old Kingdom Pyramid Texts (PT 607, 952), Weneg was a son of the sun god Re and seems to symbolize order and stability by supporting the sky and thus preventing the chaos outside the cosmos from crashing down upon the world. In this aspect he bears a different yet related role to that of Re's daughter Maat and is also similar to the Heh deities which supported the sky. Weneg was also said to be a judge of other gods, again perhaps paralleling the judicial role of the goddess Maat.

*The god **Wadj-Wer** (at right), his body covered in symbolic waves, in a procession of deities bringing offering-hieroglyphs into the sanctuary of the mortuary temple of Sahure, Abusir, 5th dynasty. Egyptian Museum, Berlin.*

This category of deities includes a number of gods who overlapped considerably in both their mythology and worship. In some cases deities were revered in both child and adult forms, though this is relatively infrequent, and the so-called 'child deities' usually represented the young offspring of major deities. As such these child gods often played a role relating to the divine conception and birth of the king and some were associated with the mammisis or 'birth houses' of later temples.

Horus the Child

The name 'Horus the Child' was given to a number of related forms of divine infant. Most of these were the son of Osiris and the goddess Isis whom she bore in the papyrus marshes of Chemmis in the northern Delta and raised in secret there in fear of the god Seth. Occasionally, however, the infant god was included in temple groupings as the child of other divine parents – as at Medamud where he was the son of Montu and Raettawy. Already in the Pyramid Texts the god is referred to as 'the child with his finger in his mouth'; and in this form he was known as Har-hery-wadj or 'Horus upon his

(Above right) King Iuput in the guise of **Horus the Child** *seated upon the lotus flower which rose from the primeval waters of creation. Detail of faience plaque, 23rd dynasty. Royal Museum, Scotland.*

(Left) Cippus or amuletic plaque of Horus depicting **Horus the Child** *grasping noxious creatures and standing upon the heads of crocodiles beneath a mask of Bes. Such magical stelae symbolized the god's power to protect from, and to heal, the bites and stings of wild creatures. Ptolemaic Period. Egyptian Museum, Cairo.*

papyrus plants' and sometimes as 'Horus hidden behind the papyrus' in reference to the myth of his origins. The god was most commonly called Harpa-khered (Greek Harpokrates), which translates as 'Horus the Child' and was often depicted in this form seated on the lap of Isis, or standing, alone, as depicted in the amuletic plaques known as *cippi* of Horus. As Harsiese, 'Horus son of Isis', the god was clearly identified in his role as the goddesses' legitimate son and heir of Osiris. This is also true of the related names Horus iun-mutef or 'Horus pillar of his mother' and Har-nedj-itef (Greek Harendotes) or 'Horus saviour of his father'.

Ihy

Mythology

Ihy was a child god, whose name was interpreted by the Egyptians themselves as 'sistrum player' or 'musician' and who personified the jubilation associated with the use of the sacred instrument (see p. 143). Another meaning of his name could be 'calf', referring to his relation to the cow Hathor who was usually held to be his mother – as at Dendera, and at Edfu where he appears as Harsomptus. Ihy was also regarded as the son of certain other deities, however, and could be associated in this way with Isis, Nephthys and even Sekhmet. While Horus was

and specifically dedicated to Hathor and to Ihy. The god plays particularly important roles in the mammisi or birth house of Nectanebo I at Dendera where his divine conception and birth – and that of the king – were celebrated, and where 'mystery plays' in 13 acts concerning the divine birth appear to have been performed. A second birth house at this site built for Caesar Augustus celebrates the divine birth of Ihy as the son of Hathor.

Neferhetep

Not as well known as the child god Ihy, Neferhetep was also portrayed as an infant deity, the son of Hathor, in the town of Hiw near Nag Hammadi. The young god's name means 'perfect in conciliation', probably reflecting the mythological fact that the raging goddess Hathor was transformed into a gentle and loving mother. Neferhetep was also viewed as a divine ram and symbol of male potency. He was said to be loved by 'wives at the sight of his beauty' in which beauty is a circumlocution for the god's phallus. The god thus functioned in two complementary aspects – as both a child and the power behind the child's conception.

Nefertem

Mythology

Nefertem is often thought of as the god of perfumes, but this association is a secondary one and he was primarily the youthful god of the lotus blossom which rose from the primeval waters according to Egyptian myth. Nefertem was thus not only identified with the blue lotus (*Nymphaea cerulea*) but also with the sun god who emerged from it, and his association with Re is common. In the Pyramid Texts he is called 'the lotus blossom which is before the nose of Re' (PT 266), showing that his association with perfume was an early and natural one. In later times Nefertem was also closely associated with Horus the son of Re and the two deities were sometimes merged. At Memphis, Nefertem came to be grouped with the pre-eminent god Ptah and his consort Sekhmet in a particularly important triad in which he was commonly viewed as their child. Other Egyptian cities also claimed Nefertem, however. At Buto he was the son of the cobra goddess Wadjet and he was also sometimes viewed as the son of the feline goddess Bastet.

Iconography

In his representations, Nefertem is usually depicted anthropomorphically as a male god wearing a lotus blossom upon his head. Sometimes this lotus headdress is augmented by two upright plumes and twin necklace counterpoises which hang at its sides. Occasionally Nefertem is also depicted as a

most commonly viewed as Ihy's father, the god was also said to be the offspring of Re. Although his mythological nature was primarily connected with music, he was also connected with the afterlife in some contexts. In the Coffin Texts and the Book of the Dead Ihy is called 'the lord of bread' and said to be 'in charge of the beer' in reference to offerings, but also possibly in allusion to ritual celebrations which involved intoxication in the worship of Hathor.

Iconography

The god was depicted as a naked boy, wearing the sidelock of youth and with his finger to his mouth. He is not always shown in diminutive size, however, and may be depicted at the same scale as his mother and other deities or the king appearing in the same scene. He may also wear the uraeus on his brow and is sometimes depicted holding the sistrum and the *menat* necklace which were his symbols and those of his mother, Hathor. Despite Ihy's usual depiction in anthropomorphic form, there is limited evidence of the god being depicted in the form of a calf.

Worship

As the son of Horus and Hathor, Ihy was one of the triad of deities worshipped at Dendera and this was his main cult site. A very early shrine in this location was rebuilt in the 4th dynasty by Khufu

*(Left) The child god **Ihy**, son of Hathor. Roman birth house, Dendera. Elsewhere, the god was sometimes regarded as the child of other deities.*

*(Below) The god **Nefertem** wearing his characteristic lotus flower headdress with the addition of twin plumes and necklace counterpoises.*

(Right) **Nefertem**, *whose
lotiform headdress symbolized
both his identity as 'lord of
perfumes' and the
regeneration and rebirth
implicit in the lotus's mythic
role in creation. 18th dynasty.
Tomb of Horemheb, Valley of
the Kings, western Thebes.*

*(Opposite above) This
painted wooden head of
Tutankhamun emerging
from the blue lotus appears to
depict the king as* **Nefertem**.
*Chapter 81 of the Book of the
Dead provides a spell for the
deceased to be reborn in the
form of the lotus of this god.
Egyptian Museum, Cairo.*

Mythology

Shed, 'He who rescues' or 'the enchanter', was a protective god venerated mainly from New Kingdom times, though he is attested earlier. He was the master of wild beasts of the desert and river as well as weapons of war so that he was believed to provide protection from dangerous animals and martial harm as well as against illness and inimical magic. Shed was connected with Horus, sometimes appearing in the form Horus-Shed, to the extent that by the Late Period he was largely subsumed by the greater god.

Iconography

Shed was depicted as a child or young man, usually with a shaved head except for the sidelock of youth, wearing a kilt and sometimes with a broad collar and with a quiver slung over his back. He usually grasps serpents and wild, symbolically noxious animals and stands on the back of one or more crocodiles – essentially the same iconographic attributes found on *cippi* of Horus.

Worship

Shed was primarily a god of popular religion without his own temples and cultic service. He is attested in personal names, and representations of the god on protective plaques, pendants, and the like, are known from a variety of contexts. Two stelae dedicated to Shed were found in a chapel in the workmen's village at Amarna, showing the god's popularity and persistence in even that restrictive period.

lion-headed god (in reference to his leonine 'mother' Sekhmet) or standing on the back of a lion (perhaps also relating to his solar connections). In a few cases, depictions of Nefertem as a lion wearing his distinctive lotus headdress also are found. The god usually wears a short kilt and may hold a *khepesh* sickle sword – perhaps in association with one of his epithets, *khener tawy* 'protector of the Two Lands'. Because of his association with the primeval creation myths Nefertem may be represented as a child seated on a lotus blossom, and a variation on this motif is found in examples which show only the head of the god emerging from the lotus – as in the famous painted wooden example found in the tomb of Tutankhamun. In these images the association of Nefertem and the infant sun god is particularly close, and such depictions might be seen as representing the king as one or the other, or even both of these deities.

Worship

Nefertem's mythological characteristics meant that he was primarily a deity of royal and divine monuments. He was not commonly worshipped and, in fact, was popularly more often feared as the son of the ferocious Sekhmet. Amuletic 'divine decrees' of the Third Intermediate Period, made when a child was born, thus often promise to protect the child from manifestations of Nefertem along with other deities who were considered potentially harmful. On the other hand, a few protective amulets depicting the god were also made in this period.

The protective child god **Shed** *depicted grasping serpents and wild animals and standing on crocodiles. Pectoral, 18/19th dynasty. Roemer and Pelizaeus Museum, Hildesheim.*

Female Anthropomorphic Deities

Amaunet

Mythology

Amaunet, whose name means 'the female hidden one', was the consort of Amun and one of the eight Hermopolitan gods (see p. 77) who represented aspects of the primordial existence before the time of creation. As this group of original powers consisted of four balanced pairs of male and female deities, and Amaunet's name is clearly derivative of that of her husband, it seems likely that she may have originally have been an artificially created complement to Amun rather than an independent deity. Mythologically, as the Pyramid Texts show, the shadow of Amun and Amaunet was a symbol of protection (PT 446), and it may have been for this reason that Amaunet entered the ideology of royal ritual as a protective, tutelary deity. The goddess appears in this role in the Akhmenu or festival hall of Tuthmosis III at Karnak and in Ptolemaic times she was shown nursing the infant figure of Philip Arrhidaeus at her breast as part of scenes depicting the king's enthronement which were carved on the wall of Karnak's inner sanctuary. In a typical contortion of Egyptian mythology, Amaunet as 'mother of Re' could also be the mother of her own consort, Amun in the form of Amun-Re.

Iconography

In representational works Amaunet is usually depicted as a goddess in human form, wearing the Red Crown of Lower Egypt and carrying a papyrus-headed staff. The exact reason for this iconography is unclear, but at Karnak she is known to have been identified with the goddess Neith whose cult centre was in the Delta region. A colossal statue of the goddess set up in the temple of Amun at Karnak in the time of Tutakhamun is the most famous and imposing known representation of this goddess. A type of vulture amulet called 'amunet' is probably not to be connected with Amaunet and, like the goddess Mut, her representations are normally anthropomorphic.

*The temple of Amun at Karnak. Through the prominence of her husband Amun the goddess **Amaunet** achieved additional stature at Karnak, which became one of her most important cult sites.*

Worship

Despite her probable origins as the female complement of Amun, at Thebes Amaunet was overshadowed by Amun's other consort, Mut, since at least the time of Senwosret I (12th dynasty) in Middle Kingdom times. However, Amaunet is known to have had her own priests at Karnak and to have found some prominence in rituals associated with the king's accession and Sed or jubilee festivals. Although she does not seem to have been widely worshipped outside the Theban area, Amaunet did maintain her identity into the later dynasties of Egyptian history as an important local goddess.

Anat

Mythology

This goddess was one of a number of deities introduced into Egypt from the Near East. She was a warrior goddess particularly associated with the region of ancient Ugarit (modern Ras-Shamra) on the Syrian Levant; and although she was given titles such as 'mistress of the sky', and 'mother of the gods', Anat's nature was primarily martial. In the West Semitic myths relating to the goddess she ruthlessly sent an eagle to slay a youth named Aquat whose bow she coveted, and when she slew the monster Mot whom she fought, she vengefully hacked and burned his body before grinding his bones and scattering them in the fields. She thus became one of the patron deities of the military exploits of the Ramessid kings. A war hound of Ramesses II was called 'Anat in strength' (one of the daughters of that pharaoh was also called Bint-Anat or 'daughter of Anat') and the goddess was said to personally protect Ramesses III in battle. Anat was often referred to as a virgin, but she had a strong sexual aspect and was said to have united with Reshep and with Baal. In Egypt Anat was considered to be a daughter of Re and, like other Near Eastern goddesses, she was sometimes equated with Hathor – especially as the Egyptian deity could herself exhibit a violent aspect to her nature. Her aggression and foreign origin led to Anat being said to be one of the consorts of Seth, while her sexual aspect also led her to be associated with the fertility god Min.

Iconography

Representations of Anat usually reflect her mythological character, and she was characteristically depicted in the form of a woman holding a shield, spear and battle axe – often with one arm raised holding one of her weapons in a threatening gesture. She normally wears a long dress and a high crown similar to the White Crown of Upper Egypt but flanked by plumes on either side. Her iconography can sometimes reflect elements of the goddess Hathor with whom she was associated.

Worship

Anat is first attested in Egypt towards the end of the Middle Kingdom, but she seems to have been favoured by the Hyksos during their period of rulership in Egypt (one of whose kings took the name Anat-her), and by Ramessid times Anat was established as a fairly important goddess in the Delta region. In the Third Intermediate Period a large precinct was dedicated to the goddess in the temple of Mut at Tanis, and the name Anat-em-heb or 'Anat in her festival' was a theophorous name taken by Egyptians analagous to the older Hor-em-heb or Amen-em-heb 'Horus/Amun in his Festival'. Although the goddess was often associated with Astarte, the cult of Anat was clearly practised independently.

*The royal craftsman Qeh and his family worship the goddess **Anat** in her typical iconography. Lower register of the stela of Qeh from Deir el-Medina. 19th dynasty. British Museum.*

Anukis

Mythology

Anukis was the goddess of the southern border region of Egypt and particularly the cataracts of the Upper Nile in the region of Aswan. She was worshipped since at least Old Kingdom times as a daughter of Re, but in Middle Kingdom times she was incorporated into the triad of Elephantine as the offspring of Khnum and Satis. The goddess's name is difficult to interpret but may mean 'embracer' with either the meaning of motherly embrace or crushing, strangling grip. It is also possible that these meanings indicate a dual nature similar to the known nature of Hathor – with whom Anukis was associated at Thebes. Like Hathor and certain other goddesses, Anukis was viewed in a mythologically maternal role towards the Egyptian king, and is sometimes given the epithet 'mother of the king'. The Greeks identified Anukis with Hestia, their goddess of the hearth.

Iconography

Representations of the goddess depict her as a woman wearing a headdress which consists of a low crown surmounted with a row of bound plumes, sometimes with streamers at the rear or a

*The goddess **Anukis** wearing the plumed headdress that is her most characteristic attribute. Detail, decorated block, temple of Dakka, Nubia. Ptolemaic Period.*

uraeus at the front. In addition to the ubiquitous *ankh*, the goddess is often shown holding a papyrus sceptre. Her sacred animal was the gazelle, and she is sometimes depicted with this animal or by means of it. In her maternal role she is sometimes shown nursing the figure of the king, as in the small Nubian temple of Beit el-Wali.

Worship

In addition to the cult centres she shared with Khnum and Satis at Elephantine and Aswan, there was a temple dedicated to Anukis a little to the south of Aswan on the island of Sehel at the first cataract. She was worshipped throughout most of lower Nubia and appears in monuments such as the temple of Beit el-Wali along with other deities of the region. The popularity of the goddess is also attested in both male and female personal names such as 'beloved of Anukis' and '[he] of Anukis'.

Astarte

Mythology

Astarte was the West Semitic counterpart of the Babylonian goddess Ishtar (the Sumerian Inanna) worshipped in Mesopotamia. Like Ishtar, she had both a benevolent and a terrifying aspect – she was a goddess of love and fertility, but also of war. This latter aspect was dominant in the goddess's Syro-Canaanite manifestation – she appears as a war goddess in the Hebrew Bible (I Samuel 31) and entered Egypt in this guise during the New Kingdom where she was particularly linked to the military use of chariots and horses. She is mentioned on the Sphinx Stela set up by Amenophis II (perhaps her first appearance in Egyptian texts) as being delighted with the young prince's equestrian skill and, like the Syrian goddess Anat, was believed to protect the pharaoh's chariot in battle. She was adopted into the Egyptian pantheon as a daughter of Re (or sometimes Ptah) and wife of the god Seth with whose fearsome and bellicose nature she could easily be equated. According to the fragmentary 19th-dynasty story of Astarte and the Sea, the goddess seems to have been involved in thwarting the demands of the tyrannical sea god Yam, though the details of this myth are lost to us. While the sexual aspect of Astarte does not seem to have been as pronounced in Egyptian religion as in her Canaanite homeland, it was probably not entirely absent in her Egyptian mythology.

Iconography

In Egypt, Astarte was usually portrayed as a naked woman on horseback brandishing weapons and wearing an Atef Crown (see p. 121) or a headdress with bull's horns. According to the Classical writer Philo, Astarte wore the horns of a bull as a symbol of domination; but Mesopotamian and Syrian gods

*Ostracon with the image of
an unidentified goddess in
the form of a female winged
sphinx and with a complex
crown may well depict
Astarte in one of her
Near Eastern forms. New
Kingdom, from Deir
el-Medina.*

and goddesses commonly wore horns as a sign of their divinity, so this attribute may not have had any special significance with Astarte. A number of depictions of an otherwise unidentified goddess wearing a horned helmet – as on ostraca found at the workmen's village of Deir el-Medina – may well represent this goddess.

Worship

A formal temple of Astarte existed in the Ramessid capital of Pi-Ramesse in the Delta, and there were doubtless a number of temples where the goddess was incorporated into the existing cult, such as that found at San el-Hagar, the ancient Tanis, where Astarte is known to have been worshipped along with the Egyptian deities Mut and Khonsu. While there is not a great deal of evidence from Egypt of the popular veneration of Astarte – as opposed to expressions of her tutelary role as a military deity – votive stelae showing worship of the goddess are known, and the appearance of her image or name on scarabs and ostraca may also indicate a level of popular acceptance.

Baalat

Baalat was goddess of the Canaanite and West Semitic area and feminine counterpart of the storm god Baal. Baalat means 'lady' or 'mistress' and like the word *baal* is often connected with a locality as in the title 'Baalat Gebel' – 'lady of Byblos'. In Egypt, the goddess was associated with Hathor probably because they were both linked with the products and resources of the region to the northeast of Egypt and also because of the Canaanite deity's proclivity for sexuality. At Dendera Hathor was in fact described as residing at Byblos. In the small temple of Hathor located at Serabit el-Khadim in the Sinai, a sandstone sphinx was dedicated with both the name of Hathor in hieroglyphs and the name of Baalat in an early Semitic alphabetic script. Worship or recognition of Baalat in Egypt may have gone back as far as the time of the cedar wood trade with Lebanon during the reign of the 4th-dynasty king Sneferu. However her assimilation with Hathor meant that she was rarely regarded as an independent deity and was probably of most interest to Egyptians working or trading in the outlying regions where she was commonly found.

Hathor

'Lady of Fragrance...
Sovereign, revered one...
The Two Lands are under your sway.'

From a hymn to Hathor

Mythology

One of Egypt's greatest goddesses, Hathor may possibly have originated in predynastic or early dynastic times, though most of the evidence for her dates to later periods. While she appears infrequently in the Pyramid Texts, she is of great importance in the Coffin Texts and later religious literature and is eventually found in so many contexts that only the most important can be considered here.

Mother or wife of Horus: The name Hathor was written as a composite hieroglyph showing a falcon within the hieroglyphic sign representing a walled building or courtyard and literally means 'the house of Horus', relating to the goddess's mythological role as mother of the ancient falcon god. Though this may not have been her original name, it clearly became one of the most important aspects of her identity and it is as the mother of the god or as his consort that Hathor was worshipped in her main cult centre at Dendera and elsewhere. Hathor was also protective and healing in this role, with her healing aspect probably a result of the myth in which the goddess restored the sight of Horus after his eye had been injured by Seth.

Sky goddess: From the written form of her name – as the house of Horus – Hathor may also be seen as the sky in which the great falcon lived or, alternatively, as the womb, metaphorically referred to as 'house', from which he was born. In this form, Hathor was both a solar sky-goddess and a goddess of the primeval sky-waters (see below), and she may also have functioned as a personification of the night-time sky or the Milky Way, though this aspect of the goddess is less clear. But her connection with the sky is obvious, and in the Pyramid Texts she is equated in this guise with the clothing of the ascendant king who states 'My kilt which is on me is Hathor, my plume is a falcon's plume and I will ascend to the sky…' (PT 546) – referring to both Hathor and Horus as sky deities.

Wife or daughter and 'eye' of Re: Hathor was closely connected with the sun god Re whose disk she wears and whose wife, 'Eye' or daughter she was said to be. It has been suggested that the goddess was 'created' as a consort for the sun god as he rose to power at the beginning of the Old Kingdom, which fits well with much of the evidence we have of a relatively unknown goddess who is suddenly propelled into importance. Thus, Hathor played an important role in the royal sun temples of the later Old Kingdom, and her mythological relationship with the sun god was firmly established. As the 'Golden One' she was the resplendent goddess who accompanied the sun god on his daily journey in the solar barque, and she could also be feared as the vengeful 'Eye' of Re as seen in the story of the narrowly averted destruction of the human race by Hathor in her rage. In the Pyramid Texts Hathor assists the king in this role of 'Eye', however (PT 705) – preserving him by enabling his daily rebirth with the sun.

Cow goddess: Although Hathor is most probably not the cow-deity depicted at the top of the Narmer Palette as is often stated (see Bat), or the deity whose standard was the skull of a cow mounted upon a pole in predynastic times, an ivory engraving from the 1st dynasty depicting a recumbent cow inscribed 'Hathor in the marshes of King Djer's city of Dep' seems to reflect an early use of bovine imagery for the goddess. In any event, Hathor's bovine form is central to her developed persona and it is in this form that she must be related to the primeval cow goddess Mehet-Weret, whom she seems to have assimilated by Middle Kingdom times. In her bovine form Hathor also protected the king and acted as a royal nurse, symbolically suckling the monarch even as an adult. The so-called 'seven Hathors' found in the Book of the Dead and elsewhere were aspects of the goddess usually depicted as seven cows (see p. 77).

Goddess of women, female sexuality and motherhood: Hathor was often described as the 'beautiful one' and was inextricably associated with love and female sexuality as well as with motherhood. Not surprisingly, the Greeks identified Hathor with Aphrodite and the goddess was especially venerated by Egyptian women. Mythologically, Hathor was perhaps chief among those goddesses who represented the female creative principle who were called the 'hand of Atum', in reference to the story of Atum copulating with himself at the time of

(Above) **Hathor** emerging from a papyrus thicket at the base of the mountain, a motif particularly common in representations of the goddess from western Thebes.

(Left) **Hathor** in her bovine form protects the high official Psamtik in a manner reminiscent of the ancient motif of the king protected by the Horus falcon. 26th dynasty. Egyptian Museum, Cairo.

creation. Her overt sexuality is seen in the story which recounts how Hathor cheered the dejected god Re by exposing herself so that the great god laughed and rejoined the company of the gods. One of her names was 'mistress of the vagina', and Hathor was associated with all aspects of motherhood and believed to assist women in conception, labour and childbirth.

Mother or wife of the king: A particularly important aspect of Hathor's maternal nature is the role she played as the mother of the king, which was often expressed by means of her identity as the nurturing bovine goddess discussed above. The Egyptian king was called the 'son of Hathor' perhaps both in this sense and also in the sense that Hathor was the mother of the falcon god Horus whose incarnation the reigning king was. Hathor was also the 'wife' of the king from an early date, and already in the 4th dynasty we find the king's chief wife acting as her priestess and probably being viewed as the earthly manifestation of the

Queen Nefertari (right) greeted by the goddess **Hathor** in her fully anthropomorphic guise. 19th dynasty. Tomb of Nefertari, Valley of the Queens, western Thebes.

Hathor *in the guise of 'Mistress of the West', and with the headdress-symbol of Imentet, embraces the king in the afterlife. 18th dynasty. Tomb of Horemheb, Valley of the Kings, western Thebes.*

goddess. The relationship between Hathor and the king is particularly clear in the famous sculptural works from Menkaure's valley temple at Giza depicting Hathor with the king, which depict the goddess both in the role of a wife stood next to her husband and as a seated mother figure. Much later, in New Kingdom times, Hathor still remained a potent deity with whom royal wives were associated.

Goddess of foreign lands and their goods: In addition to her purely Egyptian roles, Hathor was also made a goddess of foreign lands as far apart as Byblos in the Lebanon in the north and Punt (probably northern Eritrea) in the south. As the patroness of foreign regions she oversaw trade and the acquisition of many mineral and other resources won from the deserts. In the Sinai, for example, the Egyptians mined turquoise, copper and malachite from the beginning of the Old Kingdom till New Kingdom times, and it was Hathor who acted as the protector and patroness of these remote mining areas. At such sites in the Wadi Maghara and later at Serabit el-Khadim and elsewhere, Hathor was specifically worshipped as 'the mistress of turquoise'. By extension, based on the similarity of colour, Hathor was also called 'mistress of faience'.

Goddess of the afterlife: Women aspired to be assimilated with Hathor in the afterlife in the same manner that men desired to 'become' Osiris, but the goddess's relationship to the deceased applied to men and women alike. From quite early times, especially in the Memphite region, she was worshipped as a tree goddess, 'mistress of the sycamore', who supplied food and drink to the deceased; and from at least the 18th dynasty she served as the patron deity of the Theban necropolis, where she protected and nurtured royalty and commoners alike, either in the form of the cow or as the anthropomorphic 'mistress of the west' who was often depicted welcoming the deceased to the afterlife with purifying and refreshing water. She was considered to receive the dying sun each evening and so it was a desire of the deceased to be 'in the following of Hathor'.

Goddess of joy, music and happiness: Although closely related to Hathor's aspect as a goddess of fertility, sexuality and love, her role as a provider of pleasure and joy was independent in itself. In a similar manner, while Hathor's relationship with music was clearly cultic in cases such as the ritual use of her rattle-like sistrum, it was also present in the use of music for the purposes of popular festivity and pleasure. Hathor was also associated with alcoholic beverages which seem to have been used extensively in her festivals, and the image of the goddess is often found on vessels made to contain wine and beer. Hathor was thus known as the mistress of drunkenness, of song, and of myrrh, and

Faience 'naos'-type sistrum decorated with the human-bovine face of **Hathor**. *26th dynasty. British Museum.*

it is certainly likely that these qualities increased the goddess's popularity from Old Kingdom times and ensured her persistence throughout the rest of Egypt's ancient history.

Iconography

Hathor was most often represented in anthropomorphic form as a woman wearing a long wig bound by a filet, or with a vulture cap with a low modius, surmounted by a sun disk between outward curving cow horns. In this form, in late representations, she is often indistinguishable from Isis, who took over many of her attributes and can only be identified by inscription. In her guise as mistress of the west Hathor wears a falcon perched upon a pole which served as the hieroglyphic sign for 'west'. Often she is depicted in a turquoise or red sheath dress or in a

143

form in the Theban area where we find monarchs such as Amenophis II, Hatshepsut and Tuthmosis III depicted crouching under the belly of the cow goddess drinking from her udder, or standing before her bovine image. In the same area we also find Hathor depicted as a cow emerging from a papyrus thicket at the foot of the western mountain of Thebes. Usually only the head and neck of the cow are depicted in this form of the goddess and the motif is clearly expressed in the elegant gilded head of a cow found in the tomb of Tutankhamun which doubtless represented this aspect of Hathor. When depicted in the form of a pillar, Hathor's image was a fusion of bovine and human characteristics. The capital of the pillar was formed as an essentially female face, but it was triangular in shape to incorporate the face with a cow's ears and a wig which curls at each side – perhaps in imitation of the bicornate uterus of the cow. In some contexts Hathor could also be represented in other zoomorphic forms – primarily as a lioness, or as a serpent, and even in plant form as a papyrus plant or sycamore tree.

Worship

The origins of the worship of Hathor are difficult to pinpoint. If she is not the goddess represented by the standard of the 7th Upper Egyptian nome, as seems likely, then the site later called Diospolis Parva (modern Hiw) was not a cult centre of the goddess from the Predynastic Period, as is sometimes suggested. The ivory artifact of the 1st dynasty mentioned above seems to show the antiquity of Hathor's worship, however. A temple of the goddess which continued through Roman times was first built at Gebelein (called by the Greeks Aphroditopolis) in the 3rd dynasty; and in the Old Kingdom several temples of the goddess are mentioned in the annals recorded on the Palermo Stone. The southern side of the valley temple of Khafre (Chephren) at Giza is known to have been dedicated to Hathor, and the title 'priestess of Hathor' becomes common from the 4th dynasty on. As time progressed, temples dedicated to Hathor were built throughout Egypt and also beyond Egypt's borders in Nubia, the mining regions of the Sinai, Byblos and other areas of Egyptian influence and control. In Egypt proper, important temples to Hathor were established at Atfih (also called Aphroditopolis by the Greeks), at Cusae, Deir el-Medina, and Dendera, her greatest cult centre. The annual high point of the developed cult of Hathor was the sacred marriage which took place between the goddess and Horus of Edfu in the third month of the summer season. Fourteen days before the appearance of the new moon, the statue of the goddess was taken from her shrine at Dendera and began the procession to the temple of Horus some 70 km (33 miles) to the south. Eventually, on reaching Edfu during the day before the new moon, the statues of Hathor

*The architectural use of **Hathor**-headed columns such as this is known to have occurred from Middle Kingdom times and may have originated earlier. Ptolemaic Period. Temple of Isis, Philae.*

garment combining these colours, and at Edfu she is specifically called 'mistress of the red cloth'. She is one of the few goddesses to be depicted carrying the *was* sceptre, and she may hold a papyrus stem or sistrum as a personal attribute. But the goddess could also be represented in bovine form as the 'great wild cow', as a woman with the head of a cow, or as a composite human-bovine face. Hathor was particularly venerated in fully bovine

144

and Horus participated in various rituals before being placed in the birth house where they spent the night together. For the next 14 days the celebrations which followed this divine marriage represented one of the greatest religious festivals of ancient Egypt in which royalty, nobles and commoners alike participated.

From the 18th dynasty to the end of the Dynastic Period Hathor-head amulets are common. Amuletic figures depicting a walking or seated goddess holding a papyrus stem start to appear in the Third Intermediate Period and may represent Hathor or Isis, though those showing the goddess with a cow's head certainly depict Hathor. In addition to these amulets and charms, many items of daily use, such as mirrors, perfume containers and cosmetic items, were decorated with the figure or symbols of Hathor according to her various roles. She was also commonly represented on *ex voto* objects, such as statues, stelae and offering vessels, which were left at her shrines and sacred areas as gifts and as requests for specific blessings. In her role as deity of sexuality and fertility, wooden and stone phalli were dedicated to Hathor and in at least one of her festivals a model phallus was carried in procession in formal reference to this aspect of her nature.

However, just as Hathor simply cannot be delimited in any of the individual forms or aspects described above, her worship was also often diverse and difficult to generalize. It must also be remembered that the worship of Hathor was so widespread that she was often regarded as a form of the indigenous deity in localities where she originally had no cult of her own. In this way, at Thebes Hathor was identified with Mut, and at Elephantine with Sothis. Despite the fact that by the end of Egypt's history Hathor was often assimilated with the goddess Isis, there remain many instances where the ancient deity still maintained her identity and continued to be venerated by the Egyptians with great affection.

Heret-Kau

A little known goddess whose name means 'she who is over the spirits', Heret-Kau seems to have been associated with the afterlife, but her exact nature and roles are uncertain. She was invoked in the foundation rituals of certain Lower Egyptian temples along with Neith and Isis, and a priest of the goddess is attested in Old Kingdom times, though little more is known of her cult.

Iat

A minor goddess of milk, this deity's name resembles *iatet,* an Egyptian word for milk. Iat was naturally associated with the nursing of infants and also, perhaps by extension, with their birth. She is mentioned in these ways in the Pyramid Texts where the king states 'my foster-mother is Iat, and it is she who nourishes me, it is indeed she who bore me' (PT 131). The goddess is seldom mentioned in Egyptian texts, however, and little is known about her.

Imentet

The goddess of the western regions of the dead, Imentet is recognized by the hieroglyphic sign for 'west' upon her head. She personified the necropoleis of the western side of the Nile Valley and is

The goddess Hathor depicted in the form of **Imentet** *(left), Goddess of the West, with Re-Horakhty. The falcon symbol on the head of the goddess represents the hieroglyphic sign for 'west'. 19th dynasty. Tomb of Nerfertari, Valley of the Queens, western Thebes.*

depicted in various tombs welcoming and giving water to the deceased. Yet although she had an independent iconography, Imentet often appears to be no more than a manifestation of Hathor or Isis.

Isis

'Mighty one, foremost of the goddesses
Ruler in heaven, Queen on earth…
All the gods are under her command.'

From an inscription at Philae

Mythology

The origins of Isis, who in the later periods of history was to become Egypt's most important goddess, are shrouded in obscurity. Unlike the situation with so many deities, no town in Egypt claimed to be her place of origin or the location of her burial and there are actually no certain attestations of her before the 5th dynasty. Yet she is clearly of great importance in the Pyramid Texts where she appears over 80 times assisting the deceased king. In the funerary texts of later periods her protective and sustaining roles were extended to nobles and commoners and her power and appeal grew to the point that she eventually eclipsed Osiris himself and was venerated by virtually every Egyptian. As time passed, and her importance grew, Isis merged with many other goddesses including Astarte, Bastet, Nut, Renenutet and Sothis, but her most important native syncretism was with Hathor from whom she took many of her iconographic attributes and mythological characteristics. Compared with some of Egypt's early cosmic goddesses, the mythological roles played by Isis are relatively restricted, yet they are immensely important roles which together personified her as a goddess of great power whose relationship with her followers was a personal one extending from this life into the afterlife itself.

Sister-wife of Osiris: According to the theology of the Heliopolitan sun cult, Isis and Osiris were both the children of Geb and Nut (see p. 18), but Isis became the wife of her brother and assisted him in ruling Egypt during his mythological kingship on earth. The myths concerning the two deities are extensive, and the fullest account is found in Plutarch's *De Iside et Osiride*, but after Osiris' death and dismemberment at the hands of his enemy Seth, Isis, along with her sister Nephthys, mourned inconsolably and began to search for her husband. Eventually the goddess found her husband's scattered parts and reunited his body (or in another version, she found his body enclosed in the trunk of a tree). Through her magic Isis revivified the sexual member of Osiris and became pregnant by him, eventually giving birth to their child, Horus. This underlying mythological role as the wife of Osiris is the basis of the importance of the goddess in all of her other aspects.

Mother and protector of Horus: A number of myths elaborate how Isis fled from Seth to the marshes of the Delta where she gave birth to her son Horus (see p. 201) at Khemmis or Akh-bity which means 'papyrus thicket of the king of Lower Egypt'. The Egyptians made literally hundreds of thousands of statues and amulets of the infant Horus nursing on his mother's lap in celebration of this mythic mother-child relationship showing the importance of the goddess's role as mother of Horus. After the birth of Horus various dangers threatened the young god, but throughout them Isis steadfastly cared for her son. She gained healing for him in one instance from a potentially lethal scorpion sting, which became the mythological basis for her healing powers and those associated with the so-called *cippi* or healing plaques of Horus the child. Isis continued to nurture and protect Horus until he was old enough to avenge his father and gain his rightful inheritance as king of all Egypt.

***Isis** nursing her son Horus, one of the most commonly depicted motifs in Egyptian art of the later periods. Bronze statuette. Ptolemaic Period, c. 300 BC. Egyptian Museum, Cairo.*

Mother of the king: As the wife of Osiris and mother of Horus, Isis was also the symbolic mother of the king who symbolically was the incarnation of the latter god. As early as the Pyramid Texts it is said that the king drinks milk from the breasts of his 'mother' Isis (PT 2089, etc.), and pharaohs of the New Kingdom and later periods had themselves depicted verbally and visually as the son of Isis. Because the goddess's name was written by means of the hieroglyphic sign for 'seat' or 'throne', it is possible that she originally was the personification of the power of the throne. Though many scholars feel that this may have been a later development, some have stressed that among some African tribes the throne of the chieftain is known as the mother of the king, and this anthropological insight fits well with what we know of the goddess.

Goddess of cosmic associations: Although not originally a cosmic goddess, the great importance of Isis nevertheless led to several cosmic associations being made for her. She assumed the role of the 'Eye' of Re and according to Plutarch she was also venerated as a moon goddess, though it is more difficult to find substantiation for this claim. Isis was, however, closely equated with the star Sirius, just as Osiris was equated with the constellation Orion. In this role she merged with the goddess Sothis and was sometimes called Isis-Sothis. At the height of her development, as may be seen in the hymns dedicated to her in her temple at Philae, Isis was also ascribed powers of cosmic proportions.

One hymn, which is not atypical, states that 'She is the Lady of Heaven, Earth and the Netherworld, having brought them into existence…'; and in a late aretalogy or list of her virtues, Isis is made to say, 'I separated the Earth from the Heaven, I showed the paths of the stars, I regulated the course of the sun and moon.'

Great of magic: Magic is central to Isis' many roles, for it is through magic that Osiris was revived, Horus conceived and protected, and the deceased – whether royal or commoner – assisted in the afterlife. The magic of Isis was also invoked in many spells for protection and healing – often imploring the goddess to come to the aid of a child or individual as if he or she were Horus himself. Most of the myths relating to the goddess stress her magical ability and one in particular – in which she learns the true name of Re – stresses her position as the greatest of the gods in terms of magical knowledge and power. In this myth Isis creates a snake which bites Re, and the stricken sun god is only healed of the snake's venom when he reveals his true name to her and thus further enhances her power.

Mourner, sustainer and protector of the deceased: Along with her sister Nephthys, Isis represents the archetypal image of the mourner in Egyptian literature and art. Both goddesses are mythically equated with the kite, a bird of prey with a particularly shrill piercing cry which has been thought to have been suggestive of the cries of women wailing

*The conception of Horus by **Isis** in the form of a hawk flying above the deceased Osiris. Isis is attended by the birth goddess Heket in the form of a frog at the foot of the funerary bier. Roman Period. Western roof chapel, temple of Hathor, Dendera.*

*The enthroned **Isis** (centre) and her son Horus receive offerings from the king. The goddess's headdress incorporates both the hieroglyphic sign for the throne and the horned sun disk. Roman Period. Temple of Hathor, Dendera.*

in mourning. The kite is also essentially a scavenging rather than hunting bird of prey that often wanders looking for carrion, and it is in this form that Isis was said to have searched for her murdered husband. The goddess was more than just a mourner, however, and through her great power Isis was able to function as the protector and sustainer of the deceased in the afterlife. Even in the Pyramid Texts she is said to care for the deceased, as she did for her own son Horus, and in the later periods of Egyptian history Isis becomes the supreme deity in this capacity, caring for the deceased in a personal way based on her character as a devoted mother.

Iconography

Isis is represented anthropomorphically in the form of a woman wearing a long sheath dress and crowned with either the hieroglyphic 'throne' sign which represents her name or, beginning in the 18th dynasty and most commonly in the later dynastic periods, with the horns and solar disk that

she appropriated from Hathor. The attributes she frequently holds, the sistrum rattle and *menat* necklace, were also taken over from Hathor, but Isis often holds only the generic *ankh* sign and papyrus staff commonly depicted with other goddesses. While her most commonly depicted representational pose shows her standing upright, Isis is also depicted kneeling – often with her hand resting on the *shen* or eternity sign. In either of these positions the goddess may be shown in the guise of a mourner with one hand lifted to her face. Often her arms are outstretched and placed around the seated or standing figure of Osiris and sometimes her arms are winged. She is depicted in this manner on the sides or corners of royal sarcophagi of the 18th dynasty and in statues or representations where she shelters and supports Osiris. In one known instance a figure of Isis protecting an image of herself personifies the protective nature of the goddess. Isis may also be represented as a scorpion, in fully avian form, as a kite, and as a mother goddess she may be depicted as a sow or in bovine form – in the latter case an analogue of Hathor or as the mother of the Apis bull. Finally, Isis could also be depicted in the form of a tree goddess, as in the tomb of Tuthmosis III in the Valley of the Kings where she appears as a personified tree, nursing the king at her breast which descends from one of the tree's branches. Amuletic depictions of Isis – usually in anthropomorphic form – or the symbol often called the Isis knot and known by the Egyptians as the *tyet*, were frequently placed on the mummy from New Kingdom times, and the goddess's protective power was doubtless utilized in amulets carried by many Egyptians in life also.

Worship

For a good part of Egyptian history it seems that Isis was not usually associated with any particular locality or worshipped in her own temples. Rather she was incorporated into the temples of other deities with whom she was associated. There are minor exceptions such as the chapel of Isis 'Mistress of the Pyramid' constructed at Giza in the 21st dynasty. However, the first important temple known to have been dedicated to the goddess, the Iseion – her temple at Behbeit el-Hagar in the eastern Delta – was not begun until the reign of Nectanebo II in the 30th dynasty, and only completed under Ptolemy III. Even here, as in her other later sanctuaries, Isis was venerated along with Osiris and Horus as was probably the case in earlier shrines which existed on the site. Other important chapels and temples of Isis were built at Dendera where the goddess was honoured by Augustus with a small independent sanctuary. This was at Deir el-Shelwit just south of Thebes where a small temple was also constructed for her in Roman times, and in her most famous temple on the island of Philae which was begun by Nectanebo I and grew under a series of Ptolemaic rulers and Roman emperors. The hymns inscribed there identify Isis with many other goddesses and show that she had successfully absorbed them as 'Isis in all her manifestations'. She was thus invoked in many spells of the later dynasties often tailored to her own character, as in spells and love charms to make a woman love a man as Isis loved Osiris, or to make a woman hate her present partner as Isis hated Seth.

Her influence was amazingly widespread. There was a temple of Isis at Byblos, where the goddess was equated with the local form of Astarte, from quite early times, though it is not known for certain whether the myth of Osiris' body being washed ashore at that site and the subsequent visit of Isis predates actual Isis worship at Byblos or not. Later, the worship of Isis became widespread in the Graeco-Roman worlds as one of the Eastern 'mystery religions', and the Classical writer Apuleius left a detailed description of the initiations into her cult. Evidence of veneration of the goddess has been found as far apart as Iraq and England, with temples being built to Isis in Athens and other Greek cities and later in many parts of the Roman Empire as well as in Rome itself. The cult of Isis rivalled those of the traditional Greek and Roman gods, and its importance and persistence is seen in the fact that her worship continued at Philae until the 6th century AD – long after most of Egypt and the wider Roman world had been converted to Christianity.

The goddess **Isis-Aphrodite** combined the great Egyptian deity with the Greek goddess of love in a form that became popular throughout much of the ancient Mediterranean world. Terracotta figurine, c. 100 BC. University of Leipzig Museum.

*This grey granite statue of **Iunit**, spouse of the Theban god Montu, is the first known representation of this goddess. 18th dynasty. Luxor Cachette statue. Luxor Museum.*

Iunit

A goddess of mainly localized importance in the Theban region, Iunit was incorporated into the local ennead of Karnak in New Kingdom times. Along with the goddess Tjenenyet, she was venerated as the consort of the ancient falcon war god Montu (see p. 203) in the town of Armant (Hermonthis) a little to the south of Thebes. Her name means 'She-of-Armant', and although the goddess first appears in reliefs dated to the reign of Mentuhotep III of the 11th dynasty, it is thought that she may have been worshipped there from very early times. It is perhaps possible, though not likely, that she is the goddess of the same name mentioned in the Pyramid Texts (PT 1066). The female deity Raet, also known from the Theban region, seems to be related to Iunit and may possibly represent a solar aspect of the goddess of Armant.

Iusaas

Iusaas was a Heliopolitan goddess whose name seems to mean 'she comes who is great' and who functioned as a feminine counterpart of the male solar-creator principle personified by Atum. Because of these associations Iusaas is depicted in anthropomorphic form as a woman with a scarab beetle upon her head. Like Nebet-hetepet (see p. 156) whom she resembles in function and who may be a different form of the same goddess, Iusaas played an important theological role as the embodiment of the female creative principle but was not important in terms of cultic activity or worship.

Khefthernebes

A minor goddess, Khefthernebes was a divine personification of the region of the Theban necropolis in New Kingdom times. She was overshadowed, however, by other female deities of the region such as Imentet, Meretseger and Hathor.

Maat

Mythology

The goddess Maat personified the concepts of truth, justice and cosmic order (Egyptian *maat*). She is known to have existed at least from the Old Kingdom and is mentioned in the Pyramid Texts where she is said to stand behind the sun god Re (PT 1582, *passim*), though it is not until the New Kingdom that we have evidence of her being called the 'daughter of Re'. The goddess was also associated with Osiris – said to be 'lord of *maat*' at an early date – and in later times she was subsumed to

some extent by Isis, although according to Egyptian mythology the husband of Maat was usually said to be the scribal god Thoth. As the daughter of Re Maat was also the sister of the reigning king who was the 'son of Re', and the relationship of the goddess with the king was a vital one. Both the monarch's legitimation and the efficacy of his reign were ultimately based upon the degree to which he upheld *maat* and it was common therefore for kings to style themselves 'beloved of Maat'.

Her role was multifaceted but embraced two major aspects. On the one hand, Maat represented the universal order or balance – including concepts such as truth and right – which was established at the time of creation. This aspect is the basis of her relationship with Re – for she is the order imposed upon the cosmos created by the solar demiurge and as such is the guiding principle who accompanied the sun god at all times. The order represented by Maat must be renewed or preserved constantly, however, leading to the ritual presentation of Maat discussed below. As a natural corollary of her identity with right balance and harmony Maat also actively represented the concept of judgment. In the Pyramid Texts the goddess appears in this role in dual form, as 'the two Maats' judging the deceased king's right to the thrones of Geb (PT 317), and in the later funerary literature it is in the 'Hall of the two Truths' (the dual form of Maat) that the judgment of the deceased occurs. The gods themselves, acting as the judges of the divine tribunal, are called the 'council of Maat'.

Iconography

Maat was almost always depicted in fully anthropomorphic form as a goddess wearing a tall feather on her head. The feather alone could represent the goddess, however, as could the hieroglyphic sign also used to write her name which resembled a builder's measure or the plinth upon which statues of the gods were placed. In representations of the king presenting Maat to the gods, the diminutive image of the goddess is sometimes depicted in such a manner as to form a rebus of the name of the king himself. This is the case when Ramesses II presents the goddess holding a 'User' staff and crowned with a solar disk of Re in addition to her own tall plume in order to spell the king's throne name: User-Maat-Ra. In the vignettes from the funerary papyri and in other depictions Maat is featured in the ceremony of the weighing of the heart of the deceased on the scales of judgment. Usually the heart is depicted being weighed against the feather of Maat or in some cases a small image of the crouching goddess, and the figure of Maat sometimes surmounts the balance scale itself.

Worship

A small temple to Maat was built within the precinct of the Montu temple at Karnak but such

*(Right) The image of **Maat**, with outspread wings and kneeling on a hieroglyphic sign which could signify 'mourn', was utilized at the entrance to a number of later New Kingdom royal tombs. 19th dynasty. Tomb of Siptah, Valley of the Kings, western Thebes.*

*(Below) This gilded silver image of an unknown king presenting the image of **Maat** represents the classic ritual of royal responsibility and adherence to order, justice and truth. 19th dynasty. Louvre, Paris.*

*The pharaoh Horemheb stands between the goddess **Maat** and the god Ptah, who, like certain other gods, could be called 'Lord of Truth'. 18th dynasty. Tomb of Horemheb, Valley of the Kings, western Thebes.*

sanctuaries for the formal worship of the goddess are uncommon and Maat is usually depicted in the temples of other deities. Even the title 'priest of Maat' is often regarded as an honorific that may have been given to those who served as magistrates or who dispensed judicial decisions on her behalf and who apparently wore small golden images of the goddess as a sign of their judicial authority. Theologically, the most important act of veneration for the goddess was the king's ritual presentation of a small figure of Maat in the temples of the gods. In the New Kingdom Maat was offered especially to Amun, Re and Ptah, though she was also sometimes presented to her husband Thoth and was in effect offered to all the gods. Erik Hornung has pointed out that the equivalence of the presentation of the goddess with all other offerings can be seen in epithets of Maat such as 'food of the gods' and 'clothing' and 'breath', as well as in other statements which affirm that the gods 'live on Maat'. Likewise Emily Teeter has shown that most examples of the king presenting Maat are essentially identical to those in which the king presents food, wine or other sustenance to the gods. At another level, the offering of the image of the goddess was also a tangible expression of the king's offering of his own

work of maintaining *maat* in preserving order and justice on behalf of the gods.

Merhyt

A goddess associated with the Nile and with water, Merhyt may have also represented the two halves – north and south – of the Nile Valley, though little is known of her actual roles.

Merit

Merit was a minor goddess of music who was nevertheless credited as having helped in the establishment of cosmic order by means of her music, song and the gestures associated with musical direction.

Meskhenet

Mythology

A goddess primarily associated with childbirth, Meskhenet also affected other aspects of a person's

Mythology

Mut was the great mother and queen of the gods who ruled in Thebes. Her origins are somewhat uncertain and while she is not known in textual or representational sources before the end of the Middle Kingdom, she may have been established in the Theban region or elsewhere at an earlier date. Some Egyptologists believe that Mut was virtually 'invented' as a wife for Amun while others feel that she was more likely a minor or little known deity who rose to prominence alongside the god. At some point, however, Mut displaced Amaunet, the original consort of Amun, to become the god's chief wife and the adopted mother of Khonsu in the great Theban triad. The goddess's name, which was written with the hieroglyphic depiction of the griffin vulture (*Gyps fulvus*), may possibly represent her earliest form, but this is doubtful as the word *mut* and the vulture used to write it mean 'mother' and this deity was regarded both generally as a mother goddess and as the mother of the king in particular. She was also identified with the Egyptian queen, and in the New Kingdom queens usually wore headdresses made in the form of the vulture which were also symbolic of divine motherhood.

From at least New Kingdom times, however, the primary mythological aspect of Mut was the lioness. In this form she was the southern counterpart of the northern lioness goddess Sekhmet and

life according to Egyptian belief. Beyond presiding over an individual's birth, the goddess was said to decide the life destiny of the child. The Westcar Papyrus describes how the goddess assured the infants Userkaf, Sahure and Neferirkare, the first three kings of the 5th dynasty, that they would all come to rule Egypt. Meskhenet also played a role in the afterlife. She is often depicted in funerary vignettes close to the scales upon which the deceased's heart was weighed – in order to assist in the rebirth of the individual entering the afterlife.

Iconography

The iconography of this goddess depicts her in the form of a rectangular brick (upon which ancient Egyptian women squatted to give birth) with the head of a woman at one end. She may also be depicted anthropomorphically as a woman with a brick upon her head, though this form is less commonly found. A symbol having two loops at the top of a vertical stroke which was used to represent the goddess almost certainly depicted the stylized uterus of the cow.

Worship

Although without a formal cult, Meskhenet was an important household deity and is mentioned in a number of known hymns and prayers. A text in the temple of Esna mentions four protective Meskhenets associated with the creator god Khnum, but apart from this there are few instances of the goddess's presence in temple settings except in ritual birth scenes.

*Head of the goddess **Mut**, detail of a calcite pair statue of Amun and Mut from the Luxor Cachette. Reign of Tutankhamun, reinscribed in the 19th dynasty. Luxor Museum.*

was also related to the cat goddess Bastet – with whom she was joined as Mut-Bastet. Her leonine aspect also made her one of the goddesses regarded as a savage 'Eye of Re' along with Sekhmet, Tefnut and others. She was associated with Re in other ways and part of a ritual in her honour asserts that she was present 'at the splitting of the *ished* tree together with Re in Heliopolis'. Mut was also associated with the god Ptah of Memphis. Unlike most of Egypt's other major goddesses Mut played relatively little part in funerary beliefs, and her mythological sphere of influence was mainly centred on the world of the living. Nevertheless, she is described in some versions of Chapter 164 of the Book of the Dead as a goddess who delivers souls and bodies from 'the abode of the demons which are in the evil chamber', showing her power could also extend to the netherworld. A final aspect of Mut's absolute and rather terrifying power is seen in the fact that by the latter part of the New Kingdom rebels and traitors who plotted against the king were destroyed by fire in the brazier of Mut – perhaps portraying a goddess who not only protected the person of the king but also the state itself with a power that was as fierce as it was final.

Iconography

Although the earliest known representation of Mut – dating to around 1700 BC – depicts her as a lioness-headed goddess, her primary representational form in later times was anthropomorphic. In this female human form Mut is depicted wearing a dress often brightly coloured in red or blue and marked with a pattern suggestive of feathers. She is distinguished by the vulture headdress surmounted by either the White Crown of Upper Egypt or the Double Crown of the combined Two Lands – the only goddess usually depicted in this composite crown. In this form she may be depicted standing or enthroned – often holding a papyrus or lily-headed staff – with Amun and Khonsu (see illus. p. 30) or, in seated representations, nursing an infant to symbolize her motherly role. She is represented in this manner in many amulets, though these can usually only be distinguished from similar amulets of Isis by the presence of the crowns or an inscriptional label. Because of her leonine aspect Mut was sometimes depicted as lion-headed and is in essence linked with Sekhmet in the many famous lion-headed statues of that goddess that were placed in the precincts of the temple of Mut at Karnak. Interestingly, this leonine aspect is also mirrored in some images of Amun, as in one of the side chapels of the temple of Khonsu at Karnak where he was depicted in lion-headed, ithyphallic form. In some vignettes to Chapter 164 of the Book of the Dead, beginning in the 21st dynasty, Mut is also depicted as a composite deity with outstretched wings, an erect phallus and three heads – those of a vulture, lion and human. These

somewhat bizarre images represented an aggressive deity 'mightier than the gods'.

Dedications to the goddess in the milder form of cat statuettes were extremely common, and a well-known informal New Kingdom painting which shows a cat with its arm around the neck of a goose perhaps also playfully suggests the familial relationship between Amun – whose sacred animal was the goose – and Mut in her feline form. It is interesting, however, that although Mut maintained her position as consort of Amun, in 'official' representations the relationship between the deities appears more familial than sexual. In sexual or fertility-related scenes Amun is portrayed with other 'younger' goddesses such as Isis and Hathor, but in formal scenes of power or matters of state it is Mut who is enthroned as the mature mother figure and powerful queen of the gods.

Worship

In Middle Kingdom texts Mut is called 'mistress of Megeb', a location in the tenth nome of Upper Egypt close to modern Qaw el-Kebir, but little more is known of her association with this area. She is also known to have had sanctuaries at Heliopolis and at Giza, and a large precinct at Tanis, in addition to her presence at Thebes. Yet although she was depicted along with her husband Amun on most of the major walls of the Great Temple at Karnak,

*(Opposite) The goddess **Mut**, in lion-headed form, with the notched palm-branch of recorded time. Luxor Temple.*

*(Left) Gold bracelet with image of winged **Mut** from Meroe. National Collection of Egyptian Art, Munich.*

*(Below) The goddess **Mut** with horned sun disk, temple of Khonsu, Karnak. As the mythological mother of Khonsu, Mut played a part in the cult of that god along with Amun, his mythological father. 20th dynasty.*

and in chapels and representations in many other temples throughout Egypt, Mut maintained a level of independence, and the goddess's main cult centre was her own 'Isheru' precinct to the south of Karnak Temple. The major part of her temple was constructed during the 18th dynasty, much by Amenophis III (who also set up the many statues of Sekhmet around its precincts), though construction was continued by rulers of later periods through Ptolemaic times. Mut participated in many of the great festival processions with her husband Amun and was transported in her own sacred barge for these occasions. She also exercised independent power in her own cultic rituals and ceremonies such as the important 'Festival of the Navigation of Mut' held on the great Isheru lake. Another of her important temple rituals both at her Isheru precinct and in her other sanctuaries was that known as the 'overthrowing of Apep', the inimical serpent who threatened the sun god. In this ritual wax models were made representing the physical enemies of Egypt which were identified by name before being destroyed. Mut is known to have had a temple oracle to which worshippers brought problems, and the 'Great Mother' was represented in many votive statues and amulets showing a high degree of personal veneration of the goddess.

Nebet-hetepet

A relatively minor Heliopolitan goddess whose name means 'mistress of the offering' or 'mistress of contentment', Nebet-hetepet was a feminine counterpart of the creator god Atum and her identity was similar to that of the goddess Iusaas also venerated at Heliopolis. Both goddesses personified the female principle represented by the hand with which Atum was said to grip his phallus in bringing the world into existence. Nebet-hetepet could be associated with Hathor and was venerated at several sites, but was primarily little more than a logical complement to the masculine deity of creation.

Nehemtawy

A minor goddess known mainly as the consort of the serpent deity Nehebu-Kau or of Thoth, Nehemtawy usually appears in anthropomorphic form and was frequently depicted in the shape of a goddess nursing an infant on her lap. In representations of this type she can usually only be distinguished from other nursing goddesses such as Isis and Mut by her headdress which is usually in the form of a sistrum. Little is known of the worship of the goddess other than that she was venerated with Thoth in his cult centres, especially that of Hermopolis in Middle Egypt.

*(Right) Bronze statuette of the goddess **Neith** in characteristic pose. Originally the goddess would have held an ankh and staff. Late Period–Ptolemaic era. Harer Collection, San Bernardino.*

Neith

Mythology

Neith is one of the most ancient deities known from Egypt. There is ample evidence that she was one of the most important deities of the prehistoric and Early Dynastic periods and, impressively, her veneration persisted to the very end of the pharaonic age. Her character was complex as her mythology continued to grow over this great span of time, and although many early myths of the goddess are undoubtedly lost to us, the picture we are able to

recover is still one of a powerful deity whose roles encompassed aspects of this life and the beyond.

Warrior goddess: While this aspect of her personality was perhaps overstated in some older studies of Egypt's deities, it is undeniable that Neith was associated with weaponry – either in a context of hunting or warfare or possibly both – from very early times. Her earliest emblems consisted of crossed arrows and bows and she was called 'mistress of the bow' and 'ruler of arrows'. Early Egyptian theophoric names such as 'Neith fights' and 'Neith is victorious' also underscore this bellicose aspect of the goddess's character, and from Old Kingdom times Neith could appear as one of the manifestations of the fierce 'Eye of Re'. In the Ramessid story known as the 'Contendings of Horus and Seth', Neith is a wise counsellor to whom Re himself appeals for help, though her aggressive nature is seen in her threat that she will grow angry and make the sky fall to the earth if her advice is not followed. The ancient Greeks identified Neith with Athena, probably primarily because of her warlike aspect, though there were other aspects of Neith which supported this association.

Creator goddess: In her cosmogonic role Neith was also identified with the waters of Nun which preceded creation, and with the process of creation itself. As such she was called 'great cow' or the 'great flood', and closely associated with the creator deity Mehet-Weret. The earliest extant reference to this role appears on the sarcophagus of the 19th-dynasty king Merenptah where Neith is said to be the creative force present at the very beginning, yet the idea was doubtless much older. In Roman times, texts inscribed in the temple of Khnum at Esna attempted to claim Neith as an Upper Egyptian deity who emerged from the primeval waters to create the world before travelling northward to found her Delta city of Sais. These same texts claim that Neith created both Re and the sun god's arch-enemy Apophis making her the original demiurge. Neith was also considered to have created mankind, and in the 'Contendings of Horus and Seth' she is specifically called Neith 'the eldest, mother of the gods, who illuminated the first face'.

Mother goddess: The metaphors of creation and birth clearly overlap and as mother of the gods, Neith is naturally seen as an archetypal mother figure. In the New Kingdom she was regarded as the mother of humans as well as gods, and a text dating from the 6th century BC states that it was she who invented birth. Amenophis II claims that he is one 'whose being Neith moulded' and in a similar manner it is Neith, along with the goddess Serket (another deity associated with motherhood), who supports the bed in which the queen and the god Amun embrace in the theogamies depicted in Hatshepsut's temple at Deir el-Bahri and in Luxor Temple. Already by Old Kingdom times Neith was regarded as the mother of the crocodile god Sobek and thus 'the nurse of crocodiles'. Although no male deity was firmly celebrated as the partner of Neith and it is sometimes said that she may have been a neutral, almost sexless deity not unlike the Near Eastern virgin goddess Anat or the Greek Athena, the evidence of Neith as a mother goddess militates against this view.

Goddess of Lower Egypt: Neith was certainly the most important goddess and perhaps the most important deity of Lower Egypt. Although she was sometimes called 'Neith of Libya', this reference may simply refer to the proximity of the Libyan region to the goddess's chief province in the western Delta. Her frequent representations wearing the Red Crown of Lower Egypt indicate that Neith came to personify the northern, Delta region or acted as tutelary goddess of the crown of that area. In the Pyramid Texts her aggressive nature is tied to this role in the statement, 'May the terror of you come into being…like the Net [Neith]-crown which is on the King of Lower Egypt' (PT 724). The temple of Neith at Sais was sometimes called the 'house of the bee' and the bee became an important monarchial symbol incorporated into the developed royal titulary often associated with Lower Egypt.

Funerary goddess: From Old Kingdom times (though rarely at first) Neith was associated with Egyptian funerary beliefs and rituals. In the Pyramid Texts she is said to watch over the deceased Osiris along with Isis, Nephthys and Serket (PT 606), and eventually the four goddesses were each assigned one side of the coffin with the responsibility of watching over the four canopic guardians known as the sons of Horus. In this role Neith was usually placed at the east side of the coffin as the protectress of Duamutef, guardian of the stomach of the deceased. Spells of the Coffin Texts equate the deceased with Neith in the underworld and also identify her as one of the judges of the dead (CT Spell 630). In the later 'Book of that which is beyond' Neith aids the king and Re himself in the underworld journey. Because Neith was also the inventor of weaving according to Egyptian myth, she was naturally associated with the funerary process as provider of the mummy bandages and shrouds.

Iconography

The first representational evidence for Neith is the early form of her emblem (two crossed arrows mounted on a pole) which occurs in predynastic times. The first anthropomorphic representations of the goddess herself occur somewhat later, in the Early Dynastic period, and these representations make Neith one of the earliest Egyptian deities

*Two-dimensional representation of **Neith** wearing the Red Crown mirrors the pose of the sculptural representation opposite. Detail, painted coffin. Egyptian Museum, Cairo.*

*The goddesses **Neith** (at left) and Nephthys before dual images of Osiris. Above her head, Neith wears one of the distinctive symbols used to write her name from early times. 20th dynasty. Tomb of Khaemwaset, Valley of the Queens, western Thebes.*

depicted in human form. At first, the goddess wears two bows on her head, and she is not depicted wearing the Red Crown of Lower Egypt, the region with which she was most closely associated, until the 5th dynasty when she appears this way in the temple of Userkaf at Abu Ghurob. Her representations frequently depict Neith carrying only the *was* (power) sceptre and the *ankh* (life) symbol, but in her guise as warrior goddess she frequently holds a bow and arrow or a harpoon. Later in history Neith could also be portrayed in zoomorphic form. Herodotus records seeing the image of the goddess as a kneeling cow with a sun disk between its horns during her festival at Sais, and a bovine form of her image was also used at Esna. The goddess could also appear in serpentine form as protectress of the king or of Re, as may be seen in the Book of the Dead (BD 185) and in the gilded wooden cobra found in Tutankhamun's tomb. In her guise as mother goddess and as the mother of Sobek, Neith is shown in the nursing motif, and amulets show the goddess as a woman standing, suckling a small crocodile at each breast, or as a woman with a crocodile's head. At Esna Neith was associated with the Nile perch which could represent her because,

according to myth, she turned herself into such a fish to swim in the primeval waters.

Worship

Neith's prominence in early dynastic times – as seen in 1st-dynasty labels, funerary stelae, and in the names of her priestesses and the contemporary queens such as Neithotep and Merneith – suggest the goddess was worshipped from the beginnings of Egyptian culture. In fact, the earliest portrayal of what is thought to be a sacred shrine in Egypt is associated with Neith. Her symbol stands in the enclosure of a reed-built sanctuary on an ebony label from Abydos which seems to depict a visit made by the 1st-dynasty King Aha to a sanctuary of Neith. Yet widespread depictions of Neith's standard on early pottery indicate the goddess was venerated over a considerable area, and she was doubtless the most important goddess of the Early Dynastic Period. This pre-eminence may have eventually been challenged, however, and the 5th-dynasty King Userkaf is believed to have re-emphasized the cult of Neith after the later rulers of the 4th dynasty had supplanted her with Hathor. Nevertheless, there is ample evidence that

(Above) **Nut** swallows the disk of the sun which travels through her body to be reborn the following day. The figures before the goddess tow the barque of the sun towards her. Detail, Book of the Day. 20th dynasty. Tomb of Ramesses VI, Valley of the Kings, western Thebes.

(Right) **Nut**, 'Mistress of Heaven', offers purifying water – in the form of wave-like lines which issue from her hands – to the deceased king on his entrance to the afterlife. 18th dynasty. Tomb of Tutankhamun, Valley of the Kings, western Thebes.

Qadesh

Mythology

Qadesh was a Syrian goddess of sacred ecstasy and sexual pleasure. Her Semitic name would seem to mean 'holy' and despite her Near Eastern orgins, the goddess was thoroughly assimilated into Egyptian religion in New Kingdom times to the extent that she was worshipped as part of a popular divine triad along with the fertility god Min and the Asiatic god Reshep. Qadesh was often linked with Hathor whom she resembled in some ways and with the inherently sensual Near Eastern goddesses Anat and Astarte, both of whom were known in Egypt.

Iconography

In Egyptian representations Qadesh is almost invariably depicted as a naked woman – shown frontally – holding lotus blossoms in her right hand and snakes or papyrus stems in her left hand, all of these being symbols of eroticism and fertility. Her similarities to Hathor meant that the iconography of her hairstyle and headdress sometimes approximate those of the Egyptian goddess. Frequently Qadesh is depicted standing on the back of a lion and in some representations she is flanked by Min on her right and Reshep on her left, the two gods usually being depicted standing on plinths or shrines which elevate them closer to the same height as the leonine-borne goddess.

Worship

In the Near East the cult of Qadesh involved the simulation of a sacred marriage between the goddess and her consort Reshep by her followers. It is not known whether similar rites were enacted in Egypt, where the cult of Qadesh was established at least as early as the 18th dynasty, but the goddess seems to have been fairly widely venerated. Her image is found on a good many 19th-dynasty votive and funerary stelae and she was worshipped in temples at Memphis and other locations.

Raet

By at least the 5th dynasty a female counterpart had been assigned to Re, the sun god, and the simple name of the goddess – the feminine form of the name Re – indicates that she was created to complement the sun god rather than having been a deity with an independent prior existence. In the Pyramid Texts the goddess is called Raet and though a fuller variant of her name was Raettawy, 'Raet of the Two Lands', it is uncertain at what point this form was first used. In later times she was addressed by the expanded titles 'Raet of the Two Lands, the lady of heaven, mistress of the gods', parallel to the superlative titles of her husband. Nevertheless, the goddess played a lesser role in Egyptian mythology than Hathor who was also viewed as the wife or daughter of Re. Raet is therefore not frequently represented pictorially and is usually depicted in a Hathor-like form as a woman wearing a solar disk with horns and a uraeus, sometimes with the addition of two feathers above the disk. A festival of Raet was held in the fourth month of the harvest season, and she was venerated, along with Montu and Harpokrates, in the Graeco-Roman temple of Medamud.

Renpet

A minor goddess who personified the year, and was recognized by the notched palm branch which was the hieroglyphic sign for 'year' which she wore on her head. Renpet was quite frequently depicted in temple and other scenes but had no important cult.

Satis

Mythology

The Upper Egyptian goddess Satis guarded the southern frontiers of Egypt in historical times and was also connected with the Nile. Her link with the upper reaches of the Nile perhaps caused her to be

*Upper section of the stela of the royal craftsman Qeh from Deir el-Medina showing the goddess **Qadesh** flanked by her consort, the Asiatic god Reshep (right), and the Egyptian fertility god Min (left) who was associated with the eastern desert regions. 19th dynasty. British Museum.*

associated with the annual inundation and with Elephantine in the area of Aswan which Egyptian mythology sometimes identified as the source of the Nile. Her name is first attested on stone jars found beneath the Step Pyramid at Saqqara (3rd dynasty), and by the 6th dynasty she is mentioned in the Pyramid Texts as purifying the deceased king with four jars of water from Elephantine. As 'mistress of Elephantine' Satis became the consort of Khnum and thus mother of Anukis, though a relatively early connection with the Theban god Montu is also known for Satis and the original consort of Khnum appears to have been the goddess Heket. When Khnum was identified with Re, Satis became an 'Eye of Re' and the goddess then sometimes assumed some of the characteristics of Hathor, the goddess more usually depicted in this mythological role. Satis was identified with the star Sirius, called Sothis, which heralded the Nile inundation each year. The Greeks identified Satis with Hera, the wife of Zeus.

Iconography

Satis is almost always depicted as a woman wearing the conical White Crown of Upper Egypt to which are attached antelope horns or plumes and a uraeus. Usually she wears a simple sheath dress and may carry an *ankh* or *was* sceptre as signs of her divinity rather than personal attributes. Early writings of her name use a hieroglyph representing a shoulder knot in a linen garment, but later writings use an animal skin pierced by an arrow. This latter symbol could have been assimilated from Anukis the huntress goddess who came to be seen as her daughter. The symbol is sometimes depicted with the goddess in representational works.

Worship

The principal cult centre of Satis was at Elephantine where her shrine was built on an early predynastic

*(Left) Silver amuletic statuette of **Satis**. Third Intermediate Period, 21st–24th dynasty. Harer Collection, San Bernardino.*

*(Right) **Satis** (at right) embraces Tuthmosis III. 18th dynasty. Carved block, temple of Satis, Elephantine.*

site. Research by Ronald Wells has shown that elements of the temple of Satis were carefully aligned with the position of the star Sothis or Sirius in the night sky, tying the goddess in this manner to the star's rising and the annual inundation of the Nile. It has also been pointed out that the goddess's temple was situated at a point where the waters of the inundation might be heard before they became visible in the lower reaches of the Nile, so that her function of protector of the borders could also be tied to that of guardian of the Nile's flood and its resultant fertility.

Serket

see p. 233, *Invertebrate and Insect Deities* section

Seshat

Mythology

Seshat (literally, 'the female scribe') was the goddess of all forms of writing and notation, including record keeping, accounting, and census taking as well as being 'she who is foremost in the house of books': the patroness of temple libraries and other collections of texts. The goddess is known from as early as the 2nd dynasty when she is attested assisting King Khasekhemwy in the ritual 'stretching the cord' ceremony, as Seshat was also the 'mistress of builders' and it was she who established the ground plan on the founding or expansion of every sacred structure. Beginning in the Old Kingdom Seshat is also found recording herds of different types of animals seized as booty, and from the Middle Kingdom she records the names of foreign captives in addition to their tribute, and in New Kingdom temple scenes she records the king's regnal years and jubilees on the leaves of the sacred ished or persea tree. Along with Nephthys, Seshat was said to restore the members of the deceased in the afterlife. The goddess was also associated with some few other deities, mainly the god Thoth whose sister, consort or daughter she was variously said to be. In New Kingdom times Seshat was parallelled by the goddess Sefkhet-abwy whose characteristics and attributes seem to be virtually identical to her own. It is unlikely, therefore, that she is really anything but a form of Seshat.

Iconography

Seshat was depicted in anthropomorphic form as a woman often wearing a leopard skin over her robe and with a headdress consisting of a headband with a tall extension upon which was an obscure emblem resembling a rosette or seven-pointed star. This 'star' is often surmounted by a bow or crescent moon-like symbol resembling downturned horns, which was itself sometimes crowned by

After his death Apis fused with Osiris, becoming the composite god Apis-Osiris or Osirapis (and later, in Hellenistic times, the anthropomorphically-depicted god Serapis). In this context the living Apis bull itself was sometimes called the *ba* of Osiris, and the process of assimilation with other deities also led to the composite Osiris-Apis-Atum-Horus. In some funerary texts Apis was said to thresh the grain in the afterlife, but it is usually his power and virility which are tied to the deceased – so that in the Pyramid Texts the deceased king claims the surging power of the bull's phallus as one of the ways in which he is said to be able to rise up to the heavens (PT 1313).

Iconography

Apis is usually represented as a walking bull which, in post-New Kingdom times, was depicted with a sun disk (occasionally a lunar disk) between his horns – often with a uraeus rising from its base. One of the most important markings of the Apis bull was a white triangular blaze on its forehead which is often represented in silver on statues of the god. Apis also had special wing-like markings on his back called by Herodotus an 'eagle' but representing the hawk's or vulture's wings. In many depictions of the bull a rectangular cloth with a decorative diamond pattern is also shown on its back. In the latest periods Apis was represented on coffins in the form of a sacred bull running with the mummy of the deceased as it was taken to the tomb. Amulets of Apis in the form of a standing bull are rare, but votive bronzes of the bull, decorated with its distinctive markings, are quite common from the Late Period. Representations of Apis as a bull-headed man are known but are also rare, and there is an unusual class of scarab amulets with the head of a bull on the body of the beetle – probably relating it to the funerary aspect of Apis.

Worship

The 5th-dynasty Palermo Stone indicates that Apis was worshipped as early as the reign of Den in the 1st dynasty. The god is known to have been especially venerated at the site of Memphis throughout most of Egyptian history, and according to the

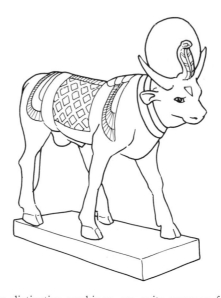

*Bronze statuette of the **Apis** bull showing stylized 'eagle's wings' and blanket on the bull's back as well as the sun disk and uraeus common on later images. Late Period. British Museum.*

*Huge calcite embalming table used in the mummification of the divine **Apis** bulls. 26th dynasty. Ptah temple complex, Memphis.*

3rd-century writer Aelian, the god's cult was established in that location by Menes and continued until Roman times which clearly reflects a tradition of great antiquity for the Memphite cult of Apis. According to the Pyramid Texts and the Book of the Dead, the divine bull was also worshipped at Sais and Athribis in the Delta.

In Memphis the Apis bull was kept in special quarters just south of the temple of Ptah where it was adored by worshippers and entertained by its own harem of cows. In addition to its participation in special processions and other religious rituals, the animal was utilized in the delivery of oracles and was regarded as one of the most important oracular sources in Egypt.

According to the Classical writers Herodotus and Plutarch, when the Apis bull reached its 25th year it was killed with great ceremony. It was then embalmed and buried in a great granite sarcophagus – some weighing as much as 70 tons – in the vast subterranean galleries of the Serapeum at Saqqara. The funeral ceremonies were extensive and it was said that in the Late Period, at the height of its worship, Egypt mourned for the deceased Apis as for the death of the pharaoh himself. The cow which had produced the Apis bull, known as the Isis cow, was also taken to Memphis at the time of the bull calf's selection and also kept under special circumstances to be eventually buried in the 'Iseum' not far from the Serapeum.

Bat

Mythology

Bat was an early cow goddess whose name means 'female spirit' or 'female power' and who appears to have been an important deity of the late predynastic and early historical times. It is difficult to pinpoint Bat's emergence in Egypt and it has been suggested, in fact, that she may have been imported from Mesopotamia. If, as seems likely, she is the goddess depicted on several predynastic objects (including the Narmer Palette), then her nature was almost certainly that of a celestial cow goddess. In any event, there are relatively few mythological references to her, and the earliest written evidence for the goddess is found in the Pyramid Texts which mention 'Bat with her two faces' – alluding to the double image of the goddess as seen in representations of her on sistra (see Hathor) and elsewhere. It has been pointed out that the mythology which developed around Bat may somehow have stressed the unity of Egypt, as her image is represented at the centre of a 12th-dynasty pectoral flanked by the reconciled Horus and Seth.

Iconography

Bat is seldom depicted in Egyptian art, though her iconography was distinctive and was an important

influence on the cult of Hathor. The goddess is depicted having a human head with bovine ears and horns – which grow from her temples rather than from the top of her head, and which curve inwards (rather than outwards as do Hathor's) giving the head a lyre-like appearance. Her head is often shown atop a pole or a 'body' resembling either a necklace counterpoise or a type of garment knot, so that the total image is suggestive of a sistrum or sacred rattle (see Hathor).

If Bat is the deity depicted at the top of the Narmer Palette, and also on the king's belt on that monument, she may also be the deity represented on an even earlier palette depicting a bovine head with outstanding ears taking the form of stars with stars attached to the tips of the horns and at the top of the head. This celestial-related iconography would also apply to the heads on the Narmer Palette which appear to look down on the depicted scenes from above.

In the Middle Kingdom the iconography of Bat was almost completely absorbed into that of Hathor, yet her particular image survives on many Hathoric columns.

Worship

Whatever the situation regarding this goddess's early history, as the chief deity of the 7th Upper Egyptian nome (the area around modern Nag Hammadi, where her cult centre was known as 'the mansion of the sistrum') Bat was an important local goddess for many hundreds of years. Eventually, however, in Middle Kingdom times, she was subsumed by Hathor, the greater goddess of the adjacent 6th nome of Upper Egypt, who took on her identity and attributes as an aspect of herself.

Buchis

Mythology

The sacred bull known to the Greeks as Buchis (in Egyptian *bakh*, *ba-akh* or *bakhu*) was worshipped in the area of Armant, the ancient Hermonthis, and elsewhere in the region of Thebes. The burial ground of these bulls, known as the Bucheion,

(Right) Limestone stela depicting a king offering to the **Buchis** bull associated here with Montu. Ptolemaic Period, c. 181 BC. Egyptian Museum, Cairo.

lies at the desert's edge at Armant, and although ravaged through time their discovery in 1927 revealed an impressive cemetery which seems to have functioned from New Kingdom times. Archaeological excavation presently provides evidence for well over 600 years of use from at least the time of Nectanebo II (c. 360 BC) to the time of the Emperor Diocletion (c. AD 300). The burial place of the cows who were the successive Buchis bull's mothers, known locally as the Baqariyyah, is also known at Armant. The legends of the Buchis bull were also long lasting, and as late as c. AD 400 the Roman writer Macrobius described the sacred animal with fanciful embellishments including the assertions that the bull changed colour every hour and had a coat of hair which grew backwards.

Iconography

Although, according to one ancient author, the Buchis was an animal with a white hide and black face, it seems the bull could be of other colouring (perhaps the basis of the statement by Macrobius above), and it is not always easily distinguished from other sacred bulls. Amuletic images are particularly difficult to identify, but depictions of the bull god are known on stelae and from various other contexts from the 19th dynasty on.

Worship

Buchis was associated with Re and Osiris and particularly with the Theban god Montu with whom he was identified directly. As a result, although never as important as the Apis bull of Memphis or the Mnevis bull of Heliopolis, Buchis was highly revered in the Theban region and was worshipped not only at Armant but also at Thebes itself, and at the outlying sites of Tod and Medamud. It is unlikely that a separate bull was maintained at all of these locations and more probable that a single sacred animal travelled from site to site and was represented by a statue during times of its absence from any one sanctuary. As was the case with other sacred bulls, Buchis delivered oracles at his cult sites but was also famous for curing diseases, especially those of the eye. The Buchis bull was also renowned for its ferocity, which may have been a result of its association with the warlike Montu, and inscriptions at Medamud show that the animal participated in fights with other bulls which were staged in a special arena.

Hesat

Hesat was a cow goddess with a number of mythological associations. Her name may mean 'the wild one'– and as the wild cow she may have been worshipped from very early times. Already in the Pyramid Texts she appears as the mother of Anubis (PT 2080) and of the deceased king (PT 1029) who is characterized as her son in the form of a golden calf. She was also the divine nurse of the living king. The goddess was said to suckle a number of divine bulls and in particular was the mythical mother of the sacred Mnevis bull, and in

some texts, the Apis bull. At Heliopolis, the mothers of the Mnevis bulls were buried in a special cemetery dedicated to Hesat. Hesat also provided milk for humanity and was often named with Tenemit, the goddess of beer, through her power to quench thirst through the 'beer of Hesat'. In the Ptolemaic era Hesat was associated with Isis, and the goddess was honoured in the form of the sacred Isis-Hesat cow.

Mehet-Weret

Mythology

An ancient cow goddess whose name means 'Great Flood', Mehet-Weret was said to have risen from the waters of creation and to have given birth to the sun god Re whom she placed, as a solar disk, between her horns. This image of the cow who raises the sun disk into the sky also equates Mehet-Weret with the heavens and she is clearly viewed as a sky goddess in the Pyramid Texts, where the goddess represents the waterway of the sky which was sailed upon by the sun god and the king (PT 1131). The goddess of the great flood was closely associated with Neith and often identified with her. In later times she was also associated with Hathor as we see in the Book of the Dead (Spell 186), where both are referred to as the 'Eye of Re' (see p. 206). She could also be linked with Isis.

*(Above left) Bronze statuette of the cow-headed goddess sometimes called **Mehet-Weret** but more usually Isis, the mother of the Apis bull. Late Period. Petrie Collection, University College, London.*

*Wooden images of the sky cow Isis-Mehet, or **Mehet-Weret**, from one of the funerary beds of Tutankhamun. 18th dynasty. Egyptian Museum, Cairo.*

Iconography

This goddess was almost invariably represented in bovine form. In the vignettes of the New Kingdom funerary papyri and in tomb paintings she is depicted as a sacred cow with the sun disk between her horns, kneeling on a reed mat and often wearing a ceremonial collar and decorated blanket and with a sceptre or flail rising from her back as a sign of her power and divinity. She is almost certainly the deity identified as Isis-Mehet (with Mehet probably being an abbreviation of Mehet-Weret) portrayed in the giant funerary couch of Tutankhamun made in the form of two slender cows each with a sun disk between its horns.

Worship

As a conceptualization of primeval creation Mehet-Weret appears to have had no independent cult of her own, though her importance as a power in the area of creation-birth-rebirth meant that she was commonly incorporated into funerary literature and representations.

Mnevis

Mythology

The divine bull of Heliopolis which was known to the Egyptians as Mer-Wer (though the oldest form of the name as it appears in the Coffin Texts is Nem-Wer) and called by the Greeks Mnevis was originally an independent deity who was incorporated into the worship of the sun god at an unknown early date. Manetho claimed that the god's cult was introduced in the 2nd dynasty, but he appears in only a minor capacity as the 'bull of Heliopolis' in the Pyramid Texts. Yet at some point Mnevis came to be regarded as the *ba* or 'power' of Re and a manifestation of the combined Re-Atum and as such gained considerable importance. According to Plutarch the Mnevis bull was second only to the Apis bull of Memphis and was also accorded great respect and privileges. He provided oracles in the same manner as the more famous Apis, being regarded as the 'herald' who made known the sun god's wishes and decisions. Like the Apis bull, Mnevis is also mentioned on the Rosetta Stone as one of the recipients of Ptolemy V's largesse. In a clear effort to enhance the stature of Mnevis, the priests of Heliopolis claimed Mnevis to be the father of Apis. Although there are some known links between Mnevis and Osiris – as in dual names such as Mnevis-Osiris and Mnevis-Wennefer – these may be simply the result of an abstract fusion of the solar and netherworld deities rather than being based on any direct mythological association.

Iconography

As with the other sacred bulls of Egypt, there was only one Mnevis bull at any one time and the

the god is primarily from later times. In the 23rd dynasty Osorkon III erected an important temple to him in the northern part of the main Bastet sanctuary at Bubastis, his mother Bastet's sacred town, and he was also worshipped in the town of Aphroditopolis in Upper Egypt. From these cult centres the god's worship spread southwards, and he is well represented in the Graeco-Roman temples of Upper Egypt as at Dendera, Edfu and Philae, and in Nubia where he appears at sites such as Dabod and Dendur. Worship of Mahes is also attested in the outlying oases of Bahariya and Siwa. In the practice of magic and popular religion Mahes is mentioned in amuletic papyri of the late New Kingdom, and in the Late Period he was frequently depicted in small amulets of glazed composition and sometimes of bronze.

Mekhit

Mekhit was a lioness goddess of which relatively little is said in Egyptian mythology. Like the better known Sekhmet and Tefnut, Mekhit was one of the deities who could symbolize the vengeful Eye of Re' (see p. 206), though she may have also been associated with the moon. The goddess was

the consort of Onuris and shared that deity's cult centre at This near Abydos.

Menhyt

A lesser-known lioness goddess, Menhyt was worshipped in the area of Edfu in Upper Egypt and also in the Delta region where she was associated with the goddess Neith at Sais and also with Wadjet, the tutelary deity of Lower Egypt with whom she is linked in the Coffin Texts. Menhyt could function as the uraeus on the brow of the sun god so that, as with many leonine deities, she was also regarded as a solar figure.

Mestjet

A lion-headed deity known from only a single inscription, Mestjet was one of the many forms of the fierce 'Eye of Re' and as such provides a clear example of the multiple manifestations of certain deities. The stela on which the goddess's name occurs dates to the 21st dynasty and was found at Abydos, indicating that Mestjet was a specific form of the 'Eye' worshipped in that particular region.

(Below left) **Mekhit**, *the lioness consort of the god Onuris. Detail from a Late Period bronze dyad. Musée des Beaux-Arts, Budapest.*

(Below) Stela depicting the veneration by a woman and her daughter of the lioness-goddess **Mestjet**, *a form of the 'Eye of Re'. 21st dynasty.*

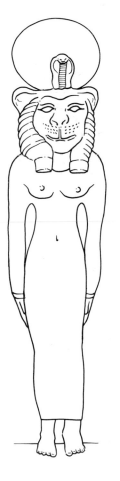

Mut

see p. 153, *Female Anthropomorphic Deities* section

Pakhet

Mythology

A fierce lioness goddess whose name means 'she who scratches' or 'tearer', Pakhet is known from Middle Kingdom times when she is described as a night huntress with sharp claws in the Coffin Texts. Pakhet was believed to instill terror in her enemies and must be grouped with the other leonine deities whose nature was, like Sekhmet, primarily aggressive. She was called the 'goddess at the entrance of the wadi', probably referring to the lion's habit of frequenting watering areas at the edge of the desert. The goddess was associated with a form of Horus as her partner, and identified with certain other goddesses such as Weret-Hekau, Sekhmet and Isis. Pakhet the huntress was naturally identified by the Greeks with their own goddess of hunting, Artemis.

Iconography

Pakhet was not widely depicted in Egyptian art, but she most often appears in combined anthropomorphic-zoomorphic form as a lioness-headed woman. She has no special iconographic attributes, but amulets depicting a lioness goddess standing over the prostrate figures of captives usually appear to represent Pakhet.

Worship

The worship of Pakhet was somewhat localized and her chief realm of influence was the area near Beni Hasan in Middle Egypt. A rock-cut chapel to the goddess carved out of the limestone cliffs by Hatshepsut and Tuthmosis III at that location is known by the Greek name Speos Artemidos (the cave of Artemis) due to Pakhet's association with that Greek goddess. A whole cemetery of sacred cats was dedicated to Pakhet in this area, though most of the burials appear to date to the Late Period. There is no surviving evidence for a cult for the goddess at Beni Hasan before early New Kingdom times, though it is probable that Hatshepsut honoured an established local deity and a formal cult of the goddess certainly seems to date to as far back as Middle Kingdom times. Amulets of the goddesses were worn in life, probably both for protection and fecundity.

Ruty

Mythology

The twin divine lion gods known as Ruty (Egyptian *ru.ty,* 'the pair of lions') were linked from early times with the Heliopolitan deities Shu and Tefnut (PT 447), but because lions typically inhabited the desert margins to the east and west of the Nile Valley, the animals came to be associated with the eastern and western horizons. The general identification of leonine deities with the sun god strengthened this association, and in the 17th chapter of the Book of the Dead Ruty thus became the double lion over whose back the sun rose each day. The twin lions were associated with a number of deities, however. In the Pyramid Texts they may be equated with Atum (PT 2081) and in the Coffin Texts we find associations with Geb, Nut, Re and other gods (CT I, 8; II, 204; II, 175; etc.). In the Book of the Dead they are equated collectively with Atum and also, individually, with Re and Osiris.

Iconography

Although Ruty could be depicted as a single lion or lion-headed god, the twin deity was most frequently shown as two lions, often positioned back to back and with the sun disk or horizon hieroglyph (*akhet*) depicted between them. Because the two animals respectively faced the sunset and sunrise they could thus replace the mountains on either side of the horizon hieroglyph in some representations. The well-known ivory headrest found in the tomb

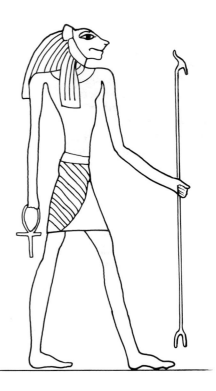

The twin lion deities called **Ruty** *may be depicted as two figures or as a single god with the dual name. 21st dynasty. Detail, relief from Tanis.*

of Tutankhamun which has a figure of the air god Shu supporting the head of the king is flanked by small images of the lions of the eastern and western horizon, so that the king slept symbolically between the guardians of yesterday and tomorrow.

Worship

The original cult centre of Ruty was perhaps Nay-ta-hut, the Greek Leontopolis (modern Tell el-Yahudiya) in the Delta, but in the Old Kingdom the lion pair was also aligned with Heliopolis and may have been venerated at a number of other sites. Although an essentially cosmic deity, Ruty also entered popular religion. In amuletic form the two lions linked the wearer with the daily regeneration of the sun and thus had significance in both every-day life and in funerary contexts.

Sekhmet

Mythology

Sekhmet was the most important of Egypt's leonine deities. As with many Egyptian goddesses, she had two distinct aspects to her personality – on the one hand a dangerous and destructive aspect, and on the other a protective and healing aspect. Her name means 'powerful' or 'the female power-ful one' and well suits the nature of the goddess as expressed in destructiveness, though it had equal implications for her other aspects. From early times Sekhmet was regarded as the daughter of Re and

she became one of the most important manifesta-tions of the 'Eye' of the sun god. In the version of the 'Eye' myth applying to Sekhmet (and also to Hathor), when Re became old and his human subjects began to plot against him he sent the fearsome goddess to punish them – leading to the near destruction of all humanity. Because Sekhmet was said to breathe fire against her enemies she was adopted by many Egyptian kings as a mili-tary patroness and symbol of their own power in battle, and bore martial titles such as 'smiter of the Nubians'. Even the hot desert winds were said to be the 'breath of Sekhmet'. The leonine goddess was also directly associated with plagues (often called the 'messengers' or 'slaughterers of Sekhmet'), and this too could be tied to the king's power. A passage in the Middle Kingdom story of Sinuhe states that the fear of the king overran foreign lands like Sekhmet in a time of pestilence. On the other hand, Sekhmet's power was used to protect the king in an almost motherly manner, and as early as the Pyramid Texts it is stated that the goddess conceived the king (PT 262, 2206). The goddess also had power to ward off pestilence and could function as a healing deity, even being called 'Sekhmet, mistress of life'. Sekhmet was associated with a number of other deities. She was regarded as the consort of Ptah and mother of Nefertem at Memphis where she eventually absorbed a number of other, more minor deities as 'mistress of Ankhtawy'. Sekhmet was often closely associated with Hathor – especially as the Eye of Re – and

Granite statue of the goddess **Sekhmet** *depicted as a lioness-headed woman. New Kingdom. Egyptian Museum, Cairo.*

Some of the hundreds of statues of **Sekhmet** *originally set up in the area of the temple of Mut at Karnak. New Kingdom.*

was also linked with the Theban goddess Mut, becoming in effect an aggressive manifestation or counterpart of that goddess, as well as being linked with Pakhet, the lioness goddess of Middle Egypt, and the cat goddess Bastet, among others.

Iconography

Sekhmet was most frequently depicted in semi-anthropomorphic form as a lioness-headed woman. She often wears a long wig and usually has a solar disk balanced atop her head in this aspect. The long dress worn by the goddess is frequently coloured red, and one of Sekhmet's epithets was 'mistress of red linen' symbolizing either her native Lower Egypt or her warlike nature. Sometimes her garment has a rosette pattern over each nipple, and while this has been suggested to reflect patterns in the shoulder hair of lions it is perhaps more likely that the pattern reflects an astronomical symbolism of the 'shoulder star' of the constellation Leo, which is marked in Egyptian astronomical paintings. During the reign of Amenophis III, hundreds of statues of Sekhmet were set up in the area of the temple of Mut to the south of the Great Temple of Amun at Karnak, and in the king's mortuary temple in western Thebes. These impressive statues, which were carved from hard black granite or diorite, often show the goddess either seated or standing with a papyrus sceptre – the symbol of her native Lower Egypt. Depictions of lion-headed goddesses wearing the Double Crown usually represent the fusion of Sekhmet and Mut. Sekhmet could also be depicted in fully zoomorphic form as a lioness, though this is relatively uncommon. The leonine head of the goddess (or that of certain other feline deities) was also represented on many examples of the so-called aegis – a metal collar surmounted by the head of a deity – which was used from New Kingdom times in cultic ceremonies for the propitiation of the divine.

Worship

Although the main cult centre of Sekhmet was at Memphis, the goddess had temples in many other areas. A sanctuary was built in her honour at Abusir (where she appeared in reliefs as early as the 5th dynasty), and she is represented in numerous temples up through the Graeco-Roman Period. Her association with other deities led to further cult centres, and there was a specific temple to the combined Sekhmet-Hathor, for example, at Kom el-Hisn in the western Delta. The priests of Sekhmet are known to have been organized for the cultic service of the goddess from Old Kingdom times and also appear to have played an important role in the magical aspect of medicine in later times, reciting prayers and spells over the sick along with the physical ministrations of the physicians. The formal rite of 'appeasing Sekhmet' was also performed by her priests to combat epidemics. In popular religion, the 'seven arrows of Sekhmet' which were believed to bring bad fortune were particularly feared, and many spells and charms were utilized for protection against the wrath of the goddess and her messengers. A spell called 'The book of the last day of the year' was recited over a piece of cloth which was worn around the neck at the potentially dangerous time of year's end, and on New Year's Day itself many Egyptians exchanged presents often in the form of amulets of Sekhmet or Bastet in order to pacify these goddesses. Statues of the goddess can still inspire feelings of awe or apprehension, and the famous statue of Sekhmet which now stands in the temple of Ptah at Karnak was broken early in the 20th century by local people who feared that it might harm their children.

Seret

The leonine goddess Seret is only meagrely attested, but a 5th-dynasty inscription shows that she had a presence in the 3rd Lower Egyptian nome. This area was inhabited by a predominantly Libyan population in early times, and it is possible that the goddess was of Libyan origin. Seret is sometimes called a 'goose goddess', but this is an error based on a misunderstanding of the writing of her name.

Shesmetet

The leonine goddess Shesmetet is generally believed to be a form of Sekhmet or Bastet but she may have originated as an independent deity, and it is possible that her epithet 'lady of Punt' reflects an origin in this African area to the south of Egypt. Shesmetet is attested in Egypt from the Early Dynastic Period, however, and is found in the Pyramid Texts (PT 262, 2206) where she is said to give birth to the king. In later funerary texts she also acts as the mother of the deceased. Shesmetet was associated with, or considered a personification of, the *shesmet* girdle – a belt with an apron of beads which was part of the attire of kings of the Early Dynastic Period and Old Kingdom and also worn by certain deities such as the god Sopdu. The goddess was depicted in leonine form or as a woman with the head of a lion, and her potential ferocity meant that she was invoked as a protective deity in popular religion and in magical spells.

Tefnut

Mythology

According to the Heliopolitan theology Tefnut was the daughter of Atum and the sister-wife of Shu, but she is a somewhat enigmatic deity. Her role in the cosmic scheme is usually said to be that of goddess of moisture and Tefnut certainly is associated with moisture in certain ways – she created 'pure water' for the deceased king from her vagina, for example (PT 2065), but her central identity may lie elsewhere. The goddess's name has no certain etymology, though it has been suggested to be an onomatopoeic representation of the sound of spitting as this is mythologically one of the ways in which the divine pair Shu and Tefnut were said to be created by Atum, and her name was represented by a pair of lips, spitting, in late texts. But the earliest evidence for Tefnut's original nature is found in the Pyramid Texts where James Allen has shown that it is perhaps possible that she represents the atmosphere of the lower world just as Shu represents the atmosphere of the upper – as it is said

that 'the earth (Geb) is held up under Nut (the sky) by your arms, Tefnut' (PT 1405). According to one story Shu and Tefnut were said to be created in the form of two lion cubs which also gave the goddess a distinct leonine identity. Tefnut was thus an 'Eye of Re', and a late papyrus tells how she quarrelled with the sun god and taking leonine form flew in a rage to Nubia from where she was eventually persuaded to return by the god Thoth.

Iconography

Tefnut could be depicted in fully anthropomorphic form but was most often represented as a lioness or lioness-headed goddess in reference to her leonine associations. In human or semi-anthropomorphic form, she may wear a long wig and a solar disk and uraeus atop her head. Like other leonine goddesses, Tefnut was frequently represented on cultic aegises and counterpoises, sometimes together with her brother-husband Shu in an unusual dual-headed design. The goddess could also be depicted as a rearing serpent upon a sceptre, and sometimes as a lion-headed serpent.

Worship

The main cult centres of Tefnut were at Heliopolis where she had a sanctuary as one of the members of that city's great Ennead, and at Leontopolis (modern Tell el-Muqdam) in the Delta where she was worshipped with her brother-husband Shu in the form of a pair of lions. Amulets and plaques of Tefnut are known from the Late Period, but popular veneration of the goddess was probably mainly localized around her cult centres.

Tutu

A somewhat obscure apotropaic god venerated mainly in the Graeco-Roman Period, Tutu was called 'he who keeps enemies at a distance' and was believed to provide protection from hostile manifestations of deities and demons. The god was said to be the son of Neith, and was depicted in the form of a walking lion or as a composite deity with human head, the body of a lion, the wings of a bird and a tail which was a snake.

HIPPOPOTAMINE DEITIES

The hippopotamus was viewed quite ambivalently in ancient Egypt. The male animal was regarded as dangerous and destructive and was therefore often associated with the god Seth. The female hippopotamus, however, while possessing the same strength and destructive potential, was regarded benignly as a protective force and a symbol of motherhood. Already in the Old Kingdom there were at least three names or distinct forms of the female

*The goddess **Tefnut**, depicted here with a large uraeus atop her head, was usually portrayed in leonine or leonine-human form but she could also be represented as a serpent, or as a lion-headed serpent.*

hippopotamus deity: Ipet, Reret and Taweret. Generally their characteristics were similar and it is often impossible to tell them apart, yet it is not always clear whether they should be viewed as differing forms of the same goddess or as separate, if largely conflated, deities.

Ipet

Mythology

The benign hippopotamus goddess Ipet was a protective and nourishing deity. In the Pyramid Texts the king asks that he may nurse at her breast so that he would 'neither thirst nor hunger...forever' (PT 381–82) and in later funerary papyri she is called 'mistress of magical protection'. Her name means 'harem' or 'favoured place' and under the epithet Ipet-weret, 'the great Ipet', the goddess fuses to some degree with Taweret 'the great one', but she nevertheless maintains some independent characteristics. Ipet appears to have had a strong connection with the Theban area and it is possible that the goddess may have served as a personification of that city. In Theban theology she was considered the mother of Osiris and as a result her afterlife associations are clear in the funerary texts in which she appears.

Iconography

Ipet, like the other deities in this section, was usually depicted as a fusion of hippopotamus, crocodile, human, and lion, though the hippopotamine aspect of her appearance is primary. She was depicted as a female hippopotamus, usually standing upright on legs which have the feet of a lion. Her arms are often human in appearance though they usually terminate in leonine paws and she was also depicted with large pendent human breasts and the swollen belly of a pregnant woman. The back and tail of the goddess are those of a crocodile and sometimes this aspect is shown as a complete crocodile stretched over her back. Sometimes her representations appear to be apotropaic in nature, and in the vignettes of funerary papyri (as in Spell 137 of the Book of the Dead) the goddess is shown holding a torch and lighting incense cones to provide light and heat for the deceased.

Worship

Ipet was particularly venerated in the region of Thebes. She appears as a protective figure on the back of a statue of a 17th-dynasty ruler of the area, and although in most areas there was no cult associated with the goddess, a temple of Ipet was built just west of the temple of Khonsu within the complex of the Great Temple of Amun at Karnak in the Late Period and Ptolemaic times. According to Theban beliefs it was at this place that the goddess rested when she gave birth to Osiris.

*The constellation called 'Isis', '**Reret-weret**' or other names. Tomb of Pedamenope, western Thebes.*

Reret

Mythology

The name Reret means 'sow', and under that name or Reret-weret 'the great sow', or in the form of Nebet-akhet 'mistress of the horizon' (an epithet also given to Taweret), the hippopotamus goddess represented one of the constellations of the northern sky as visualized by the Egyptians. This seems to have been the constellation we now call Draco in which the ancient pole star, Thuban, is situated; and in this role the stellar hippopotamus seems to have secured the 'imperishable' circumpolar stars which revolved around her. Perhaps due to her celestial associations Reret (and sometimes her other hippopotamine counterparts) was identified with the goddesses Nut and Hathor and was also seen as a protectress of the sun.

Iconography

The basic iconography of Reret – as a composite hippopotamus goddess with pendulous breasts and swollen belly – does not usually differ from that of her counterparts, though in astronomical contexts she takes on some specific attributes. While Reret may hold the knife, torch, *sa* or *ankh* signs found with all forms of the hippopotamus goddess, in astronomical paintings such as that on the ceiling of the tomb of Sethos I in the Valley of the Kings, she is frequently depicted holding a mooring post – sometimes in the form of a crocodile – to which is tethered one or more of the northern, circumpolar

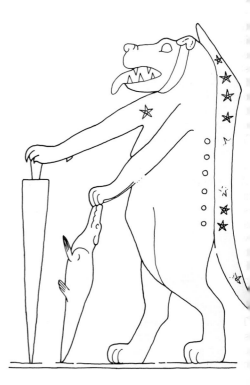

constellations in the form of an ox. There are also variants which show the goddess holding a rope attached to a foreleg which symbolizes the same constellation. In these depictions marks on the chest or arm of the hippopotamus may have represented the ancient pole star Thuban.

Worship

Unlike Ipet, Reret does not seem to have enjoyed the service of a cult in her own name; and unless she is viewed as only a form of Taweret, neither did she have amulets or other evidences of popular veneration.

Shepet

Shepet was a female hippopotamine deity who appears to be a form or name variant of Reret or Taweret. In some cases, as in the Roman birth house at Dendera, the goddess appears with typical 'Taweret'-like iconography but with the head of a crocodile.

Taweret

Mythology

Taweret (Egyptian 'the great [female] one'), along with her counterparts, is attested since Old Kingdom times. She is the most commonly encountered form of the Egyptian hippopotamus goddesses and had a number of mythological associations. Sometimes the hippopotamus goddess was equated with Isis – for example, in some of the Late Period *cippi* – though the connection between the two deities is not always clear. More frequently Taweret is equated with Hathor whose headdress she often shares. In the vignette accompanying Book of the Dead Chapter 186 in the Papyrus of Ani she stands together with the Hathor cow and seems to be identified with that goddess directly, as only Hathor is mentioned in the spell. An unusual stela in New York's Metropolitan Museum of Art shows Taweret offering before an image of Mut (sometimes seen as a form of Hathor) with the features of Tiye, wife of Amenophis III, a queen who seems to have associated herself with the hippopotamine goddesses for some reason. Because the male hippopotamus was associated with Seth in Egyptian religion, Taweret was called the 'concubine of Seth' who, according to Plutarch, had become one of the 'followers of Horus'. However, Taweret was also said to be the consort of the god Bes.

Iconography

Taweret is depicted with pendulous breasts and the swollen belly of a pregnant woman. The goddess usually wears a female wig which may be surmounted with a feathered headdress, a modius, or

with horns and solar disk. She is usually shown with her mouth open or her lips pulled back to reveal rows of teeth in a grimace which perhaps emphasizes her protective function. The main attributes of the goddess are the *sa* symbol of protection, the *ankh* symbol of life, and the torch, the flame of which was intended both to dispel darkness and to expel inimical forces. Usually the *sa* symbol is the largest of these attributes and is placed on the ground before the goddess who rests one or both paws upon it. Variants of Taweret include forms of the goddess with the head of a cat or the head of a human woman, as seen in a carved wooden unguent jar in the form of Taweret (or Ipet) but with the features of Queen Tiye. A small faience figure (probably a copy of an 18th-dynasty object) is known of much later – Ptolemaic – date which follows this same form, but with the more pronounced facial features of the Amarna Period.

Worship

Although she appears in some late temple scenes as a protective deity and there is a temple dedicated to

(Above left) **Taweret**, 'The Great One', stands with sa hieroglyphs of 'protection'. 26th dynasty. Egyptian Museum, Cairo.

(Above) Wooden statuette of Queen Tiye, wife of Amenophis III, in the form of **Taweret**. 18th dynasty. Egyptian Museum, Turin.

*The deceased worships **Taweret** and the goddess Hathor, in bovine form, who emerges from the hill representing the western necropolis of Thebes. The two deities, associated with childbirth and love respectively, and both having ties to the afterlife, were sometimes juxtaposed. Vignette to Spell 186, Book of the Dead of Userhatmose. 19th dynasty. Egyptian Museum, Cairo.*

the related goddess Ipet (Opet) at Karnak, Taweret was one of the Egyptian deities who regularly had no formal cult. Nevertheless, judging by the number of images of the goddess that have survived, Taweret appears to have been one of the most popular of Egyptian household deities. The goddess is one of the earliest recognizable apotropaic deities and she is widely represented on amulets from Old Kingdom times onward. She was represented on beds, head-rests and other small items of furniture as well as on cosmetic items such as unguent pots and spoons, and on various items with fertility significance such as the so-called 'paddle dolls'. Faience vases, similar to the small jars in human form which were made to hold mother's milk, were made in the shape of the goddess with pouring holes at the nipples, probably to hold milk for magical use. Interestingly, large numbers of Taweret amulets were found in the excavated houses of Akhenaten's capital at el-Amarna, and Bes and Taweret images decorated some of the rooms there. In a similar manner, some of the houses in the workmen's village at Deir el-Medina in western Thebes contained a room with a bed-shaped altar and wall paintings depicting Bes, Taweret and naked women which may have been associated with childbirth rituals. In her role as a protective deity, Taweret spread through Egyptian trade to the wider Mediterranean world, eventually entering the iconography of Minoan Crete, for example, where her form remains recognizable despite her modified role as a goddess of water.

CANINE DEITIES

Egyptian religion embraced a number of canine deities from ancient times. Some of these deities were clearly represented by the wolf while others – such as Anubis himself – were more generic and exhibit qualities of both the dog and the jackal. Regardless of their specific origin, canine deities frequently represent mortuary and afterlife concerns and almost all were eventually associated in some way with the cult of Osiris. In some cases, however, the connection between certain canine deities and the person of the king is clear.

(Above) Early slate palette representing unidentified canid. Oriental Institute Museum, Chicago.

*(Right) The **Anubis** animal exhibits features of both the jackal and the dog and may represent a hybrid of the two. Egyptian Museum, Cairo.*

Anubis

Mythology

Before the rise of Osiris, Anubis was the most important Egyptian funerary god. Originally he appears to have been primarily concerned with the burial and afterlife of the king, though eventually this role was extended to incorporate all the dead. One Egyptian text derives the name of Anubis from a verb meaning 'putrefy', and his name was also linked to a word for 'king's son', perhaps in relation to Osiris, but these are probably later, contrived etymologies, and the original meaning of the name is unsure. The god's association with the dead probably originated in the habit of desert canines scavenging in the shallow graves of early cemeteries, and, as was common in Egyptian protective magic, the form of the threat was then utilized in order to provide protection for the dead. During the Old Kingdom the prayers carved on funerary stelae and on the walls of the mastaba tombs were addressed directly to him, and in the Pyramid Texts he is mentioned dozens of times in connection with the king's burial. Eventually the cult of Anubis was assimilated to that of Osiris who was said to be the father of Anubis who in turn was said to have wrapped the body of the underworld god, thus tying his role in mummification to the worship of Osiris. Differing myths have survived regarding the parentage of Anubis, however. In the Coffin Texts he is the son of the cow goddess Hesat, and also the son of Bastet. According to other stories he was the son of Seth or of Re and Nephthys while Plutarch records the tradition that he was the son of Nephthys but by Osiris and was subsequently adopted by Isis as her own son.

The central, mortuary character of Anubis is well illustrated in the epithets which were given to him. There were many of these, but some of the most frequently used titles of the god summarize much of his essential nature.

Foremost of the westerners: Because the majority of the Egyptians' cemeteries were located on the western bank of the Nile – the symbolic direction of the setting sun and the underworld – the deceased were referred to as 'westerners'. Thus, the epithet *khenty-imentiu,* 'foremost of the westerners', refers to the role of Anubis as the leader of the dead. The title was taken from the earlier canine deity of that name that Anubis superseded at Abydos.

Lord of the sacred land: The epithet *neb-ta-djeser* or 'lord of the sacred land' is similar in signifying the supremacy of Anubis over the desert areas where the necropoleis were located. The word *djeser* is often translated pure, so this epithet sometimes appears in translation as 'lord of the pure land'. In addition to this general epithet Anubis also bore many titles relating him to specific areas in Egypt such as 'lord of the White Land', meaning the area of Gebelein.

He who is upon his mountain: Anubis *tepy-dju-ef,* 'who is upon his mountain', is a title probably based on the image of the jackal god watching over the burials of the dead from the heights of the desert cliffs overlooking the necropoleis. The expression was a general one relating to the high desert areas to the west of the Nile rather than any particular mountain.

Ruler of the bows: In the Pyramid Texts there is a reference to 'the Jackal, the Governor of the Bows,…Anubis' (PT 804), which refers to the so-called 'nine bows' – nine ethnically differentiated figures depicted as literal bows or as bound captives who represented the enemies of Egypt. This expression underlies the motif used in the seal which was placed upon the entrances to the royal tombs of the Valley of the Kings in the New Kingdom and which showed the figure of Anubis crouching above the nine bows, symbolizing the god's control of evildoers who might endanger the burial or the underworld enemies of the dead.

*(Above) **Anubis** attends the mummy of the deceased. Detail, painted sarcophagus. 22nd dynasty. Egyptian Museum, Cairo.*

*(Opposite left) **Anubis** in fully anthropomorphic form. 19th dynasty. Temple of Sethos I, Abydos.*

*(Opposite right) **Anubis** in his typical hybrid form. 19th dynasty. Tomb of Tawosret, Valley of the Kings, western Thebes.*

He who is in the place of embalming: Anubis *imy-ut* – 'who is in the place of embalming' – specifically referred to the role of Anubis in the embalming process and as master of the *per wabet*, the ritual tent or pavilion where embalming was carried out. Mythologically it was Anubis who embalmed the body of Osiris and the deceased king and who then protected it along with the containers in which the internal organs were preserved – a process known to have been carried out from at least the beginning of the 4th dynasty.

Foremost of the divine booth: The epithet *khenty-seh-netjer* can symbolically refer to either the embalming booth or the burial chamber, or even to the shrine in which the coffin and sarcophagus were placed in New Kingdom royal burials. The god is often depicted in this role in his zoomorphic form atop funerary chests, and the statue of Anubis seated upon a gilded model shrine which was found in the tomb of Tutankhamun symbolized

this epithet specifically. During the Graeco-Roman Period Anubis was transformed in a number of ways and took up new roles, becoming something of a cosmic deity reigning over the earth and sky and being related to arcane wisdom as the bringer of light to humanity. In his original mortuary role he was also associated with the Greek Hekate and with Hermes Psychopompos who, in Greek mythology, conducted the souls of the deceased to the shores of the River Styx.

Iconography

The various roles played by Anubis are seen in the iconography and representation of the god. In zoomorphic form, the identity of the animal depicted in representations of Anubis is uncertain, as the term used by the Egyptians for him, *sab*, was used of the jackal and of other canines. The animal bears certain traits of the dog family such as the long muzzle, its round-pupilled eyes, five-toed forefeet and four-toed hind feet, while on the other hand, its

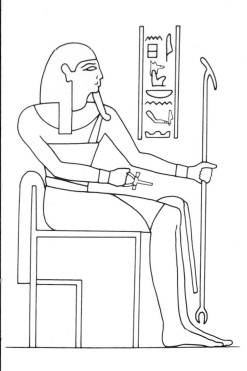

tail is wide and club shaped, and characteristically carried down, more like that of the jackal, fox or wolf. It is therefore possible that the original Anubis animal was a hybrid form, perhaps a jackal crossed with some type of dog. The black colouring of the animal was certainly symbolic and was connected with the discolouration of the corpse after its preparation for burial and the black colouration of the fertile earth which was itself a symbol of regeneration. In this animal form, Anubis is usually depicted lying on a shrine or simply as if he were doing so, with his ears erect, his legs stretched out before him, and his tail hanging down, vertically, behind him. Often he wears a collar and a ceremonial tie around his neck, and either a *sekhem* sceptre or flail (or both) may be shown rising from his back.

Anthropomorphically, the god is depicted – with rare fully human exceptions – with the head of the Anubis animal on a human body and sometimes with a tail, though usually without specific items of insignia or other iconographic attributes. He is shown performing the 'opening of the mouth' ceremony on the mummy and statues of the deceased, attending the mummy in the tomb and escorting the spirit of the deceased into the underworld. He is frequently depicted weighing the heart of the deceased against the feather of truth in the presence of Thoth and also leading the deceased before Osiris. His mythical role in protecting Isis at the time of her giving birth to Horus and his relationship with the well-being of the king led to the appearance of Anubis in the mammisi or birth-houses of the Graeco-Roman Period. In very late representations, as on the walls of the catacombs of Alexandria, Anubis could be shown dressed in the armour of a soldier in his protective role and with the lower half of his body in serpent form to reflect some of his later aspects.

Worship

Anubis was the chief deity of the 17th Upper Egyptian nome in Middle Egypt and its capital which the Greeks called Cynopolis or 'city of the dogs' (the modern el-Qeis), but his cult was recognized throughout Egypt and chapels and images of the god occur in mortuary temples and in tombs throughout the pharaonic period. The chapel of Anubis in the temple of Hatshepsut at Deir el-Bahri may have given continuity to an earlier shrine of the god in that area and provides an excellent example of the continuing importance of the god long after his assimilation into the cult of Osiris. Because he was said to have prepared the mummy of Osiris, Anubis became the patron god of embalmers, and in the Memphite necropolis an area associated with the embalmers seems to have become something of a focal point for the cult of Anubis in the Late Period and Ptolemaic times and has been termed the Anubeion by modern Egyptologists.

Masks of the god are known, and priests representing Anubis at the preparation of the mummy and the burial rites may have worn these jackal-headed masks in order to impersonate the god; they were certainly utilized for processional use as this is depicted representationally and is mentioned in late texts. The many two- and three-dimensional representations of Anubis which have survived from funerary contexts indicate the god's great importance in this aspect of Egyptian religion and amulets of the god were also common. The fragmentary royal annals preserved on the Palermo Stone show that in the Early Dynastic Period statues of Anubis were also made, which were called 'births' of the god.

Input

Input was the female counterpart of Anubis. Although she did not share the level of importance of her consort, she had her own cult in the 17th Upper Egyptian nome.

Sed

Sed was an ancient jackal-like god who may have been an independent deity or, alternatively, related in some way to the jackal god Wepwawet. The earliest textual attestation of the name Sed is found on the 5th-dynasty Palermo Stone, and he appears as the theophoric element in personal names up through the Middle Kingdom when he appears to be replaced by Wepwawet in this context. This and other evidence suggests the possibility that Wepwawet may have been an epithet of Sed in the same way that the feminine parallel Wepetwawet was an epithet of the goddess Neith, though this is uncertain. In any event, Sed was closely related to kingship ideology, and the ancient Sed festival or jubilee of the Egyptian king is thought to be named

*The importance of **Anubis** in ancient Egyptian funerary belief can be seen in the veneration accorded the god throughout much of Egyptian history. Of considerable importance long before the rise of Osiris, Anubis continued to be worshipped until the very end of the pharaonic period. 22nd dynasty. Tomb of Shoshenq. Egyptian Museum, Cairo.*

after this god. Sed was also associated with Maat in certain ways and may have been viewed as a champion of justice similar to Maat herself.

Wepwawet

Mythology

Wepwawet was possibly the oldest of Egypt's jackal gods, being already represented on one of the standards preceding the king on the Narmer Palette at the dawn of Egypt's historical period and attested by name from the 3rd dynasty. The archaeological evidence indicates that the god's origins were probably in the region of Upper Egypt, but his worship soon spread; and in the Pyramid Texts he is even said to have been born in the Lower Egyptian shrine of the goddess Wadjet (PT 1438). Wepwawet translates as 'opener of the ways', but the meaning of the god's name is susceptible to a number of interpretations. Based on the god's frequently attested warlike character, it could refer to the opening of the ways before the king in terms of military conquest. In the context of the 'adze of Wepwawet' which was used in the 'opening of the mouth' ritual, it could also refer to the magical opening of the deceased king's eyes and mouth, and in funerary texts Wepwawet also 'opened the ways' in leading the deceased through the netherworld and the king to ascension (PT 1009). The title could be even understood in a cosmic sense as he is said to open the way for the sun to rise in the sky (PT 455). As 'leader of the gods', the image of Wepwawet

Wepwawet in fully zoomorphic form on his characteristic standard. Detail, relief of Ramesses III.

went before the king and before other gods in many events and the name could possibly relate to his leading of these ritual processions. Finally, in the Memphite Theology we find the expression 'the opener of the body, Wepwawet', so that as a firstborn the god could be seen as the opener of the way of the womb. Wepwawet and Anubis are sometimes confused – even in the ancient texts – but it is clear that they were independent deities. On the other hand, Wepwawet may have been synonymous with the god Sed who was depicted as a canid atop an identical standard in early times. In a less direct manner, Wepwawet was identified with the god Horus and could also be associated with the sun god in the form of Wepwawet-Re.

Iconography

Wepwawet was usually depicted in the form of a jackal or other wild canid and occasionally as a jackal-headed man. In zoomorphic form the god may be differentiated from Anubis when colour is present, as Anubis was usually depicted as black and Wepwawet, grey. When standing, the latter animal was also characteristically depicted with its sloping back legs together rather than apart. But as a jackal-headed man the god often appears indistinguishable from Anubis and can then only be differentiated by a naming text, if not by his attributes of mace and bow. In vignettes of the 138th chapter of

King Wepwawetemsaf before **Wepwawet** *in hybrid form. Limestone stela from Abydos. 13th dynasty. British Museum.*

191

the Book of the Dead, Anubis and Wepwawet are depicted on either side of a representation of Osiris. As symbols of north and south or east and west are also usually depicted on each side, it seems clear that the two gods could have symbolic orientational significance – with Anubis often being linked to the north and Wepwawet the south. When depicted on his standard, Wepwawet usually has before him a peculiar bolster-like emblem called the *shedshed* which may have represented the royal placenta which was regarded as the king's 'double'.

Worship

In later historical times the major cult centre of Wepwawet was at Asyut in Middle Egypt which was called by the Egyptians Zauty and by the Greeks Lykopolis or 'wolf city'. The god was also venerated at Abydos in connection with Osiris. There Wepwawet went before the ritual funerary procession of the netherworld god, and on funerary stelae from this site it is common for the deceased to wish to 'behold the beauty of Wepwawet during the procession'. The god was also depicted on standards placed before the tomb in some depictions of funerary ceremonies. While infrequently found in expressions of popular veneration, Wepwawet appears in some theophoric names – as in the name of King Wepwawetemsaf of the 13th dynasty.

OVINE DEITIES

Most ovine deities were, in fact, male ram gods and the majority were tied to fairly specific locations.

Finely carved limestone head of the curved-horned 'Amun ram' Ovis platyra. 29th dynasty–early Ptolemaic Period, c. 400–200 BC. Metropolitan Museum of Art, New York.

The greatest of these was the god Khnum of the region of Elephantine, though a number of lesser ram-gods enjoyed considerable status in their own areas. Due to the similarity of the onomatopoeic name of the ram 'ba' and the *ba* spirit, a number of ram gods were worshipped as the *ba* of great gods such as Re or Osiris.

Banebdjedet

Mythology

An ancient ram god of whom little is known in terms of his origins, Banebdjedet means 'the *ba* Lord of Djedet' (the city of Mendes). Because *ba* the onomatopoeic word for ram, sounded like the word *ba* meaning spirit or soul, mythologically the god was supposed to have represented the soul of Osiris; and in the Late Period this association was widened to four manifestations – as the soul of Re, Osiris, Shu and Geb – an aspect of his nature which added considerably to his importance. As a ram god Banebdjedet was also credited with strong sexual powers and an account preserved in the temple of Ramesses III at Medinet Habu states that the god Tatenen transformed himself into Banebdjedet in order to copulate with the king's mother so as to become the father of Ramesses. The god also appears in the somewhat later story from the reign of Ramesses V which is preserved in Papyrus Chester Beatty I and which tells the story of the 'Contendings of Horus and Seth'. In this tale Banebdjedet plays an important role in counselling the gods to seek the advice of Neith whose judgment in the dispute is eventually followed. The god was made famous in the writings of the Classical authors, especially the Greek geographer Strabo, the poet Pindar and the Roman historian Diodorus of Sicily.

Iconography

Banebdjedet was depicted as either a ram or ram-headed man or, as is sometimes the case, as the head of a ram alone. From New Kingdom times he was often depicted as having four heads – two facing forward and two facing back – to symbolize his various aspects as the souls of the four gods he represented.

Worship

The main cult centre of Banebdjedet was at Mendes (modern Tell el-Rub'a) in the northeast Delta region where the god was worshipped along with his consort, the dolphin or fish goddess Hatmehyt, and his son Harpokrates. A cemetery with the sarcophagi for the burial of the sacred rams of the god has been excavated there, though little else remains of his cult. Although he was of considerable importance in the Delta region, Banebdjedet tended to be supplanted by other ram deities in southern Egypt, though the god's mythology demonstrates a wide and lasting veneration. According to the Greek poet Pindar, the ram was scandalously permitted to have intercourse with women in the course of its veneration, although this is not documented in any Egyptian sources. Ram-headed amulets of the Late Period may represent this deity, and certainly do so when they have four heads to depict the quadrapartite nature of the god.

Heryshef

Mythology

The name of the ram god Heryshef – literally 'he who is upon his lake' – has been seen as suggesting a creator god who emerged from the waters of the first primeval lake, but could just as likely refer to a feature such as a sacred lake of the god's main cult centre. The Greek historian Plutarch rendered the god's name as 'Arsaphes', translating the word as 'manliness', though this seems to be based on an apparent etymology suggested by the procreative aspect which was an essential part of the god's nature. To the Greeks Heryshef was Herakles and so his major cult site, the Egyptian Hnes, was named Herakleopolis by them. Mythologically Heryshef became associated with both Osiris and Re and was known as the *ba* of these great gods. He was also associated with Atum who was linked with the sacred 'naret' (perhaps sycamore) tree of Hnes.

Iconography

Heryshef was usually represented as a long-horned ram or a ram-headed man. In zoo-anthropomorphic guise the god was depicted in a kingly pose wearing a royal kilt but with the head of a ram. Due to his association with Osiris, Heryshef was also frequently shown as a ram or a ram-headed man wearing the Atef Crown, and due to his links with Re he was also depicted in both forms wearing the disk of the sun god.

Worship

The main centre of worship for this god was the town of Hnes or Herakleopolis Magna near the modern town of Beni Suef in Middle Egypt. The god's cult is attested at this site as early as the 1st dynasty in the records preserved on the Palermo Stone, and Heryshef is known to have risen to considerable importance during the First Intermediate Period when Hnes served as the capital of northern Egypt – though the earliest temple structures that have been found so far at this cult site date to Middle Kingdom times. The temple of Heryshef was greatly enlarged in New Kingdom times, especially by Ramesses II, and appears to have thrived down to the end of the pharaonic period. In popular

*Exquisitely formed votive image of the ram god **Heryshef** from the temple at Ehnasya. 25th dynasty. Museum of Fine Arts, Boston.*

religion, Heryshef appears on ivory wands of the Middle Kingdom and is also doubtless the deity represented by many ram or ram-headed amulets of the later periods.

Kherty

Kherty, whose name means 'lower one', was a chthonic deity, a ram-god who inhabited the netherworld and who thus could act as a deity of hostility or protection. The god appears in the Pyramid Texts (PT 1308) where he is said to be the 'chin' of the king among many deities representing the deceased monarch's body, and in the Old Kingdom he was associated with Osiris as a benevolent partner of the underworld god who could aid in protecting the king's tomb. On the other hand, Kherty also exhibited a negative side and it was said that Re himself must protect the king from Kherty's malevolence (PT 350). Kherty was usually depicted as a ram, but may also appear in the form of a bull or a lion, and in any of these forms he could have associations with the sun god Re. Kherty's ovine form also led to his association with the great ram god Khnum. The god's major cult centre seems to have been at ancient Khem or Letopolis, the modern Ausim, a little to the north of Cairo.

Khnum

Mythology

Khnum was one of Egypt's most important ram gods and was associated with the Nile and with the creation of life. Particularly linked to the first cataract, Khnum was said to control the inundation of the Nile from the caverns of that region, and as a result of this power as well as the inherent pro-creative power of the ram, the god was viewed as a personification of creative force. His association with the Nile and with its fertile soil perhaps contributed to his portrayal as a potter who was said to have shaped all living things upon his wheel. As a result of his creative ability and because the onomatopoeic word for ram – 'ba' – was similar to the spiritual aspect or *ba* of living things Khnum was held to be the *ba* of Re. The sun god was thus depicted as a ram-headed being in his netherworld representations – and Khnum himself is sometimes called Khnum-Re. In a similar manner Khnum was also held to be the *ba* of the gods Geb and Osiris. At

Esna Khnum was associated not only with the lion goddess Menhyt, but also with the goddess Neith. Khnum's association with the Nile made him 'lord of the crocodiles', probably suggesting his link to Neith who was mother of the chief crocodile god Sobek. At Elephantine he was the head of a triad including the goddesses Satis and Anukis who were also associated with the same geographic area.

Iconography

Khnum was most frequently depicted in semi-anthropomorphic form as a ram-headed god wearing a short kilt and a long, tripartite wig. Originally he was depicted with the horizontal undulating horns of *Ovis longipes*, the first species of sheep to be raised in Egypt, but as time progressed he was also depicted with the short curved horns of the *Ovis platyra* ram (the 'Amun ram') and may thus have two sets of horns atop his head. He was also called 'high of plumes' and may wear two tall feathers, or the plumed Atef Crown or the White Crown of Upper Egypt on his head. His most distinctive attribute, however, was his potter's wheel, with which he was often depicted moulding a child as a concrete representation of his creative work. This motif was naturally utilized in the mammisi or birth houses of temples where Khnum was shown forming the infant king, but the

*The god **Khnum** as a ram-headed man with the undulating horns of the* Ovis longipes *ram. Decorated red sandstone block from a temple wall. 18th dynasty. British Museum.*

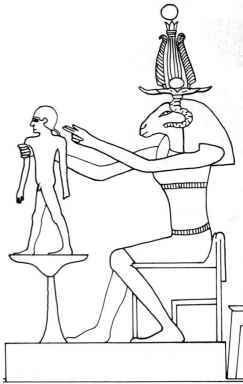

*(Below) **Khnum**, as creator, moulds an infant on his potter's wheel.*

The so-called 'Famine Stela' on the island of Sehel near Aswan contains a prayer to **Khnum**, *who is said to have ended a time of famine caused by low Nile floods. Ptolemaic Period.*

motif also appears elsewhere. Khnum may also be depicted in the fully zoomorphic form of a walking ram as in many amulets and pectoral decorations, but these representations are often extremely difficult to distinguish from those of other ram deities such as Heryshef without inscriptional evidence.

Worship

The major cult centre of Khnum was the island of Elephantine at Aswan where he was venerated since early dynastic times. Mummified rams sacred to the god and buried in stone sarcophagi have been discovered there, but little survives of early cult structures. The best preserved temple of the god is that at Esna which, although it only partially survives, provides much information about the god and his cult in the many inscriptions carved on its walls. He was worshipped as the *ba* of Geb at Herwer near the modern town of el-Ashmunein, and as the *ba* of Osiris at Shas-hotep, the modern Shutb near Asyut. Khnum's role as 'potter of mankind' led to

his widespread recognition as a god associated with childbirth, but his role as controller of the Nile also deserved veneration, and amulets of the god may have been made with either or both of these powers in mind. The so-called Famine Stela of Sehel Island near the first cataract preserves an appeal to the god at a time of famine caused by seven years of low inundations. The inscription dates to Ptolemaic times, but is a copy or forgery of a text from the time of the 3rd-dynasty king Djoser.

OTHER MAMMALIAN DEITIES

While deities taking bovine, feline, hippopotamine and ovine form represented most of the important mammalian deities of ancient Egypt, a number of more minor gods and goddesses took other animal forms. These were usually represented by actual animals such as the baboon and the desert hare, though the most important exception – the god Seth

determinative sign for many words connoting confusion and chaos at the personal, social and cosmic levels. These aspects are all reflected in Egyptian mythology. An early tradition claimed that at birth he savagely tore himself free from his mother (PT 205), and his mythical relationships are characterized by dispute and violence. According to legend he murdered his brother Osiris and then engaged in a bitter contest – lasting 80 years – with Osiris' son and heir Horus whom Seth challenged for the role of ruler. In this ongoing contest Seth put out the eye of Horus who in turn castrated Seth, doubtless an allusion to suppressing the sexual power and violence of a god associated with rape and unnatural sexual desire. Although his sister Nephthys was said to be his wife, even she left him to become a 'follower of Horus' – as did the hippopotamus goddess Taweret, also said to be a consort of Seth, along with the violent Semitic goddesses Astarte and Anat. In the Pyramid Texts (PT 1521) Seth is also paired with the sometimes belligerent goddess Neith. The god's fearsome character is seen in Egyptian funerary literature of the New Kingdom where he is said to lurk in the netherworld and to seize the soul of the deceased, and his malevolent character was thought to be expressed in this world too: in all kinds of problems and crimes, in sickness and disease, as well as civil unrest and foreign invasion. He was associated with storms and bad weather of all types and thought to be the god of the wide, raging sea. Mythologically he could be identified with other malignant Egyptian deities including the great chaos serpent Apophis, and by the Greeks with their own rebellious god Typhon.

God of strength, cunning and protective power: The character of Seth was not entirely inimical, however, as he was also held to be cunning and of great strength and these qualities could be put to good use. One of his most common epithets was 'great of strength' and his sceptre was said to weigh the equivalent of some 2,000 kg (4,500 lb). He was the lord of metals: iron, the hardest metal known to the Egyptians, was called 'the bones of

Seth'. In the Pyramid Texts it is the strength of Seth that the deceased pharaoh claims (PT 1145) and many living kings linked themselves to him. The warrior Tuthmosis III called himself 'beloved of Seth', for example, and Ramesses II is said to have fought like Seth at the great Battle of Kadesh. The strength of Seth is also utilized in representational motifs associated with kingship, as in the scenes carved on the thrones of statues of Senwosret I in the Egyptian Museum in Cairo which show Seth opposite Horus in the *sema-tawy* motif binding the symbolic emblems of the two halves of the land. Here the strength of the god as well as his juxtaposition with Horus is implicit in the scene. Even the gods utilized this god's help. Thus, although Seth could be identified with the chaos serpent Apophis, he also was the sun god's defender against the same monster, and a partially preserved myth tells how the strength and cunning of Seth were used to save the goddess Astarte from the baleful sea god Yam who had demanded her as tribute. Seth could also protect and help in other, more mundane ways. A diplomatic text which tells of Ramesses II's marriage to a Hittite princess explains how the king prayed to Seth to mitigate the severe weather conditions which were obstructing the princess's journey to Egypt, and the god's help was similarly sought by many common people for protection or the removal of adverse conditions.

Iconography

Seth was originally depicted as an animal with a curved head, tall square-topped ears, and erect arrow-like tail. In the earliest clear examples of the creature it is depicted standing, though later representations often show it in a seated or crouching stance. The god's importance is clear in his representations. A 12th-dynasty pectoral now in the Myers Museum of Eton College shows the Seth animal in this representational form, in juxtaposition with the god Horus as emblems of the two kingdoms. The close association between Seth and the rulers of the Ramessid dynasties is also seen in monuments such as the statue in the Egyptian Museum in Cairo which depicts the crouching god overshadowing and protecting a king in exactly the same manner in which other monarchs were portrayed beneath the figure of the Horus falcon. The seated Seth animal appeared on the standard of the 11th Upper Egyptian nome – in later times impaled with a knife to counteract any potential harmful effects of the image. There are also scenes showing the sun god's barque being towed by Seth animals instead of the customary jackals.

As time progressed Seth was also represented in semi-anthropomorphic form as a man with the head of the Seth animal, and this form of his iconography is particularly common in New Kingdom times. Images and amulets of the god sometimes show him wearing the White Crown of Upper Egypt, or

Despite their inimical characters, the reconciled **Seth** *and Horus may be depicted as a combined deity with the heads of both gods.*

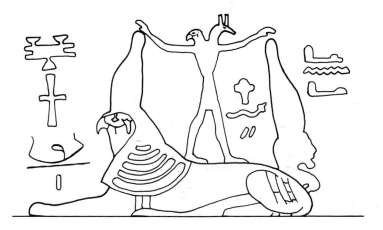

the Double Crown of all Egypt which he claimed as his own. He may also be shown fused with Horus as a two-headed deity – symbolically binding the rulership of Upper and Lower Egypt. In the later periods sculptural representations of the god in this aspect were often changed into more acceptable deities such as Thoth. Yet in some areas where his worship persisted the image of Seth was used until relatively late times. In the temple of Hibis in the el-Kharga Oasis the god is represented as a winged figure slaying the serpent Apophis, which some scholars believe may have provided the original inspiration for the Christian motif of St. George and the dragon. Besides the Seth creature itself, a number of animals such as the antelope, ass or donkey, goat, pig, hippopotamus, crocodile, and certain fish were all regarded as symbolically noxious by the ancient Egyptians, so the god Seth could also be represented in the guise of any of these abhorred creatures. Sometimes they are used as visual circumlocutions for the god, just as written texts often refer to him indirectly as 'Son of Nut' rather than by name. In the first millenium BC, in fact, the Seth animal disappeared from art and writing, and the god was most often depicted as an ass with a knife in its head to render it harmless.

Worship

Despite the odious character of Seth, the god received considerable veneration in the course of Egyptian history. Even apart from those periods in which he was elevated to a special position, Seth had cult centres in various areas, particularly in Upper Egypt where he was often regarded as a patron deity of the region, symbolically balancing Horus in Lower Egypt. The earliest cult centre of the god was perhaps at ancient Nubt, the Greek Ombos, some 30 km (19 miles) north of Luxor, at the entrance to the Wadi Hammamat, which controlled trade to the eastern desert regions; it was in this area that Seth was said to have been born. He was particularly venerated in the 5th, 10th, 11th and 19th Upper Egyptian nomes, but was also venerated in Lower Egypt, especially in the area of the 14th nome which lay on Egypt's northeastern frontier. A cult centre of the god also existed in the royal city of Pi-Ramesses in the Delta.

Although not an aspect of the veneration of the god, the sacrifice or destruction of various Sethian animals was part of the religious activity which surrounded him. From early times a red ox representing Seth was sacrificially slaughtered, and a similar ritual of 'strangling the desert bird' is also known. Perhaps the most important rituals of this type involved the hippopotamus, and as early as the 1st dynasty there is evidence for the royal hippopotamus hunt in which, in its developed form, the king hunted and destroyed a wild hippopotamus as a symbol of the victory of Horus over Seth. The destruction of the hippopotamus became

*The god **Seth**, in his role as a martial deity, teaches Tuthmosis III the use of the war-bow. 18th dynasty. Detail of a relief, Karnak.*

especially important in the later periods when widespread veneration of Seth had virtually ended.

Amulets of the god are not common, though some which are extant are finely made and were probably worn in life. Seth was frequently invoked or mentioned in magical spells, however, where his power was utilized against other inimical deities or against conditions which were relevant to the god's own mythology. Overall, however, for many Egyptians – over much of Egypt's history – Seth seems to have remained an ambivalent deity at best. Wax models were made of the god and then thoroughly destroyed in order to combat his influence, and in the Egyptian calendar the birthday of Seth was regarded as a particularly unlucky day.

Thoth

see p. 215, *Avian Deities* section

Wenet

Wenet was the patron goddess of the area of Wenu – later Hermopolis Magna – and the surrounding 15th Upper Egyptian nome. Known as 'the swift one', her sacred animal was the desert hare and the goddess was depicted as a hare, as a woman with a standard bearing a recumbent hare on her head, or even with a human body and the head of a hare. According to Plutarch the Egyptians venerated the hare on account of its swiftness and keen senses, but the animal's form was also taken by certain underworld deities and at the same time Wenet was sometimes depicted in the form of a snake, a creature with clear chthonic associations. Amulets made in the shape of the hare may have related to some aspect of the creature's nature or may have been symbolic of this goddess. Wenet's male counterpart, Wenenu, was sometimes identified as a form of Osiris or Re.

Avian Deities

Re in the form of a ram-headed falcon, and associated with Osiris, flanked by the mourning Isis and Nephthys as birds of prey. 19th dynasty. Tomb of Siptah, Valley of the Kings, western Thebes.

FALCON DEITIES

From the very earliest times the falcon seems to have been worshipped in Egypt as representative of the greatest cosmic powers. According to this view, the eyes of the soaring bird were the sun and the moon and the speckled feathers of its underside were perhaps seen as the stars. Many falcon gods existed throughout Egypt, however, and only as time progressed were a good number of these assimilated to Horus, the most important of the group. The falcon also became important as a symbol of the king and as a god of kingship from early dynastic times.

Dunanwi

Mythology

Dunanwi (Egyptian for 'he who stretches out the claws'), god of the 18th Upper Egyptian nome, may have originally been a divinity in feline or other form, but was certainly known in the aspect of the falcon for most of Egyptian history. In the Pyramid Texts Dunanwi appears in several contexts, including that of the purification ritual in which the god represents the east in accompanying Thoth, Horus and Seth who together personify the four cardinal points (PT 27, etc.). From the end of the Old Kingdom, however, Dunanwi seems to have been

assimilated with the falconiform god Nemty and is known only in that form thereafter. The falcon god Dunawi – 'he who stretches out the arms [wings]' – mentioned in the Coffin Texts (CT VI 126) appears to be a later form of the same god. Like most other local falcon gods, Dunanwi was also assimilated to Horus and, because his nome was next to that of Anubis (the 17th Upper Egyptian nome), he appears in the Late Period as the combined Horus-Anubis.

Iconography

As depicted on the standard of his nome, the falcon god stands atop the standard's pole, often with wings outstretched. In some representations the bird's own wings are clearly extended, while in others the falcon appears to have a second set of wings which are stretched in addition to those folded over its back.

Worship

The repeated mention of Dunanwi in the Pyramid Texts might indicate at least a fairly wide level of recognition of the god in early times, but after his assimilation with Nemty and eventually with Horus, his veneration was mainly limited to that of a local god of his own nome.

Horus

Mythology

Horus was one of the earliest Egyptian deities, his name attested from the beginning of the Dynastic Period, and it is probable that early falcon deities such as that shown restraining 'marsh dwellers' on the Narmer Palette represent this same god. The Turin Canon, which provides some of our most important information on Egypt's early history, specifically describes the Predynastic rulers of Egypt as 'Followers of Horus'. But Horus appears in many forms and his mythology is one of the most extensive of all Egypt's deities. The following represent only the god's most significant aspects – and each subsumes a number of forms of the deity.

Sky god: This is the original form of Horus as 'lord of the sky' which preceded all others. The Egyptian word *her* from which the god's name is derived means 'the one on high' or 'the distant one' in reference to the soaring flight of the hunting falcon (if not a reference to the solar aspect of the god). Mythologically, the god was imagined as a celestial falcon whose right eye was the sun and left eye the moon. The speckled feathers of his breast were probably the stars and his wings the sky – with their downsweep producing the winds. It was in this form that Horus was apparently worshipped at some of Egypt's earliest sites such as Hierakonpolis and in which Horus assimilated a number of other local falcon gods.

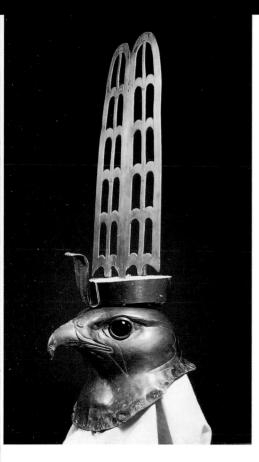

into the Osirian family in very different form – as a divine infant.

God of kingship: Horus was directly linked with the kingship of Egypt both in his falconiform aspect and as son of Isis. From the earliest Dynastic Period the king's name was written in the rectangular device known as the *serekh* which depicted the Horus falcon perched on a stylized palace enclosure and which seems to indicate the king as mediator between the heavenly and earthly realms, if not the god manifest within the palace as the king himself. To this 'Horus name' of the monarch other titles were later added, including the 'Golden Horus' name in which a divine falcon is depicted upon the hieroglyphic sign for gold, though the significance of this title is less clear. The kingship imagery is found in the famous statue of Khafre seated with the Horus falcon at the back of his head and in other similar examples. As the son of Isis and Osiris Horus was also the mythical heir to the kingship of Egypt, and many stories surrounding his struggle to gain and hold kingship from the usurper Seth detail this aspect of the god's role. Harwer (Haroeris) 'Horus the Elder' was the mature god represented in these stories who battles the typhonic Seth for 80 years until the tribunal of the gods finally awards him his rightful place on the throne of all Egypt

*(Left) Golden head of an image of the **Horus** falcon with polished obsidian eyes. From Hierakonpolis, one of the earliest cult centres of Horus. 6th dynasty. Egyptian Museum, Cairo.*

*(Below) The **Horus** falcon, as tutelary deity, protects King Khafre. Detail, one of 23 statues from the valley temple of Khafre. 4th dynasty. Egyptian Museum, Cairo.*

Sun god: As a natural outgrowth of his role as cosmic sky god Horus was also venerated more specifically as a solar god. An ivory comb of the 1st-dynasty king Djet depicts a falcon in a boat riding on outstretched wings suggesting the falcon traversing the sky as the sun god. The Pyramid Texts specifically refer to Horus in solar terms as 'god of the east' and he appeared in at least three forms in this guise. As Horakhty or 'Horus of the two horizons' Horus was the god of the rising and setting sun, but more particularly the god of the east and the sunrise, and in the Pyramid Texts the deceased king is said to be reborn in the eastern sky as Horakhty (PT 4). Eventually, Horakhty was drawn into the sun cult of Heliopolis and fused with its solar god as Re-Horakhty. As Behdety or 'he of [the] *behdet*', Horus was the hawk-winged sun disk which seems to incorporate the idea of the passage of the sun through the sky. As Hor-em-akhet (Harmachis) or 'Horus in the horizon', Horus was visualized as a sun god in falcon or leonine form. By New Kingdom times, the Great Sphinx of Giza – originally a representation of the 4th-dynasty king Khafre – was interpreted as an image of Hor-em-akhet.

Son of Isis: Horus also came to be worshipped as the son of Osiris and the goddess Isis (see Male Child Deities), though either this god was originally a separate deity with whom the ancient falcon god was fused, or the falcon deity was incorporated

Finally, as Har-semau or Harsomptus, 'Horus the Uniter', Horus fulfills this role of uniting and ruling over Egypt, though he is sometimes identified as the son of Horus the Elder and Hathor in this role – as at Edfu and Kom Ombo – and called by the name Panebtawy 'Lord of the Two Lands'.

Iconography

In his original avian form Horus was depicted as a falcon (probably the lanner – *Falco biarmicus* – or peregrine – *Falco peregrinus*) shown two-dimensionally in profile except for the tail feathers which were turned towards the viewer according to the canons of Egyptian composite perspective. Early examples sometimes show the falcon leaning forward in a lateral position but the upright stance became standard as time progressed. Sometimes the falcon is shown in direct association with the Seth animal or one of his symbols – especially in the Late Period – as in the nome sign of the 16th Upper Egyptian nome where the falcon is depicted with its talons sunk into the back of an oryx – an ancient symbol of Seth. As the hawk-winged Behdety, the god became one of the most widespread images in Egyptian art, an image perhaps foreshadowed in the comb of Djet (see above), and which became virtually ubiquitous as a motif used in the decoration of temple walls and stelae throughout Egypt. In the form of Horakhty he may appear as a falcon or even as a falcon-headed crocodile, and in fully anthropomorphic form Horus appears as an adult god or more usually as a child – the son of Isis. But it is in the combined zoo-anthropomorphic form of a falcon-headed man that the god most frequently appears, often wearing the Double Crown signifying his kingship over all Egypt.

Worship

Because Horus was worshipped in many forms – and assimilated many other gods – it is difficult to summarize the sites associated with his worship. It is clear, for example, that Horus was associated with the area of Nekhen in southern Egypt (the Greek Hierakonpolis or 'City of the Hawk') from very early times, and it seems likely that the god

*(Right) Colossal granite statue of the **Horus** falcon wearing the Double Crown of Egyptian kingship. Ptolemaic Period. Temple of Horus, Edfu.*

*(Below) Falcon-crocodile god embodying aspects of **Horus** and certain other deities. This hybrid god was worshipped in several areas of Egypt and Nubia. After Champollion, Monuments de l'Egypte et de la Nubie, 1845.*

*(Below right) Ptolemy VIII destroys a captive before **Horus-Behdety**. Ptolemaic Period. Temple of Horus, Edfu.*

pole

Horu: was in fact the falcon deity worshipped there since
ciatec the predynastic period. But Horus was worshipped
to ha along with other deities in many Egyptian temples,
least and important sites of his worship are known
from one end of Egypt to the other. For example,
Wors in the north, the falcon god was particularly ven-
Nemt erated in the Delta at the ancient site of Khem
12th a (the Greek Letopolis and modern Ausim) since at
the 12 least the beginning of the Old Kingdom and was
and w known there as Horus Khenty-irty or Khenty-khem,
and a 'Foremost One of Khem'. Chapter 112 of the Book
on the of the Dead tells how the Delta city of Pe (the his-
a theo torical Buto) was given to Horus as compensation
Kingd for his eye which was injured by Seth, thus explain-
tion to ing this important centre of the god and the site
time p of Behdet also became a centre of Horus worship
in the Delta. In southern Egypt Horus enjoyed the
attentions of his own cult along with his consort
Hathor and their son Harsomptus in the important
Ptolemaic temples at Edfu and also at Kom Ombo.
At Edfu, the god's many ceremonies included the
annual Coronation of the Sacred Falcon at the
beginning of the 5th month of the Egyptian year in
which an actual falcon was selected to represent the
god as king of all Egypt, thus uniting the ancient
falcon god with his form as Horus son of Osiris
and with the king. Further south, in Nubia, we find
temples to forms of the god at Quban (Horus of
Baki), Buhen, and Aniba (Horus of Miam) as well
as the inclusion of the god in many other monuments – as at Abu Simbel and elsewhere. As the
object of popular veneration throughout Egypt,
Horus was often represented by amulets depicting
him either as a falcon or as a falcon-headed man
(often wearing the Double Crown). His widespread
veneration is also seen in the many healing plaques
or *cippi* that aimed to utilize his power.

Khenty-irty

Khenty-irty was a falcon god of Khem or Letopolis
(modern Ausim), the capital of the second Lower
Egyptian nome. Originally worshipped as Khenty-
khem ('foremost of Khem'), the falcon god was
eventually assimilated by Horus during the Old
Kingdom. The meaning of his name Khenty-irty
has been explained in different ways but may mean
'sharp-eyed one'. Like Khenty-khety, this god's veneration was mainly localized around his cult centre.

Khenty-khety

The god Khenty-khety was a local deity of the
Lower Egyptian area of Kem-wer or Athribis
(modern Tell Atrib). In the Old Kingdom he was
largely absorbed by Horus and as a result was
frequently called Horus Khenty-khety. Also called
Horus Khenty-khai or Hor-merty, the god was

usually depicted as a falcon-headed man, often
holding two eyes representing the sun and moon,
but he could also be depicted as a crocodile due
to his early assimilation of the indigenous deity
of that form. Although found beyond it, he was
mainly venerated in his central cult area.

Montu

Mythology

Montu was the falcon-headed war god venerated
in Thebes and its surrounding areas. Although
he appears in the Pyramid Texts and in some
archaeological contexts of Old Kingdom date, it
was with the Theban rulers of the 11th dynasty
that Montu rose to importance. Three rulers of
this dynasty bore the birth name Montuhotep or
'Montu is content', and the god became a deity of
national standing worshipped in his own right,
also associated with Horus under the name 'Horus
of the strong arm'. As the Middle Kingdom progressed, Montu also began to be viewed as an
Upper Egyptian counterpart of Re of Heliopolis,
due perhaps to the similar name of his cult centre,
Iuny, with that of Iunu or Heliopolis, and the two
deities were worshipped as the combined Mont-Re.
The god was thus later equated by the Greeks with
Apollo. During the 12th dynasty, however, Montu's
importance began to wane as the god Amun rose
to power in the Theban area. Nevertheless, the war
god's popularity continued with martially vigorous rulers of the New Kingdom such as Tuthmosis
III and others who compared themselves to him
as heroes who fought 'like Montu in his might'.
Montu's consorts were the little-known Theban
goddess Tjenenyet and the solar goddess Raettawy.

Iconography

Montu was represented in a number of ways.
Originally a falcon god, other forms were applied to
him as time progressed. A ceremonial axe from the

Tuthmosis IV slays an Asiatic captive before the martial deity **Montu**, *who holds a* khepesh *sickle-sword and a symbol of the king's long reign. Ivory wrist ornament. 18th dynasty. Egyptian Museum, Berlin.*

of kingship. The god ruled on earth over his creation until according to legend he became old, then Re departed to the heavens where he continued to rule and also acted as the ancestor of the king of Egypt. In the Pyramid Texts we find the combined Re-Atum called the father of the king, and according to the legend preserved in the Westcar Papyrus, the kings of the 5th dynasty were actual sons of Re divinely begotten on the wife of the priest Re of Sakhebu. Already by the 5th dynasty, the 'Son of Re' epithet of the king's titulary had been introduced which formalized this mythical relationship for the rest of Egyptian history. Rulership under Re was synonymous with right rulership or rule according to *maat*, and we find inscriptions of the opposite which are historical condemnations – as when Hatshepsut recorded of the foreign Hyksos rulers that they were kings 'without Re'.

Iconography

Re was represented in many forms. The god could be depicted as the fiery disk of the sun, usually encircled by a protective cobra, and often given outstretched wings. Occasionally prior to the Amarna Period and in that time the solar disk was depicted with outstretched rays. While not usually represented in fully anthropomorphic form, Re was commonly depicted semi-anthropomorphically as a man with the head of a falcon, a ram or a scarab. Re was also represented in zoomorphic form as a falcon wearing the sun disk upon its head. Under the guise of his various manifestations he could also be represented as a ram or scarab beetle, a phoenix, heron, serpent, bull, cat, lion and other

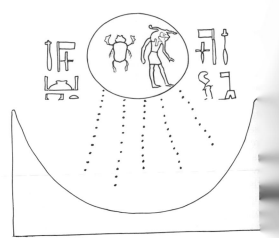

*(Right) The three major forms of **Re** combined – as morning scarab beetle, noon solar disk, and evening ram-headed man. 21st dynasty. Detail, Papyrus of Bakenmut.*

*(Below) The enthroned **Re-Horakhty-Atum**, '… great god, Lord of Heaven'. 18th dynasty. Tomb of Roy, western Thebes.*

was in fact the falcon deity worshipped there since the predynastic period. But Horus was worshipped along with other deities in many Egyptian temples, and important sites of his worship are known from one end of Egypt to the other. For example, in the north, the falcon god was particularly venerated in the Delta at the ancient site of Khem (the Greek Letopolis and modern Ausim) since at least the beginning of the Old Kingdom and was known there as Horus Khenty-irty or Khenty-khem, 'Foremost One of Khem'. Chapter 112 of the Book of the Dead tells how the Delta city of Pe (the historical Buto) was given to Horus as compensation for his eye which was injured by Seth, thus explaining this important centre of the god and the site of Behdet also became a centre of Horus worship in the Delta. In southern Egypt Horus enjoyed the attentions of his own cult along with his consort Hathor and their son Harsomptus in the important Ptolemaic temples at Edfu and also at Kom Ombo. At Edfu, the god's many ceremonies included the annual Coronation of the Sacred Falcon at the beginning of the 5th month of the Egyptian year in which an actual falcon was selected to represent the god as king of all Egypt, thus uniting the ancient falcon god with his form as Horus son of Osiris and with the king. Further south, in Nubia, we find temples to forms of the god at Quban (Horus of Baki), Buhen, and Aniba (Horus of Miam) as well as the inclusion of the god in many other monuments – as at Abu Simbel and elsewhere. As the object of popular veneration throughout Egypt, Horus was often represented by amulets depicting him either as a falcon or as a falcon-headed man (often wearing the Double Crown). His widespread veneration is also seen in the many healing plaques or *cippi* that aimed to utilize his power.

Khenty-irty

Khenty-irty was a falcon god of Khem or Letopolis (modern Ausim), the capital of the second Lower Egyptian nome. Originally worshipped as Khenty-khem ('foremost of Khem'), the falcon god was eventually assimilated by Horus during the Old Kingdom. The meaning of his name Khenty-irty has been explained in different ways but may mean 'sharp-eyed one'. Like Khenty-khety, this god's veneration was mainly localized around his cult centre.

Khenty-khety

The god Khenty-khety was a local deity of the Lower Egyptian area of Kem-wer or Athribis (modern Tell Atrib). In the Old Kingdom he was largely absorbed by Horus and as a result was frequently called Horus Khenty-khety. Also called Horus Khenty-khai or Hor-merty, the god was usually depicted as a falcon-headed man, often holding two eyes representing the sun and moon, but he could also be depicted as a crocodile due to his early assimilation of the indigenous deity of that form. Although found beyond it, he was mainly venerated in his central cult area.

Montu

Mythology

Montu was the falcon-headed war god venerated in Thebes and its surrounding areas. Although he appears in the Pyramid Texts and in some archaeological contexts of Old Kingdom date, it was with the Theban rulers of the 11th dynasty that Montu rose to importance. Three rulers of this dynasty bore the birth name Montuhotep or 'Montu is content', and the god became a deity of national standing worshipped in his own right, also associated with Horus under the name 'Horus of the strong arm'. As the Middle Kingdom progressed, Montu also began to be viewed as an Upper Egyptian counterpart of Re of Heliopolis, due perhaps to the similar name of his cult centre, Iuny, with that of Iunu or Heliopolis, and the two deities were worshipped as the combined Mont-Re. The god was thus later equated by the Greeks with Apollo. During the 12th dynasty, however, Montu's importance began to wane as the god Amun rose to power in the Theban area. Nevertheless, the war god's popularity continued with martially vigorous rulers of the New Kingdom such as Tuthmosis III and others who compared themselves to him as heroes who fought 'like Montu in his might'. Montu's consorts were the little-known Theban goddess Tjenenyet and the solar goddess Raettawy.

Iconography

Montu was represented in a number of ways. Originally a falcon god, other forms were applied to him as time progressed. A ceremonial axe from the

*Tuthmosis IV slays an Asiatic captive before the martial deity **Montu**, who holds a khepesh sickle-sword and a symbol of the king's long reign. Ivory wrist ornament. 18th dynasty. Egyptian Museum, Berlin.*

*The god **Montu** 'Lord of Thebes', with characteristic solar disk and twin plumes, escorts the 'pharaoh' Alexander the Great and offers him life. Relief scene in the inner area of Luxor Temple.*

Montu could also be represented in the form of his sacred bull, the Buchis (see p. 172), or occasionally in the later dynasties as a bull-headed man.

Worship

The main cult centres of Montu were all in the Theban region and included four important temple sites: Medamud, where a sanctuary established by Senwosret III was expanded during the New Kingdom when it was linked to Thebes by a canal, and further expanded in the Graeco-Roman Period; Karnak, where Montu had his own temple precinct to the north of the Great Temple of Amun; Armant, where the god's most important sanctuary – no longer in existence – was located; and Tod, where temples were built in the Middle Kingdom and also New Kingdom and Graeco-Roman times. It was in the Middle Kingdom temple at this last site that the rich 'Tod treasure' consisting of chests of items dedicated to Montu was found in 1936. Amulets were made of the god in the later periods and sometimes these took the form of four falcon-headed deities side by side – representing the 'four Montus' of the four Theban area sites.

Nemty

Mythology

The god Nemty (previously read as Anti) was an ancient falcon deity (Egyptian 'wanderer') whose cult was assimilated from quite early times into that of the god Horus. Nemty may also be associated with two other falcon gods mentioned in the Pyramid Texts and Coffin Texts respectively: Dunanwi and Dunawi. The Coffin Texts characterize Nemty as supervising the *henu* boat of the falcon deity Sokar, and in later texts he appears as the ferryman who transports Re and other gods. A late Egyptian myth preserved in the Ptolemaic Period Papyrus Jumilhac relates how the head of the cow goddess Hathor was cut off by Nemty – an act reminiscent of that perpetrated by Horus against Isis in the 'Contendings of Horus and Seth'. Nemty was flayed of his skin and flesh for this crime, which appears to be an etiological story explaining why the worshippers of Nemty in the 12th Upper Egyptian nome constructed their cult image of silver – the metal associated with the bones of the gods – rather than the usual gold of which the flesh and skin of the gods was said to be formed.

Iconography

Nemty is usually depicted as a falcon squatting on a curved, stylized boat which resembles a lunar crescent or even a throw stick in its simplicity. On the standard of the 18th Upper Egyptian nome, however, the boat does not appear; and in the form of Dunanwi, the god stands atop the standard's

burial of the 18th-dynasty queen Ahhotep depicts Montu in the form of a ferocious winged griffin, but this iconography was possibly influenced by Syrian sources, since most representations of the god show him in semi-anthropomorphic form with a human body and the head of a falcon. Sometimes he carries the curved *khepesh* sword as a symbol of his warlike nature. Montu usually wears the sun disk and uraeus but is distinguished from Re and other falcon deities by the two tall plumes which also adorn his head. When depicted in fully falcon form, the god is also identified by this headdress.

pole with wings outstretched. His association with Horus means that the god could indirectly be associated with Seth and, as a result, Nemty is known to have been depicted with the head of Seth on at least one occasion.

Worship

Nemty was predominantly worshipped in the 10th, 12th and 18th Upper Egyptian nomes (the capital of the 12th nome was *per nemty* 'the house of Nemty'), and was of some importance in the regions between and adjacent to these Middle Egyptian provinces on the east bank of the Nile. The god is found as a theophoric element in personal names in the Old Kingdom and Middle Kingdom, but his assimilation to Horus doubtless eroded his importance as time progressed.

'Hail to you, Re, perfect each day,
Who rises at dawn without failing…
In a brief day you race a course,
Hundreds thousands, millions of miles.'

Hymn to the Sun God (BM 826)

Mythology

The sun god Re was arguably Egypt's most important deity. Though possibly not as old as the falcon god Horus, Re was an ancient deity who coalesced with many other solar and cosmic gods through time while retaining his own position. At an early date he seems to have merged with the falcon god becoming Re-Horakhty as the morning sun, and with Atum as the evening sun. In the Book of the

*The deceased worships before a form of the sun god **Re** (left) above a register depicting tombs of the Theban necropolis. Stela of Djedamuniu(es)ankh, from western Thebes. 22nd dynasty, Egyptian Museum, Cairo.*

205

Dead we actually find Re fused with these and other deities as the composite Re-Horakhty-Atum-Horus-Khepri. Even when the god Amun rose to national supremacy in the Middle and New Kingdoms, Re was not suppressed and the two deities were brought together as Amun-Re in a process of syncretism which led to the association of most of Egypt's major gods with the powerful solar deity. Re was a universal deity who acted within the heavens, earth and underworld. In addition, the god was a prime element in most Egyptian creation myths and also acted as divine father and protector of the king. The extensive mythology pertaining to the god may perhaps best be understood in terms of these five roles.

Re in the heavens: According to Egyptian myth, when Re became too old and weary to reign on earth the god Nun ordered Nut to turn herself into a cow and to raise the god up on her back. When the goddess lifted Re high above the earth, she became the sky and Re became king of the heavens. The name Re is simply the Egyptian word for the sun and while the blazing solar orb was considered to be the visible body of Re, it was also seen as his independent 'Eye' (giving rise to expressions such as 'Re in the midst of his Eye', though the 'Eye' could also be a fierce manifestation of one of a number of goddesses) and as the vessel of his daily journey. According to this latter view, the solar god daily navigated the great celestial ocean in his *mandjet* or 'day barque' which crossed the sky from sunrise to sunset. He was said to be accompanied in this voyage by his daughter, Maat, and by various other deities. From the time of the Pyramid Texts we also find descriptions of the monarch ascending to the sky to join the entourage of the sun god. An important mythological aspect of the solar god in the heavens is found in his identity as a cosmic lion as seen in Chapter 62 of the Book of the Dead, for example, which states that 'I am he who crosses the sky, I am the lion of Re...'. The stellar constellation now known as Leo was also recognized by the Egyptians as being in the form of a recumbent lion, and as its bright shoulder star, Regulus, travels through the night sky along the ecliptic – the apparent path of the sun in the daytime sky – the constellation was directly associated with the sun god.

Re on earth: As Egyptian mythology tells how Re ruled on earth in the earliest ages there are also ample indications that the Egyptians recognized the sun's influence in the physical world. Akhenaten's celebrated Great Hymn to the Aten, for example, while directed to his own chosen solar manifestation, nevertheless speaks to the power of the sun in providing light and heat, causing crops to grow, etc. Normally this power of the sun on the earth was ascribed to Re, as may be seen in many scattered references in hymns and other texts honouring the sun god for the manifestations of his power on earth. A specific and important example of Re's influence on the earth is seen in that the god was said to direct the three seasons of the Egyptian year – thus influencing the annual inundation of the Nile and the subsequent growing and harvest seasons. Re's power on earth was also expressed in the role and position of the monarch according to Egyptian kingship ideology and in various other ways. Sacred books kept in the temple scriptoria or 'Houses of Life' were said to be emanations of Re, for example; and as the head of the divine tribunal Re decided many cases which affected life on earth.

Re in the netherworld: Just as Re travelled the sky in his day barque, at dusk he entered the underworld in the *mesketet* or 'evening barque', travelling through the nether regions (often depicted in his ram-headed form as the 'flesh of Re') before being reborn the following dawn. The funerary texts which were inscribed on the walls of the tombs of the Valley of the Kings depict this underworld journey and also the manner in which Re interacts with the underworld god Osiris during this time. The texts show a complex and evolving relationship between the two gods which ends with a kind of fusion in which Osiris is seen as the corpse or 'body' of the dual god and Re is the *ba* or 'soul', so that the combined Re-Osiris might be said to both ascend to the heavens as a *ba* in the day and be joined with his body in the earth at night. There are complex variations on this theme, however, and in the text known as the Litany of Re the sun god is said to visit multiple forms of himself in the underworld (74 are depicted in the tomb of Tuthmosis III,

for example). The sun god himself is also regenerated in the nightly cycle, but before this triumphal occurrence, the serpent Apophis, arch enemy of Re, is defeated each night with the aid of those deities that accompany Re in his barque. Just as the deceased king was said to ascend to the heavens to join Re's journey across the sky, so he also accompanied the solar god on his underworld journey.

Re as creator: According to the cosmogonic ideas developed in Heliopolis and at other sites, the sun god Re was the supreme creator who emerged from the primeval waters at the beginning of time to create every aspect of the world. There were many versions of this myth, and the solar demiurge was envisaged as coming into being upon a mound or a lotus flower rising from the waters in the form of a child, or a heron, falcon, scarab beetle or other

creature (see p. 19). Re then went on to create all living things in a manner which varies according to different versions of the myth. In one story involving a play on words Re created man (*remetj*) from his tears (*remut*) which fell to the earth, while in another, the sun god 'cut' his own phallus (possibly meaning circumcision) and the two deities Hu ('authority') and Sia ('mind') are said to have sprung from the drops of blood which fell to earth. In all versions of the story, however, it was the sun god who created other deities and human beings, and in this guise Re was called both 'father' and 'mother' of all living things.

Re as king and father of the king: In Egyptian mythology the creation of kingship and social order was synchronous with the creation of the world. Re was thus the first king as well as the creator

(Above left) The ba *'souls' of* **Re** *and Osiris showing the association of the two deities in Egyptian funerary belief. Vignette from the Papyrus of Ani. British Museum.*

(Above) Ramesses III given life by **Re**. *20th dynasty. Detail, column relief, mortuary temple of Ramesses III, Medinet Habu, Thebes.*

(Below) Vignette from the Papyrus of Heruben showing the nocturnal voyage of **Re-Horakhty** *through the netherworld, accompanied by Seth, Horus and Thoth. 21st dynasty, Egyptian Museum, Cairo.*

of kingship. The god ruled on earth over his creation until according to legend he became old, then Re departed to the heavens where he continued to rule and also acted as the ancestor of the king of Egypt. In the Pyramid Texts we find the combined Re-Atum called the father of the king, and according to the legend preserved in the Westcar Papyrus, the kings of the 5th dynasty were actual sons of Re divinely begotten on the wife of the priest Re of Sakhebu. Already by the 5th dynasty, the 'Son of Re' epithet of the king's titulary had been introduced which formalized this mythical relationship for the rest of Egyptian history. Rulership under Re was synonymous with right rulership or rule according to *maat*, and we find inscriptions of the opposite which are historical condemnations – as when Hatshepsut recorded of the foreign Hyksos rulers that they were kings 'without Re'.

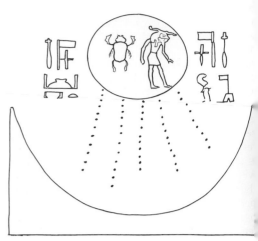

*(Right) The three major forms of **Re** combined – as morning scarab beetle, noon solar disk, and evening ram-headed man. 21st dynasty. Detail, Papyrus of Bakenmut.*

*(Below) The enthroned **Re-Horakhty-Atum**, '... great god, Lord of Heaven'. 18th dynasty. Tomb of Roy, western Thebes.*

Iconography

Re was represented in many forms. The god could be depicted as the fiery disk of the sun, usually encircled by a protective cobra, and often given outstretched wings. Occasionally prior to the Amarna Period and in that time the solar disk was depicted with outstretched rays. While not usually represented in fully anthropomorphic form, Re was commonly depicted semi-anthropomorphically as a man with the head of a falcon, a ram or a scarab. Re was also represented in zoomorphic form as a falcon wearing the sun disk upon its head. Under the guise of his various manifestations he could also be represented as a ram or scarab beetle, a phoenix, heron, serpent, bull, cat, lion and other

creatures. The combination of the beetle, solar disk and ram-headed man into one composite image was particularly common in representing Re in his morning, noon and evening forms. Re was also sometimes depicted fused with other deities as a composite god, though in the case of Amun-Re the iconography is essentially that of Amun alone (see p. 92), apart from the addition of a small solar disk to the god's crown. Clearer fusion is seen in representations of the combined Re-Osiris where, as 'Re resting in Osiris' and 'Osiris resting in Re', the god is often depicted as a mummiform figure (Osiris) with the head of a ram (Re in his night-time aspect), though Re may also be represented in this combination by the head of a falcon or scarab. Although by at least the 5th dynasty Raet or Raettawy, a female counterpart to Re, had been assigned to the sun god, he is usually depicted without a consort in his representations.

A number of solar-related images and iconographic devices were also used to signify Re in various contexts. In the New Kingdom royal tombs carved in the Valley of the Kings, elements such as sun disks, flying vultures, and yellow bands painted on the ceilings and tops of the walls of tomb passages are all used to define the path of the sun's journey through the underworld as represented by the tomb. Royal cartouches – which were themselves solar related in origin – were also sometimes utilized alongside purely solar symbols to signify the fusion of the deceased king with the sun god on this netherworld journey. Winged solar disks and other sun symbols placed under lintels and along processional routes were utilized in a similar manner in depicting the sun's symbolic passage through many Egyptian temples. Solar symbols could also be architectural in nature. The forms of the pyramid, *ben-ben*, staircase, mound and obelisk were all solar-related symbols utilized in Egyptian religious iconography that were based on concrete architectural analogues. In fact, taken together, the various solar symbols are the most prevalent elements utilized in Egyptian iconography and they are found in a wider range of contexts than any other divine symbols.

Worship

The cult of Re is first attested in the name of the 2nd-dynasty ruler, Raneb, and during the 4th dynasty worship of the god evidently reached a peak with kings taking the epithet 'Son of Re' from the time of Djedefre, and the pyramids and their associated temples being unequivocally linked to Re in various ways. By the 5th dynasty Re had become, in essence, Egypt's state god, officially recognized as the head of the pantheon. Doubtless a great temple to Re was constructed at this time in Heliopolis, though remains of this structure have never been found. But in the 5th dynasty several kings built sun temples with large masonry obelisks

in the region of their own pyramids and mortuary temples, and these solar-oriented structures may well have been modelled after the Heliopolitan cult centre and its *ben-ben* (see p. 212).

While Re's cult was centred at Heliopolis, he was worshipped universally throughout Egypt; and although there were definite high points in the importance of solar religion, Re was venerated in every age of the country's long dynastic history. Sanctuaries were constantly constructed or renewed for him, and he was included in many of the temples of other deities throughout the remainder of dynastic history. The god certainly enjoyed a kind of renaissance in the New Kingdom, beginning in the reign of Amenophis III, who constructed a number of great solar temples and courts. This reign directly preceded the ultimately aborted efforts of Akhenaten to establish the sun god, in his form of the Aten, as sole god. Despite the repudiated doctrines of the Amarna Period, solar religion continued to be of great importance during Ramessid times when Re was frequently honoured by his eponymous kings. Re also has a strong presence in New Kingdom religious literature – especially in funerary texts which successfully balanced the position of the sun god with that of Osiris. In the later periods of Egyptian history the position of the sun god is overshadowed to a large degree by other deities, yet Re remained important, and even after the close of the dynastic age, in Christian times, we find occasional texts appealing to Jesus, the Holy Spirit and the sun god Re.

Although the cult of Re was always of primary importance to the Egyptian king and in officially sponsored religion, the god was not without popular appeal and veneration. His importance is seen in non-royal as well as royal names incorporating the name of Re, and the god was represented in amulets. Many of these were made to be worn in life as a mark of veneration, in addition to the images of the god which accompanied the deceased in the funerary assemblage. Re also appears in various magical spells including those which make an ultimate threat – to stop the course of the sun in its journey. Such spells were usually aimed at attempting to cause the sun god to right some wrong and to restore balance in his creation.

Sokar

Mythology

An ancient falcon god of the Memphite region, Sokar was perhaps originally a god of craftsmanship who became associated with the necropoleis of that area and rose, in time, to considerable importance as a chthonic and afterlife deity. He is frequently mentioned in the Pyramid Texts in the afterlife context where the deceased king is said to be raised into the 'henu barque' of Sokar and

equated with the god (PT 620, 1824, 2240, etc.). Sokar is also given many epithets such as 'he of Rosetau' (the necropolis entrance into the underworld), but the meaning of the god's name is uncertain, and while the Pyramid Texts seem to explain it as being based on the words of an anguished cry of Osiris (PT 1256), this is clearly based on an association of Sokar with Osiris which occurred only after the latter god's rise to importance. Even before his association with Osiris, Sokar had became linked with the Memphite god Ptah as the combined Ptah-Sokar and also by taking Ptah's consort Sekhmet as his own. By Middle Kingdom times all three of these gods had been combined into the tripartite deity Ptah-Sokar-Osiris who remained an important funerary deity for most of the remainder of Egypt's dynastic history.

Iconography

Sokar could be depicted in various ways in addition to that of the falcon which was his original form. In the more symbolic forms he is represented by an earthen funerary mound surmounted by a falcon's head which is sometimes set in a boat, an image depicted in vignettes of the Amduat where Sokar is called 'he who is upon his sand'. As a falcon-headed man Sokar is often represented as mummiform and sometimes wears a complex conical crown with sun disk horns and cobras. In the tomb of Tuthmosis III in the Valley of the Kings he is depicted as a falcon-headed god standing on a multi-headed chthonic serpent, emphasizing his power over the nether regions and their inhabitants. The most impressive surviving example of this falcon-headed type of the god's iconography is found in the silver coffin of Sheshonq II found at Tanis. In later times his most common representation is in the form of Ptah-Sokar-Osiris, and from the Late Period onwards small statues of the combined deity were made which show him as a mummiform human-headed god standing upright on a sarcophagus-like box or pedestal, often surmounted by Sokar's falcon-head image. Ptah-Sokar-Osiris could also be represented as a squat, pygmy-like male, sometimes with a scarab beetle on his head, and the amuletic deity Pataikos appears to have been derived from these particular Ptah-Sokar-Osiris figures.

Worship

Memphis was the cult centre of Sokar and it was there, at least by early Old Kingdom times, that the great Sokar festival took place each year in the fourth month of the *akhet* season. During this the god was carried from his temple to assist the king in ceremonial activities including hoeing of the earth or the digging of ditches or canals. From New Kingdom times the Sokar festival was also celebrated with great ceremony in western Thebes where it is depicted in reliefs in the temple of Ramesses III at Medinet Habu. The festival seems

*(Above) Sethos I offers incense and a libation to the enthroned **Sokar**. 19th dynasty. Temple of Sethos I, Abydos.*

*(Below) The henu barque of **Sokar** with multiple images of the god. 19th dynasty. Detail of relief, temple of Sethos I, Abydos.*

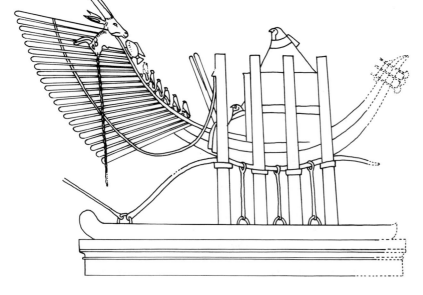

Sokar, 'Lord of the mysterious region [of the netherworld]'. 18th dynasty. Detail, wall painting, tomb of Tuthmosis III, Valley of the Kings, western Thebes.

to have stressed the continuity of the royal mortuary cult along with the resurrection of Sokar and involved the image of the god being carried in his distinctive henu barque which had a cabin signifying a funerary chest surmounted by a falcon. Outside the funerary context, veneration of Sokar is difficult to document. Amulets of Sokar are not common, but some depicting squatting, mummiform falcons may represent the god.

Sopdu

Mythology

The mythology of Sopdu is complex and presents two very different aspects of this god – he is both a cosmic falcon god similar to Horus and also, in anthropomorphic form, as a god of Egypt's eastern frontier. In the Pyramid Texts, the astral nature of the deity is stressed. The deceased king, in his role as Osiris-Orion, is said to impregnate Isis as the star Sothis and to produce Horus-Sopdu. Sopdu is also equated with the teeth of the deified king, apparently as an allusion to the curved beak of the god who is said to be 'sharp of teeth' (PT 201). On the other hand, Sopdu also gained significance as 'lord of the east' who protected Egyptian outposts in the border regions such as the turquoise mines of the Sinai Peninsula. The god thus appears in royal inscriptions where he is said to provide the various resources of the east and to be a helper of the pharaoh in controlling the native populations. As god of the Asiatic regions Sopdu was himself often associated with Near Eastern deities who were assimilated into Egyptian religion such as Baal, Reshep, Astarte, Anat and Qadesh.

Iconography

In his zoomorphic form Sopdu was depicted as a falcon crouching on a standard with two tall plumes on its head and a ritual flail held over its shoulder. This is the symbol of the Lower Egyptian nome over which the god presided, but is found in a number of representations of the god including a fine example of gilded wood from the tomb of Tutankhamun. In anthropomorphic form, as god of the eastern desert regions, Sopdu appears as a Bedouin warrior with long hair and a pointed beard. He wears a crown of two tall feathers and a tasselled or beaded *shesmet* girdle, the Egyptian name of which is perhaps related to the mineral malachite. Sopdu may carry a spear or tall *was* sceptre in one hand and an axe and *ankh* sign in the other.

Worship

As the god of the 20th Lower Egyptian nome, Sopdu's main cult centre was at Per Sopdu (the modern Saft el-Henna) in the eastern Delta. However, priests of the god are attested at a number of Egyptian sites from Old Kingdom times and he was also venerated in many eastern desert outposts such as the site of Serabit el-Khadim in the Sinai Peninsula where he was worshipped along with Hathor and certain other deities.

(Left) Gilded wooden image of the god **Sopdu** *as a falcon on a standard. From the tomb of Tutankhamun, 18th dynasty. Egyptian Museum, Cairo.*

211

It is not clear why some avian species came to represent deities in the Egyptian pantheon and others did not, and among those birds that did receive veneration there are few common characteristics. The heron, goose, vulture and ibis were the most important of these species, though other birds played occasional roles in Egyptian mythology.

Benu

Mythology

The word *benu* is related to the verb *weben* 'to rise' as well as to the *ben-ben* – the upthrust sacred stone of Heliopolis. The Benu bird was an important avian deity, originally of solar connections, which came to represent three major gods: Atum, Re and Osiris. As an aspect of Atum, the Benu bird was said to have flown over the waters of Nun before the original creation. According to this view, the bird finally came to rest on a rock at which point its cry broke the primeval silence and was said to have determined what was and what was not to be in the unfolding creation. The Benu was also said to be the *ba* of Re, and by the Late Period the hieroglyphic sign depicting the bird was used to write the name of the chief sun god. Believed to constantly rise anew like the sun, the Benu bird was called the 'lord of jubilees' which doubtless led to the conception of its long life and to it becoming the prototype for the Greek phoenix which renewed itself in a fiery death like the sun rising at dawn. According to Herodotus, in Roman tradition the bird lived for 500 years before it fashioned a nest of aromatic boughs and spices which it set it on fire to be consumed in the flames. From the conflagration a new phoenix miraculously arose, which after embalming its father's ashes flew with them to Heliopolis where it deposited the ashes on the altar of the temple of Re. Although the bird was associated primarily with Atum and Re, its connection with rebirth also led to an association with Osiris.

(Below) The grey heron or **Benu** *bird with characteristic twin plumes. Vignette from funerary papyrus, 21st dynasty. Egyptian Museum, Cairo.*

(Right) The god **Benu** *in hybrid avian-anthropomorphic form. Rarely represented in this manner, this deity was usually depicted in fully avian form.*

Iconography

The bird which first served as a symbol of solar deities in Heliopolis was probably the yellow wagtail (*Motacilla flava*) which, according to the Pyramid Texts (PT 1652), represented Atum himself. By New Kingdom times, however, the Benu was usually depicted as a grey heron (*Ardea cinera*), with long legs and beak and its head adorned with a two-feathered crest. Usually the Benu is depicted atop a stylized *ben-ben* stone as a symbol of the great solar god, but its association with Osiris meant that it was also sometimes depicted in the sacred willow of that god. The bird was also represented wearing the Atef Crown in its role as a symbol of Osiris. According to the Classical vision of the phoenix, the bird was said to be as large as an eagle, with red and gold (solar or flame-coloured) plumage. Benu could also be depicted in hybrid form as a heron-headed man.

Worship

Little is known of the formal veneration of the Benu, though its central association with the solar mythology of Heliopolis doubtless formed the basis for an important role in the cults of that area. The frequent depiction of the Benu bird in the vignettes of the 'afterlife books' as well as on heart amulets (such as that of Tutankhamun) and other objects also shows the persistence of the god's importance in funerary contexts.

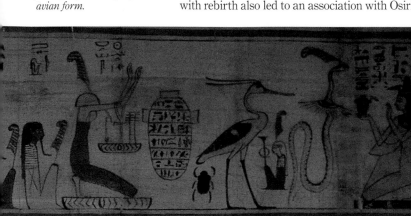

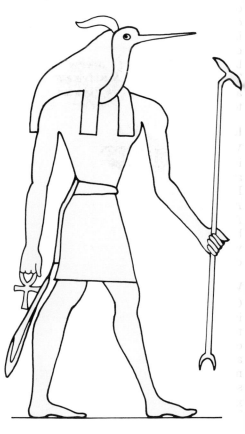

Gengen-Wer

Mythology

A primeval goose representing certain gods in their creative aspects, Gengen-Wer manifested the power of creation through his honking call or through carrying the egg from which life emerged. The god's name is based on the goose's characteristically raucous call or cackle (the onomatopoeic Egyptian word *gengen* means 'honker' and *wer* means 'great'), and he was also called by the name *negeg* or 'cackler'. According to some texts it was the honking call of Amun in the form of this god that 'awoke' the creation (e.g., Papyrus Leiden I 350, Chapter 90). The goose was also closely associated with the earth god Geb who was himself sometimes called the 'great cackler' and who, in this form, was credited with having laid the first egg from which the sun emerged as the Benu bird. The goose was also a symbol of certain other deities including Hapy and Harpokrates. According to the complex interaction of Egyptian creation mythology and afterlife beliefs Gengen-Wer is also found in descriptions of the netherworld in which the deceased is sometimes said to guard or even to be the god's egg. From the time of the Pyramid Texts the deceased aspired to fly to the heavens as a goose, and models of the bird in New Kingdom tombs are believed to represent this desire.

Iconography

Various species of geese appear in Egyptian art including the Nile goose (*Alopochen aegyptiacus*) and others which could represent Gengen-Wer. Because the goose was also used to represent Amun, its image was desecrated by the agents of Akhenaten during the Amarna Period – as in the botanical room of Tuthmosis III in Karnak Temple where the representation of this avian species was defaced.

Worship

Geese figure more frequently in Egyptian religion in the context of offerings – as food offerings given to the gods and the deceased and even as ritually offered symbols of the enemies of the gods – than as the objects of worship. Nevertheless, although not widely venerated directly, the goose was worshipped in certain localities, and a flock of sacred geese was kept on the temple lake in Amun's Great Temple at Karnak.

Henet

Henet was a pelican deity known from Old Kingdom times and venerated as a beneficial goddess. In the Pyramid Texts, for unknown reasons, she is called 'mother of the king' (PT 511), and in the later funerary texts she is said to prophesy a safe passage for the deceased through the netherworld. Henet also had a directly protective function apparently related to the pelican's ability to scoop up fish and other creatures regarded as mythologically hostile or inimical, in a manner parallel to the symbolic representations found in Egyptian tombs of the snaring and netting of those same creatures.

Nekhbet

Mythology

The vulture goddess Nekhbet 'she of Nekheb' was the chief deity of ancient Nekheb (the modern el-Kab some 80 km south of Luxor) which was the capital of the 3rd nome of Upper Egypt. The significance of the site lay in its close proximity to the town of Nekhen (the Greek Hierakonpolis and modern Kom el-Ahmar) which was an early capital of all Upper Egypt, so that the goddess was eventually adopted alongside the cobra goddess Wadjet

Celebrated depiction of bean, white-fronted, and red-breasted geese from the tomb of Nefermaat at Meidum, 4th dynasty. Several species of geese could represent the primeval deity **Gengen-Wer**.

Inlaid pectoral ornament from the tomb of Tutankhamun showing **Nekhbet** *(left) and Wadjet (right) as the tutelary deities Isis and Nephthys guarding the figure of Osiris. 18th dynasty. Egyptian Museum, Cairo.*

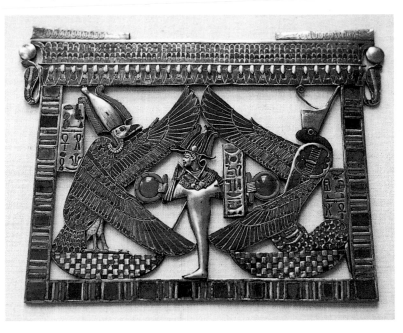

of Buto in the Delta region as one of the two tutelary deities of the united Egypt. From at least Old Kingdom times Nekhbet was identified with the White Crown of Upper Egypt and thus became closely connected with the person of the king. In this role Nekhbet was also a mythical mother of the king. The Pyramid Texts depict her as a mother goddess in the form of a great white cow, and in royal birth scenes, such as in the mortuary temple of Sahure at Abusir, Nekhbet is present as a protective nurse of the king. The Greeks thus equated Nekhbet with their goddess of childbirth, Eileithya, and called her city Nekheb Eileithyiaspolis. The Egyptians also sometimes equated or associated Nekhbet with Hathor.

Iconography

From her earliest sightings Nekhbet is often shown as a vulture (the Griffon Vulture or Lappet faced Vulture [*Gyps fulvus* or *Aegypius tracheliotus*], once more common in Upper Egypt) either standing in profile view, or with wings outstretched in direct view and only head and legs in profile. The Nekhbet vulture often holds the circular *shen* or 'eternity' hieroglyph in her claws, an iconographic element common to a variety of deities. Assimilation with her northern counterpart led to Nekhbet occasionally being depicted as a serpent (just as Wadjet may sometimes be shown in vulture form), though this fusing of the imagery of the two deities was usually for heraldic, decorative purposes and to stress their association rather than for mythological reasons. In serpent form Nekhbet usually wears the White Crown in order to maintain her identity. Egyptian monarchical symbolism utilized the image of the Nekhbet vulture in the *nebty* or 'two ladies' name of the royal titulary in which the goddesses of Upper and Lower Egypt were shown as vulture and cobra standing on woven baskets, and the two goddesses were also depicted as personifications of the crowns of the Two Lands. In anthropomorphic form Nekhbet was usually represented as a woman wearing a vulture cap, though she could also be shown wearing the White Crown of Upper Egypt.

Worship

Nekhbet had an impressively large sanctuary at el-Kab, though little has survived of this cult centre. Most of the present ruins there date to the later Dynastic Period, and only traces remain of New

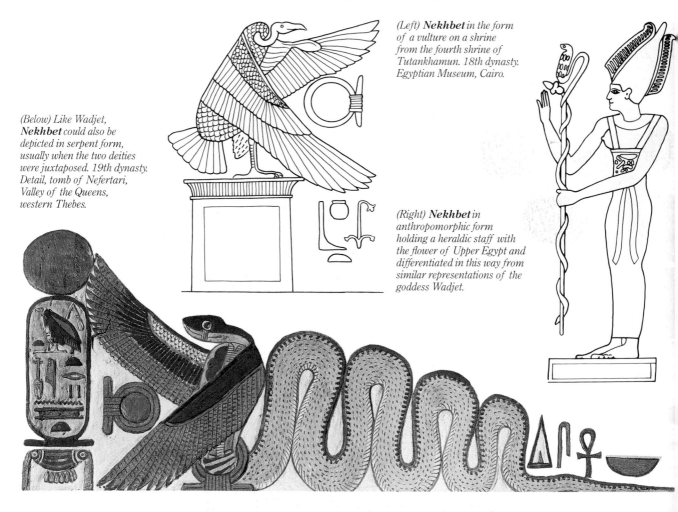

(Left) **Nekhbet** *in the form of a vulture on a shrine from the fourth shrine of Tutankhamun. 18th dynasty. Egyptian Museum, Cairo.*

(Below) Like Wadjet, **Nekhbet** *could also be depicted in serpent form, usually when the two deities were juxtaposed. 19th dynasty. Detail, tomb of Nefertari, Valley of the Queens, western Thebes.*

(Right) **Nekhbet** *in anthropomorphic form holding a heraldic staff with the flower of Upper Egypt and differentiated in this way from similar representations of the goddess Wadjet.*

Kingdom and Middle Kingdom structures. Nothing has been found of the shrines which undoubtedly stood at this site in very early times. The importance of Nekhbet in what might be called royal religion is seen in the many times she appears in a protective role alongside the pharaoh and in jewelry such as the exquisite vulture pendants found in the tomb of Tutankhamun. In the popular religion of the New Kingdom and Late Period Nekhbet was also venerated as a protectress and as a goddess of childbirth.

Thoth

Mythology

The god Thoth, or Djehuty as he was called by the Egyptians, was originally a moon god who eventually came to be associated with writing and knowledge and to preside over scribes and scholars of all types. The god appeared in two distinct manifestations, as an ibis and as a baboon, and though both were lunar-related, that of the ibis was primary. His standard, or that of the ibis that later represented him, appears on slate palettes of the Predynastic Period, and Thoth was clearly already an important deity in Old Kingdom times when he is mentioned frequently in the Pyramid Texts. There, along with the sun god Re, he is one of the 'two companions' which cross the sky (PT 128) and the gods are said to travel on the 'wing' of Thoth across the 'winding waterway' or 'river' of the heavens (PT 594–96). During the Old Kingdom Thoth was also incorporated into the prevailing solar theology along with Osiris whom he is said to protect and serve – both directly and in the person of the deceased king who became one with Osiris. Although he is called the son of Re, the legends pertaining to Thoth repeatedly reflect this linkage with the myths of Osiris and his associated gods. The legend preserved in the 'Contendings of Horus and Seth' declares that Thoth was the son of Horus and that he emerged from the forehead of Seth, who had eaten the semen of Horus on some lettuce plants. According to this story, the seed of Horus appears on the head of Seth as a shining disk which Thoth took and placed on his own head as his emblem. He was said to heal the injured eye of Horus which was associated with the Moon, and he often acted as a messenger, intercessor and conciliator between the gods.

The enthroned **Thoth** writes with brush and scribal palette – assisted by Ramesses II who holds a water pot and writing kit. As scribe of the gods Thoth 'recorded' long reigns for the Egyptian kings and also played a purificatory role in monarchical mythology. 19th dynasty. Temple of Ramesses II, Abydos.

215

***Thoth** (centre) as recorder at the judgment of the deceased. Book of the Dead of Iahtesnakht from Herakleopolis Magna. 26th dynasty. Seminar for Egyptology, Cologne.*

Importantly for his mythology Thoth was said to have invented the art of writing. He was thus the scribe of the Ennead who recorded 'the divine words' and was responsible for all kinds of accounts and records. As 'lord of time' and 'reckoner of years' he recorded the passing of time and assigned long reigns to kings. He was the patron of all areas of knowledge, and written treatises of all kinds fell under his care as lord of the 'houses of life' which functioned as scriptoria and libraries which were attached to the temples. Not surprisingly then, Thoth commanded magic and secrets unknown to even the other gods, and his select followers were regarded as possessing special knowledge as is seen in a Middle Kingdom story called 'The Magician Djedi' set in the reign of King Khufu. Thoth's record keeping also has afterlife associations, and in vignettes of the Book of the Dead he stands before the scales which weigh the heart of the deceased and records the verdict. This role gave Thoth a reputation for truth and integrity and is seen in the common assertion that a person had conducted his life in a manner 'straight and true like Thoth'.

Thoth's lunar identity remained an important aspect of his personality. The god was also often placed in juxtaposition to the sun god Re as a kind of 'night sun', and in the Late Period he acquired the epithet 'silver Aten'. In the Hellenistic Period the Greeks equated him with their own god Hermes and, based on one of Thoth's epithets, specifically as Hermes *trismegistos*, or 'three times great'. The little known goddess Nehemetawy was the consort of Thoth, though he is more often associated with the goddess of writing, Seshat, who was variously depicted as his wife or daughter.

Iconography

Although there is considerable overlapping in the iconographic use of the two forms in which Thoth was manifest – the ibis and the baboon – there are also some differences worth noting. In his purely zoomorphic forms the baboon is somewhat more prevalent in representations than the ibis, though representations of the god as an ibis-headed man are most common of all. It is impossible to know, as is sometimes suggested, if the Egyptians saw the shape of the baboon (*Papio Cynocephalus*) in the lunar disk in a manner similar to our 'man in the moon', but Thoth is depicted in baboon form in both lunar and scribal contexts. Unlike solar apes which are often depicted standing with their arms raised in adoration, Thoth as a baboon is usually shown

*The sacred ibis of **Thoth**. Wood and bronze statue. Late Period. Roemer and Pelizaeus Museum, Hildesheim.*

as a seated animal, heavily maned, resting on its rear with its legs drawn up against its body and with its paws resting on its knees. Massive, 30-ton statues in this form were set up by Amenophis III at the main cult centre of Thoth at Hermopolis. Sometimes the god is depicted with the lunar disk and crescent on his head symbolizing the moon's phases – either in statues stressing the god's role as lunar-deity or those stressing his role as patron of scribes. One famous example shows the animal squatting on the shoulders of a scribe (Ashmolean Museum, Oxford) and another, more common type shows the scribe seated before the baboon god who is raised on a pedestal (Egyptian Museum, Cairo; Louvre, Paris; etc.).

In the form of the sacred ibis (*Threskiornis aethiopicus*), whose distinctive white surrounded by black plumage and crescent-curved bill may have held symbolic significance, Thoth was depicted in many statuettes which represent the god in general without suggesting a specific lunar or scribal aspect. The ibis may be depicted standing or sitting, and a depiction of the bird perched on a standard was the usual image used to write the god's name. In underworld scenes the god is usually depicted as either an ibis-headed man or as a baboon, and scenes showing Thoth presiding over the judgment scales may depict him in either form. As an ibis-headed god Thoth also appears in many temple scenes where he may assist the gods or record matters of importance relating to the king. An important motif is that which shows him notching the palm branch which was ritually used for recording years in order to write down the great number of years granted to the king as his reign. Sometimes, as in a scene in the hypostyle hall of the Great Temple of Amun at Karnak, Thoth takes the place of Seshat in writing the name of the king – here Ramesses II – on the leaves of the sacred persea tree. Thoth also appears in an ancient purification ritual accompanying Horus, Seth and the falcon god Dunanwi who together personify the four cardinal points (PT 27). Often, however, only Horus and Thoth are depicted in this scene, pouring *ankh* or life signs over the pharaoh from sacred water jars. In one peculiar form the ibis-headed Thoth may appear naked, except for jackal-headed shoes, in his aspect as Hermopolitan creator god.

Worship

Thoth's appearance in the names of several New Kingdom monarchs (e.g., Tuthmosis – 'Thoth is born') shows important royal acceptance and patronage of the god's cult, but earlier references to offerings made in private tombs on the festival of Thoth also show the importance of this god to non-royal individuals, and his worship appears to have always had a wide base among ancient Egyptians.

It is uncertain whether the ancient Khemnu, which the Greeks called Hermopolis or 'Hermes-town' (the modern el-Ashmunein) in Middle Egypt was the original cult centre of Thoth, although it was certainly his chief centre of worship in dynastic times. It is possible that Thoth had an early cult centre in the Delta as the 15th Lower Egyptian nome had the ibis as its emblem. Thoth also had a sanctuary at el-Baqliya in the Delta, in the Dakhla Oasis in the western desert, and even in the Sinai at Serabit el-Khadim. A little to the west of Hermopolis the necropolis of Tuna el-Gebel is the site of an extensive catacomb, the Ibeum, which housed the mummified bodies of thousands of ibises, as well as many baboons, which were sold to pilgrims as votive offerings to the god. Another large burial ground for ibises and baboons was located at Saqqara, and these catacombs well illustrate the continued widespread popularity of Thoth in the religion of the later periods. In the 4th century BC the high priest of Thoth, Petosiris, renovated the cult centre of Hermopolis in the wake of the Persian invasion, and constructed a splendid tomb for himself decorated on its exterior with images of Thoth as ibis and baboon and inscribed inside with texts which show the god's great local importance. Thoth was, naturally, particularly venerated by scribes, who it is said made a small libation to the god by pouring a drop of water out of the pot in which they dipped their brushes at the beginning of each day. Amulets of the god as an ibis or an ibis-headed man – sometimes holding the divine *wedjat* eye occur, though those depicting him as a baboon were more common. These amulets were worn in life, many presumably by scribes. The wisdom and magical powers ascribed to Thoth meant that he was naturally invoked in many spells utilized in popular magic and religion.

*A scribe writes at the feet of **Thoth** as a baboon, with lunar disk, seated on a pedestal. From el-Amarna. 18th dynasty. Egyptian Museum, Cairo.*

Reptile, Amphibian and Fish Deities

CROCODILE DEITIES

The crocodile was one of Egypt's most dangerous animals and it is not difficult to see why the creature held an impressive degree of religious and mythological status. Although a number of minor crocodile deities may have existed, most of these were assimilated with the powerful god Sobek who was venerated throughout Egypt. The composite, crocodile-headed Ammut was also an important deity who must be included in this section.

Ammut

Mythology

The Ammut was a composite mythical creature whose head – and therefore most essential aspect – places her with crocodile deities. Her name meant 'female devourer' or more fully, 'female devourer of the dead'. In this role, as an underworld deity, she was also called 'great of death' and 'eater of hearts' and was supposedly the destroyer of those who had led wicked lives and who were not to be granted access into the afterlife. In the 'reality' of Egyptian myth and magic this fate was usually circumvented, but the goddess nevertheless remained a fearsome token of afterlife retribution.

Iconography

Ammut combined elements of the most dangerous animals known to the Egyptians. Her head was that of the crocodile, her neck, mane and foreparts those of the lion (though occasionally a leopard), and her rear quarters were those of the hippopotamus. It has been suggested that this composite form of land and water animals left the damned no place of escape from the goddess's wrath. Ammut appears almost exclusively in the vignettes of funerary papyri, especially illustrations of Chapter 125 of the Book of the Dead where she is shown waiting beside the scale on which the heart of the deceased is weighed against the feather of *maat* in the 'Hall of the Two Truths'.

Worship

Ammut was not worshipped in any formal cult and does not appear to have received popular veneration despite the fact that her image was doubtless recognized by many if not most ancient Egyptians. Although the name of Ammut was written with the determinative for 'deity' (see p. 26), the goddess was primarily viewed as a demonic creature to be avoided and whose power must be overcome.

Sobek

Mythology

Sobek was venerated from at least Old Kingdom times, and while the name of the god means simply 'crocodile', he was regarded as a powerful deity with several important associations. In the Pyramid Texts he is said to be the son of Neith and called the 'raging one' who 'takes women from their husbands whenever he wishes according to his desire' but who also makes green the herbage of the fields and river banks (PT 507–10) – tying him to both procreative and vegetative fertility.

*Raised relief of the god
Sobek – the most widely
worshipped of Egypt's
crocodile deities – from the
joint temple of Horus the
Elder and Sobek at Kom
Ombo. Graeco-Roman Period.*

He was, quite naturally, a god of water (it was said that the Nile issued from his sweat) and of areas such as marshes and riverbanks, wherever crocodiles were commonly found. Sobek was also said to be 'Lord of Bakhu', the mythological mountain of the horizon where it was asserted he had a temple made of carnelian. He was linked with the cults of certain other gods, such as Amun, Osiris and especially that of the sun god in the form of Sobek-Re. This association with the sun god led to his being identified by the Greeks with their own god Helios. Sobek was also associated with the Egyptian king and could act as a symbol of pharaonic potency and might.

219

Iconography

Fully or partly zoomorphic in his representations, Sobek may appear as a crocodile – often seated upon a shrine or altar – or as a man with the head of a crocodile. In either guise he often wears a headdress consisting of a sun disk with horns and tall plumes. When shown in semi-human form he may also wear a tripartite wig. The god is repeatedly associated with the colour green in his representations and called 'green of plume' (PT 507) in textual sources. His link with the Egyptian king led to the particularly fine statue of Amenophis III and Sobek now in the Luxor Museum of Ancient Egyptian Art which shows a small figure of the king protected by a much larger image of the god.

Worship

While the worship of this god is known from Old Kingdom times through to the Roman Period, it was given particular prominence during the Middle Kingdom as the names of several rulers of the 12th and 13th dynasties – such as Sobekneferu 'beautiful of Sobek' and Sobekhotep 'Sobek is satisfied' – indicate. The god's sanctuaries were numerous and widespread, but the two main cult centres of Sobek were in the area of the ancient Shedet (the Greek Crocodilopolis and modern Medinet el-Fayum) in the Fayum region which was the home of the 12th-dynasty rulers, and at Kom Ombo in Upper Egypt where he and his consort Hathor and son Khonsu shared a temple with Horus. Other important cult sites were located at Gebelein and Gebel el-Silsila. His temples were usually provided with pools containing sacred crocodiles which were mummified when they died. While apotropaic amulets of crocodiles are known from virtually all periods, amulets of crocodiles or crocodile-headed men wearing sun disks and plumes clearly represent the god and seem to have been worn in life.

(Left) Calcite pair statue of **Sobek** *with Amenophis III. 18th dynasty. Luxor Museum.*

(Right) Isis and Nephthys as serpent deities, from the tomb of Montuherkhepeshef, Valley of the Kings, western Thebes. 19th dynasty.

SERPENT DEITIES

Of great importance in Egyptian religion, various serpent deities represented both benign and malevolent powers. While the fearsome serpent Apophis was the nemesis of the sun god himself, a daily threat to the solar barque, the powerful Mehen protected Ra. Both male and female deities were represented in serpent form and ranged from deities known only from mythological contexts to the serpent goddess Meretseger, who was actively worshipped in ancient Thebes.

Apophis

Mythology

Apophis was the great adversary of the sun god Re and the embodiment of the powers of dissolution, darkness, and non-being. The huge serpent was believed to have existed from the beginning of time in the waters of primeval chaos which preceded creation and it was thought that he would continue to exist in an endlessly malevolent cycle of attack, defeat and resurgent attack. The god is not attested before the Middle Kingdom and seems to have come into being in the uncertain and fearful times which followed the pyramid age. It is the New Kingdom funerary texts which provide most of the evidence for the god's mythology. According to these various mythic accounts, as the sun made its nightly voyage through the underworld and each morning as it emerged, the solar barque was attacked by the great serpent whose terrifying roar echoed through the underworld. Apophis was sometimes equated with Seth, the god of chaos, yet in some texts the aid of that same god was enlisted in defeating the serpent. It was said that each night Apophis hypnotized Re and the entourage who sail with him except for the god Seth who resisted the serpent's deadly stare and repulsed him with the thrust of a great spear. The serpent was also said to hinder the passage of the solar barque by means of its coils which are described as 'sandbanks', and also by gorging the waters of the underworld river in order to attempt to strand the barque of Re.

Other deities and the dead themselves were also involved in the cyclic defeat of the great serpent in the various stories, most notably in the Book of Gates, by Isis, Neith and Serket and by various deities, some in the form of monkeys, who successfully capture the monster with magical nets. He is then restrained by deities including the earth god Geb and the sons of Horus, and his body cut into pieces – only to revive in the ongoing cycle. In some versions of the myth the sun god was in fact encircled or swallowed by the serpent who later disgorged him as a metaphor of rebirth and renewal. Apophis may thus bear many epithets ranging from evil lizard, opponent and enemy to world encircler and serpent of rebirth.

Iconography

In the vignettes of the funerary texts and in other settings in which he is depicted, Apophis is shown as a large serpent, sometimes with tightly compressed, spring-like coils to emphasize his great size. Almost invariably Apophis is shown restrained, dismembered, or in the process of being destroyed, often by multiple knives. Only a relatively few scenes transcend this pattern. A scene painted

221

within the tomb of Ramesses VI in the Valley of the Kings shows the serpent with twelve heads above its back representing those it has swallowed who are freed from the monster – if only briefly – when it is vanquished; and in private tombs and funerary papyri, another scene of a different type is found where Re or Hathor appear in feline form in order to slay the chaos serpent by cutting it up with a knife. There are also a number of temple scenes (at Dendera, Deir el-Bahri, Luxor and Philae) which depict the king striking a circular ball-like object which represents the evil 'eye of Apophis'.

Worship

Although the god was neither worshipped in a formal cult nor incorporated into popular veneration, Apophis entered both spheres of religion as a god or demon to be protected against. Like the god Seth, Apophis was associated with frightening natural events such as unexplained darkness, storms and earthquakes as well as his underlying threat to the very stability of the cosmos, so magical texts and rituals were produced to combat these things. The so-called Book of Apophis was a collection of these magical texts and spells dating to the late New Kingdom, though the best preserved example – the Bremner-Rhind Papyrus in the British Museum – was produced in the 4th century BC. These spells for the 'overthrowing of Apophis' provided protection from the powers symbolized by this deity or from snakes which could be viewed as minor yet dangerous manifestations of the monster. During the Late Period when such a ritual book was read in temples daily to protect the world from the threat of the sun god's arch enemy, a wax model of the serpent was cut into pieces and burnt with fire. Other spells used to protect against Apophis involved drawing a picture of the serpent on a piece of papyrus, then sealing it in a box which was spat upon and set on fire.

Denwen

Denwen was a serpent god with dragon-like ability known from Old Kingdom times. In the Pyramid Texts Denwen was said to have the power to cause a fiery conflagration which would destroy the gods, but the serpent was thwarted from this act by the deceased king.

Kebehwet

Kebehwet was a celestial serpent (assuming a derivation of her name from the word *kebhu*, 'firmament') who is mentioned several times in the Pyramid Texts. She was said to be the daughter of Anubis and the king's 'sister' and one whom he loves. The Pyramid Texts also somewhat enigmatically identify Kebehwet with the king's middle or hindparts (PT 1749, etc.), and assert that she refreshed and purified the heart of the deceased monarch with pure water from four *nemset* jars (PT 1180) and that the goddess helped open the 'windows of the sky' to assist the king's resurrection (PT 468). Her ministrations were eventually extended to all of the dead, but the goddess was never a very important deity.

Mehen

Mythology

The coiled serpent god known as Mehen protected the god Re on his nightly journey through the underworld. The earliest known mention of the god is in the Coffin Texts of the Middle Kingdom where there is reference to 'the mysteries of Mehen' (CT 493, 495), which may have involved specific rituals related to the veneration of the serpent deity. The same texts also assert that the god is a warden of criminals – primarily meaning the enemies of Re – and it seems that the deceased for whom the spells were inscribed was thought to assist in this work of Mehen.

Iconography

The Coffin Texts (CT 758–60) tell how the serpent god exists as nine concentric rings which are 'roads of fire' encircling and protecting the sun god and Peter Piccione has shown that the so-called 'coiled serpent board game', examples of which have survived from the Predynastic Period through to the

*(Opposite) Scene from the third hour of the Book of Gates showing the serpent **Mehen** protectively encircling the cabin of the sun god who passes through the underworld in his evening form, accompanied by the gods Sia and Heka. Beneath the sun god's barque, the great serpent Apophis is also shown. 19th dynasty. Tomb of Ramesses I, Valley of the Kings, western Thebes.*

*(Below) The deceased king encircled by the protective serpent **Mehen**. At the right and left of this image an enigmatic text states 'He WhoHides the Hours'. Detail, second gilt shrine of Tutankhamun. 18th dynasty. Egyptian Museum, Cairo.*

Old Kingdom in Egypt, was based on this image of Mehen. Later, in the New Kingdom, Mehen is extensively represented in the vignettes of the 'Underworld Books' such as the Amduat. There the god is depicted as an immense serpent, often shown coiled around or above the shrine-like cabin of the boat of Re, protecting the sun god from evil and especially from the inimical underworld serpent Apophis.

Worship

As with most of the more bizarre denizens of the underworld Mehen was primarily the subject of myth rather than an object of ritual worship.

Meretseger

Mythology

Goddess of the pyramidal peak which lies at the heart of the Valley of the Kings in western Thebes, Meretseger presided over the whole Theban necropolis. Sometimes called Dehenet-Imentet 'the peak of the West' after her dwelling place, her more usual name was Meretseger 'she who loves silence', which was an apt one for the goddess of the lonely and desolate region uninhabited except by the deceased and, temporarily, by those workmen who constructed the tombs there.

Iconography

Although Meretseger was identified with the peak of the Theban royal necropolis, the hill itself rarely enters the goddess's iconography. Instead, she is usually represented as a coiled serpent, as a rearing cobra – sometimes with a woman's head, as a snake-headed woman, or occasionally, as a scorpion with a female head. The serpent and scorpion were among the few creatures to inhabit the remote desert site and these were seen, therefore, as fitting symbols for the manifestation of the goddess. In her various forms, the goddess may wear a disk with horns, a modius with uraeus, or other attribute upon her head.

Worship

Because she was worshipped primarily by the workmen of the royal necropolis, Meretseger's cult is attested from much of the New Kingdom but seldom later – when the Theban necropolis ceased to be used for royal burials. A good many stelae dedicated to the goddess have been found in the workmen's village of Deir el-Medina; and some of these, imploring the goddess's forgiveness, are among the most poignant of Egyptian religious texts (see p. 50). Meretseger was believed to strike those guilty of crimes with loss of sight or poisonous stings and bites, but a number of stelae record the goddess's forgiveness and the recovery of the workmen.

*The protective and assistive deity **Nehebu-Kau**, in the form of a serpent-man, feeds the deceased. Detail of a cartonnage mummy case. Louvre, Paris.*

Nehebu-Kau

Mythology

First attested in the Pyramid Texts, the serpent god Nehebu-Kau whose name means 'he who harnesses the spirits' was regarded as a benign and helpful deity. He assisted the deceased king in various ways and seems to act as an intercessory on his behalf in that several spells record the king's desire that his 'good name' be told to Nehebu-Kau who will 'raise up this good utterance…to the Two Enneads' (PT 1708). The god is said to be the son of the scorpion goddess Serket, though an alternative tradition claimed that he was the son of the earth god Geb and the serpent harvest goddess Renenutet. His chthonic origins and serpentine nature – coupled with the 'seven cobras' he is said to have swallowed – are the sources of Nehebu-Kau's considerable power. This is seen in later texts which assert that Nehebu-Kau is not subject to any harmful magic and cannot be harmed by water or fire. The god's consort was said to be Nehemtawy.

Iconography

Although he is called a 'great serpent, multitudinous of coils' in the Pyramid Texts and may be depicted in this manner, Nehebu-Kau was frequently represented as a man with a serpent's head and tail. In serpent form he is sometimes depicted

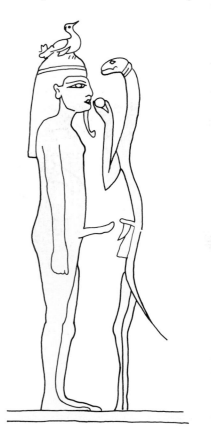

Nehebu-Kau in hybrid or semi-anthropomorphic form, as a man with the head of a serpent. This type of representation of the deity tends to appear in later contexts, while earlier depictions more frequently show the god in fully serpent form.

on the sides of divine thrones, doubtless as a protective deity, and in his semi-anthropomorphic form he is often depicted on amulets and plaques with his arms raised before him holding an offering pot.

Worship

The cult of Nehebu-Kau was practised at Herakleopolis Magna (modern Ihnasya el-Medina) and probably in other locations, and a feast of the god is known to have been celebrated since at least Middle Kingdom times on the first day of the first month of the winter season. The powerful nature and assistive qualities of Nehebu-Kau also led to his use in many amulets, and it is probably fair to assume that he was quite widely venerated in popular religion. While the god appears on amulets of late New Kingdom times, most date to the Third Intermediate Period and later.

Renenutet

Mythology

Although serpentine in form, Renenutet (Egyptian for 'snake who nourishes') was a popular and beneficent deity. Protective in nature and of a nurturing rather than venomous disposition, she was a goddess of the harvest and a divine nurse. In the Old Kingdom Renenutet was venerated as a guardian of the king in this life and in the beyond, being identified, like Wadjet, with the flame-breathing royal uraeus (PT 302) and also the king's robe 'of which the gods are afraid' (PT 1755, 1794). In the latter aspect she came to be sometimes associated with the bandages of the mummy. Her aspect as a

goddess of fertility and harvest is clearly denoted in her epithets 'lady of the fertile land', 'lady of the threshing floor' and 'lady of the granaries', and her role in this area may have originated in the imagery of the serpent who protects the crops from the rats and mice which threatened standing crops and stored grain alike. Renenutet was also identified with the household and family life in her role as provider, nourisher and as a nurse of infants.

The interrelationships of the goddess with other deities were extensive. In the Fayum Renenutet came to be linked with Sobek and Horus as a member of a triad named by the Greeks Hermouthis, Sekonopis and Ankhoes. As a grain goddess she was identified as the mother of Osiris in his form of the child Nepri, and in the Book of the Dead Renenutet is said to be the mother of Horus by Atum and thus came to be identified with Isis, with whom she shared the trait of divine nurse. Her associations with children also identified her with Meskhenet as a birth goddess and with Hathor whose headdress she wore. In the New Kingdom Litany of Re she appears in the underworld as the 'Lady of Justification' and in this form she may be associated with the goddess Maat. Finally, in the Late Period, like the god Shay, Renenutet was associated with the idea of fate and destiny, deciding not only the length of an individual's life but also many of its events.

Iconography

The iconography of Renenutet is most frequently that of an erect cobra with a sun disk and horns atop its head, often with two tall plumes surmounting the solar disk. The goddess may also be depicted anthropomorphically as a woman or a woman with a snake's head, standing or enthroned

New Kingdom shrine, now lost, of the serpent goddess **Renenutet**. *The shrine was doubtless typical of many local shrines dedicated to this deity. After Champollion,* Monuments de l'Égypte.

and sometimes holding or nursing a child which may be her son Nepri or a more generalized infant. In vignettes of the Litany of Re Renenutet is depicted as a mummiform being with the head of a cobra, though this is a specialized iconography not usually applied to the goddess. Sometimes she is the object of veneration of minor gods as in a granary at Karnak where the god Hapy was shown presenting offerings to her. Terracotta figures of the Ptolemaic Period depict the goddess as a form of Isis with a snake's head rising from a woman's body or with a woman's head atop a snake.

Worship

While amulets depicting the goddess show she may have functioned as a protective deity, it was as a goddess of fecundity that Renenutet was most widely venerated, and the goddess was popular among agricultural workers especially. The festivals of Renenutet were celebrated in the last month of the season when crops were sown, and in the following month, the first month of the summer season when they began to ripen. From Middle Kingdom times onwards we have evidence of the cult of the goddess in the Fayum where large scale crop production was accomplished, and her cult in the city of Dja (modern Medinet Madi) was particularly strong. She was also evidently venerated at Terenuthis (Kom Abu Billo) in the Delta, and in the New Kingdom we find evidence of her worship

at Giza, Abydos, and especially at Thebes. We know Renenutet was honoured in shrines erected in harvest fields and vineyards, and during the harvest and the pressing of grapes offerings were made before her image. Shrines dedicated to the goddess were also placed in magazines and granaries where the harvested crops were stored. The affection of the ancient Egyptians for this goddess is clear. As a much loved deity Renenutet even survived the pagan era in that she was ultimately transformed into the Greek Thermouthis who was later venerated as a Christian saint.

Wadjet

Mythology

The cobra goddess Wadjet was associated with the Nile Delta region from early times and became the tutelary deity of Lower Egypt in juxtaposition to her counterpart, the vulture goddess Nekhbet of Upper Egypt. Her name means 'the green one' which may refer to the natural colour of the serpent or perhaps to the verdant Delta region which she inhabited. Perhaps because she was associated more with the world of the living, the goddess does not play an important role in the Pyramid Texts, though references to the crown as a goddess do give her the epithet 'great of magic' (PT 194, 196). She was certainly closely linked to the king, both in

*Classic hieroglyphic form of the goddess **Wadjet** as a serpent on a basket, along with the vulture of the goddess Nekhbet, representing the 'Two Ladies' name of the king which symbolized the tutelary position of these goddesses over Upper and Lower Egypt. 12th dynasty. Chapel of Senwosret I, Karnak.*

the 'two ladies' or 'two goddesses' title of his royal protocol and as a protective deity in the form of the royal uraeus worn on the monarch's crown or headdress. In later texts she is called the 'mistress of awe' and 'mistress of fear', as mythologically the royal serpent spat flames in defense of the king; and military inscriptions (such of those of Ramesses II regarding the great Battle of Kadesh) describe her as slaying the monarch's enemies with her fiery breath. In the cycle of myths relating to Horus as represented in the temple of Hathor at Dendera, Wadjet acts as the young god's nurse when he is raised in the Delta site of Khemmis, giving her an association with Isis who usually took this role. Wadjet was also associated with a number of leonine goddesses as an 'Eye of Re', and like them she is sometimes said to be the mother of the god Nefertem.

Iconography

Usually Wadjet assumed the form of the erect cobra with hood extended in the creature's pose of readiness to strike, and it is in this form that the goddess is represented as the uraeus which protected both king and gods and was often shown attached to the solar disk – even during the Amarna Period when the depiction of most non-solar deities was avoided or proscribed. The raised serpent is often shown seated along with the vulture Nekhbet on two baskets, an iconography known from the

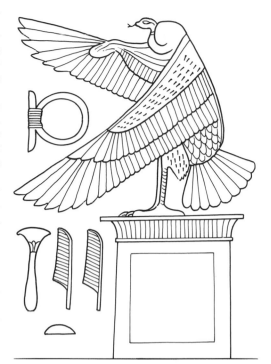

Wadjet as a serpent-headed vulture, in iconographic parallelism with her Upper Egyptian counterpart, the vulture goddess Nekhbet. Detail from the roof of the fourth gilt shrine of Tutankhamun. 18th dynasty. Egyptian Museum, Cairo.

1st dynasty. Because of the connection between Wadjet and Nekhbet some fusion of their iconographies took place, and the serpent Wadjet may be shown as a vulture or as a serpent with wings, just as a cobra depicted wearing the White Crown usually represents Nekhbet. It is possible that some depictions and amulets in the form of a papyrus sceptre or column, especially when surmounted by a cobra, are also meant to represent the goddess due to the similarity of the Egyptian word for papyrus with her name. As an 'Eye of Re' Wadjet can appear in fully leonine form and can thus also be depicted as a cobra with a lion's head – a form which may represent her or other 'Eye' goddesses. Amulets of Wadjet in various forms were quite common beginning in the Saite Period (724–712 BC).

Worship

The major cult centre of Wadjet was in the region of the ancient towns of Pe and Dep which came to be called Buto (modern Tell el-Fara'in) in the northwestern Delta. Her shrine was called the *per-nu* or 'house of flame' and is attested from predynastic times, eventually becoming representative of all the local shrines in its region. Royal sarcophagi patterned after the distinctive form of the *per-nu* shrine are known from the Old Kingdom, and the burial mastaba of the 4th-dynasty monarch Shepseskaf seems to have been constructed in this shape. In the New Kingdom several royal sarcophagi of the later 18th dynasty take this form, as does the innermost of the four funerary shrines of Tutankhamun. Many coffins and sarcophagi were

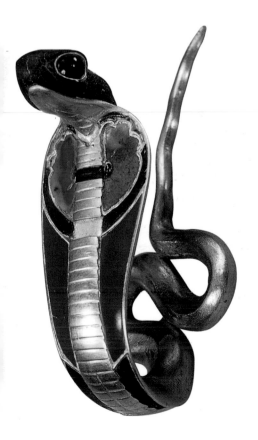

*Inlaid golden uraeus of Senwosret I representing **Wadjet** as the protective serpent who mythologically spat flames of fire against the king's enemies. 12th dynasty. From Lahun, Egyptian Museum, Cairo.*

227

also made in the shape of the *per-nu* throughout the later periods, as were other funerary containers, showing that the Lower Egyptian shrine had become thoroughly associated with the funerary sphere to an extent that was often seemingly independent of direct associations with Wadjet herself. Yet the goddess was often incorporated in funerary decoration, and this provides much of the evidence for her veneration.

Wepset

The serpent goddess Wepset, whose name means 'she who burns', appears to be one of the various identities of the fiery uraeus (see Wadjet) who guarded gods and kings, and also of the fearsome 'Eye of Re'. She is first attested in the Coffin Texts as the 'Eye', and in New Kingdom afterlife texts she is said to destroy the enemies of Re-Osiris. Wepset is usually represented in serpent form, though in the Graeco-Roman temples of Nubia she appears in anthropomorphic form as a goddess wearing a uraeus on her head, sometimes with horns and sun disk, or even with the head of a lion linking her to other 'Eye' goddesses such as Hathor and Tefnut. Although no temple of Wepset has been found at the site, known texts claim that the island of Biga was a cult centre of the goddess, and she appears in other temples of that area and Lower Nubia.

Weret-Hekau

The name Weret-Hekau, which means 'great of magic' or 'great enchantress' as it is sometimes translated, was applied to several goddesses. In the Pyramid Texts the name is associated with the divine uraeus (see p. 227) and with the crown of Lower Egypt as manifestations of the goddess Wadjet, and the name was in fact written with the determinative sign of a serpent. In later times the name is found applied more widely and also takes on a more independent nature. Weret-Hekau is mentioned several times on the objects from the tomb of Tutankhamun, particularly on a small shrine which contained an image of the goddess as a rearing serpent with the head of a woman who is depicted nursing the king, a maternal role which is found in the Pyramid Texts for the uraeus goddess (PT 1107–09).

Yam

A Semitic god, Yam is best known in Canaanite sources from Ugarit and elsewhere which show he was a tyrannical, monstrous deity of the sea and other bodies of water. He was known also in Egypt as a minor foreign god, and a fragmentary papyrus

*Cobra-headed goddess representing **Weret-Hekau** or 'Great of Magic', a name associated with several serpent deities.*

indicates that in his mythology his demands of tribute from other gods were thwarted by the goddess Astarte. In Canaanite myth he was finally defeated by the god Baal, and in Egyptian sources by Seth with whom Baal was identified. The mythological battle may have been representative of winter sea storms which calmed in the spring. Yam is not clearly described in the ancient sources and has no clear iconography though he appears to be serpentine in form. He may have had a great (sometimes seven-headed) sea monster in his following or he could himself have been that monster. Unserved by any Egyptian cult, he may still have been a god known and feared by Egyptian seafarers.

AMPHIBIAN AND FISH DEITIES

Hatmehyt

Mythology

A minor fish goddess, Hatmehyt was worshipped in the Delta city of Mendes but does not seem to have played a part in any major mythic cycle and little is known of her. Her name means 'she who is before the fishes'; this could suggest either pre-eminence – being foremost among fish deities – or temporal primacy, as the one who was before in the primeval world. Lack of mythological examples would perhaps suggest the former meaning as the most likely. Hatmehyt was eventually incorporated into the cult of Banebdjedet, the ram god of Mendes, as the consort of that more powerful god.

Iconography

Hatmehyt was depicted as a woman wearing a fish emblem upon her head, or in the form of a fish. It has sometimes been thought that the goddess's emblem was a dolphin, but it is now believed that the creature represented is the common Nile *Schilbe* fish.

Worship

The Delta city of Mendes, chief cult centre of Hatmehyt, doubtless contained a temple of this goddess at some time. Despite her eventual assimilation into the cult of the ram god of Banebdjedet, Hatmehyt does not seem to have been venerated much beyond the Delta, perhaps because fish, which were regarded as taboo in many areas, were seldom viewed as divine symbols. Usually she is represented as a woman with a fish on her head. Amulets on the Schilbe fish, which represented the deity, first appear early in the 26th dynasty.

Heket

Mythology

A frog goddess who assisted in fashioning the child in the womb and who presided over its birth, Heket is first attested in the Pyramid Texts where she assists the deceased king in his journey to the sky (PT 1312). Her connection with birth is first apparent in the Middle Kingdom story preserved in the Westcar Papyrus, however, in which the goddess 'hastened the birth' of the three kings who inaugurated the 5th dynasty. Also from this time, the

term 'servant of Heket' may have been applied to midwives in Egyptian society. Mythologically, Heket's life-giving power caused her to be associated with the Osiride family of deities and with the afterlife, and she was regarded as the wife of Haroeris/ Harwer and venerated as a female complement of Khnum.

Iconography

Heket was represented as a frog or as a woman with a frog's head. While temple representations tend to utilize the partially anthropomorphic form, amulets of the goddess are usually zoomorphic.

Worship

The main cult centre of Heket was at Herwer (perhaps modern Hur near el-Ashmunein), and the remains of a temple of the goddess have been found at Qus. She also appears in the temples of several other deities and was depicted receiving an offering of wine from Sethos I in his temple at Abydos, for example, and mentioned in the tomb of Petosiris (*c.* 300 BC) at Tuna el-Gebel, showing her cult was still strong. In less formal contexts Heket appears along with other deities on ivory 'wands' of the Middle Kingdom, and she appears in amuletic form from New Kingdom times.

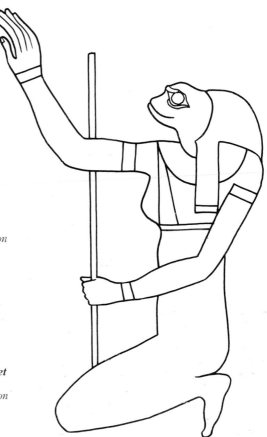

(Left) The frog birth-deity **Heket**. *Detail of a scene showing the goddess's attendance on the conception of Horus by Isis and the deceased Osiris. Roman Period. Temple of Hathor, Dendera.*

(Right) Detail of a scene depicting the goddess **Heket** *in semi-anthropomorphic form assisting in the creation of human children. 30th dynasty. Mammisi of Nectanebo, Dendera.*

Invertebrate and Insect Deities

Hededet

Hededet was a scorpion goddess whose characteristics resemble Serket in many ways but who was associated in the later periods with Isis. Like both of these goddesses, Hededet (in Egyptian *Hedjedjet*) can symbolize motherly qualities; and amulets in the form of a seated goddess with a scorpion on her head and nursing a child are likely to represent Hededet.

Khepri

Mythology

Khepri was the form of the sun god which represented the solar disk rising on the eastern horizon. As such he was one of the three forms or aspects of the solar deity who was 'Khepri in the morning, Re at midday and Atum in the evening', though it is impossible to know whether the god originally functioned in this carefully delineated role or whether he was accorded the position when, at some point, he was fused into the Heliopolitan cult of the sun. The name of the god in its earliest known occurrences, *kheprer,* is simply that of the scarab or dung beetle (*Scarabaeus sacer*) which the Egyptians visualized as a symbol of the god due to the beetle's habit of rolling a ball of mud or dung along the ground in a manner suggestive of the god pushing the solar disk across the sky. The female scarab beetle also lays her eggs in a similar ball from which the young eventually emerge as though spontaneously. The biology of the insect thus seems to underlie the name of the god as Khepri suggests the Egyptian verb *kheper*: 'develop' or 'come into being'. As the 'developing one' Khepri was the god of the first sunrise at the dawn of creation, and was thus linked with Atum as Atum-Khepri. To some extent Khepri also represented the sun in a general way and he could be linked with the solar god Re, though his identity as the morning sun remained primary and his essential mythological role was that of raising the sun from the horizon into the body of the sky goddess Nut. The god could therefore be said to be swallowed by Nut each evening and to travel through her body in the night hours to be reborn each morning. As a god who was constantly reborn Khepri was also directly associated with the concept of resurrection.

In this regard it has been suggested that the underground tunnels of the insect take the same form as the vertical shaft and horizontal passage found in Old Kingdom mastaba tombs, and that the pupae of the insect resemble the bandaged mummy of the deceased, though there is no indication that the Egyptians themselves recognized such similarities, for these types of embellishments to the lore of the scarab were recorded by Classical writers such as Plutarch and Horapollo.

Iconography

Khepri is most commonly represented in the form of the scarab beetle with varying degrees of stylization of the insect's anatomy. Painted and inlaid works often colour the insect blue or utilize lapis lazuli inlay to symbolically stress the beetle's association with the heavens, though in the vignettes of funerary texts the scarab is invariably shown black as in nature. The beetle may be shown alone or pushing the solar disk ahead of it; and although in nature the insect usually propels its mud ball with its hind legs, Egyptian depictions prefer to show the ball being pushed in a forward manner by the insect's front legs. The vignettes of funerary papyri and other scenes show the god standing on a boat being lifted by the god Nun as the personification of the primeval watery chaos towards the heavens in representation of the creation event. The body of the insect was occasionally fused with that of

other creatures such as the falcon or vulture, with the body of the scarab often being united with avian legs, tail and wings. Sometimes, as in the 4th-century BC tomb of Petosiris at Tuna el-Gebel, the insect is depicted with the Atef Crown of Osiris in order to unite the solar and netherworld realms in one image. Khepri was also depicted in semi-anthropomorphic form as a man with a scarab beetle as his head, as may be found in the tomb of Nefertari in the Valley of the Queens, and representations of this type sometimes unite the mummiform body of Osiris with a scarab head in the same kind of linkage indicated by the Atef-crowned beetle. A final variant on the image of the god is that which fuses the head of a ram on a scarab body in order to represent the joining of Atum-Khepri as the creator sun god or the combined rising-setting sun.

Worship

As with many related cosmic deities, Khepri was not accorded a cult of his own, though examples of colossal stone statues of the beetle god (such as the example now preserved beside the sacred lake in the temple of Amun at Karnak) suggest that the god was honoured in many Egyptian temples and might have represented the concepts of creation and the ongoing solar journey which were symbolically incorporated into temple architecture. On a much smaller scale, scarab beetle amulets are known from the 5th dynasty, and scarabs used as seals appear in the First Intermediate Period and were produced in great numbers from Middle Kingdom times onward. The undersides of these scarabs were incised with the owner's names and titles, with the names of deities or kings used for their protective value, or simply with decorative designs. Egyptian kings even used the undersides of scarabs as a medium for the recording of victories and other important events, with those of Amenophis III recording events as varied as the

Colossal scarab beetle on a large plinth erected by Amenophis III and later moved from that king's mortuary temple in western Thebes to Karnak Temple's sacred lake. 18th dynasty.

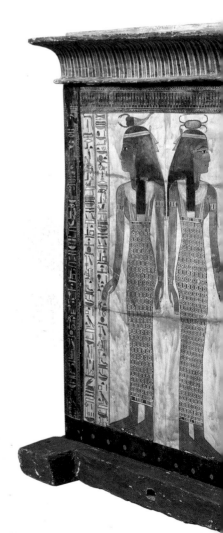

king's lion hunting expeditions and the arrival of a new princess for his harem. Other types of scarabs included 'heart scarabs' placed on the mummy of the deceased and scaraboids which fused the basic form of the scarab with the image of some other creature. The scarab was, in fact, the most popular of Egyptian amulets, and while Khepri may not have enjoyed the widespread services of a formal cult, his utilization as a potent symbol of creation and resurrection made him an almost ubiquitous deity in ancient Egyptian culture.

Sepa

The centipede god Sepa, sometimes called 'the centipede of Horus', is attested from Old Kingdom times through to the Graeco-Roman Period. He was linked with the gods of Heliopolis, particularly with Horus and with Osiris, sometimes appearing as Osiris-Sepa. In addition to his myriopodic form, Sepa could be represented with the head of a donkey or as a mummiform god (relating to his association with Osiris) with two short horns on his head. He was viewed as a protective deity having the power to prevent snake bites and was honoured with a festival from early times. A temple of the god was situated in Heliopolis.

Serket

Mythology

Serket was a scorpion goddess known from the 1st dynasty whose protective role is attested from at least the Old Kingdom when she appears in the Pyramid Texts – both alone and in the company of other goddesses – guarding the deceased king. Her importance as a protective deity is seen in texts such as that in which the king claims 'My mother is Isis, my nurse is Nephthys…Neith is behind me, and Serket is before me' (PT 1375). Along with these same goddesses – Isis, Nephthys and Neith – Serket became one of the four protective deities who

*Stuccoed, painted and varnished wooden outer sarcophagus or funerary sled of Khonsu, son of Sennedjem, showing **Serket** with the goddess Neith on one end, with Thoth, Anubis and other figures (including Isis and Nephthys mourning the mummy of the deceased) on its long side. 19th dynasty. Egyptian Museum, Cairo.*

*The enthroned goddess
Serket, given the
designations 'Lady of
Heaven, Mistress of the
Sacred Land [the necropolis]'.
19th dynasty. Tomb of
Nefertari, Valley of the
Queens, western Thebes.*

guarded coffins and the canopic chests and jars in which embalmed internal organs were placed, with the specific canopic responsibility of protecting the god Qebesenuef (see p. 88). She is often paired with Neith as Isis is with Nephthys. Her funerary role was a primary one, and she is sometimes called 'mistress of the beautiful house' referring to the embalming pavilion.

The full form of her Egyptian name – *Serket hetyt* – means 'she who causes the throat to breathe' and appears to be euphemistic of the fact that the scorpion can be fatally dangerous, and the goddess may heal just as she might destroy. Serket also fulfilled the role of a mother goddess, in which aspect she was called 'Serket the great, the divine mother'. Historically the scorpion was

regarded as a symbol of motherhood in many areas of the Near East, and as early as the Pyramid Texts Serket is said to nurse the king (PT 1427). In the New Kingdom scenes which record the 'divine birth' of Amenophis III in Luxor Temple and that of Hatshepsut in her mortuary temple, Serket is present with Neith supporting the god Amun and the queen on the marriage bed. She also appears with Nephthys in the mythological story of the birth of Horus when the two goddesses assist Isis in guarding the infant god after he is stung or bitten. In the same myth Isis is accompanied by seven scorpions which are emanations of Serket, and which protect Isis and her unborn child but also punish a woman who refuses to give her shelter. According to Egyptian mythology,

Serket was herself the mother of the serpent god Nehebu-Kau.

Iconography

Serket is usually represented in anthropomorphic form as a woman wearing a scorpion with raised tail atop her head. Almost always – as in the writing of the scorpion hieroglyph in the goddess's name and elsewhere – the creature is not drawn completely for protective, magical reasons, having its sting and often its legs or claws omitted. This is the standard depiction of the goddess when she appears in funerary contexts as, for example, in the graceful gilded statue which guarded the canopic chest in the tomb of Tutankhamun. In settings such as this the goddess stands with outstretched arms both protecting and embracing her charge. In her aspect of divine mother, however, Serket may be represented quite differently with the body of a woman, armed with knives, and with the heads of both a lioness and a crocodile. In funerary scenes Serket could be shown in fully zoomorphic form as a rearing cobra, and the goddess could also be represented in leonine form, as well as in the form of the scorpion. Amulets and images of the later dynasties which show a scorpion with the head of a woman wearing horns and solar disk may represent Serket with the attributes of Isis, Isis in scorpion form or simply a fusion of the two goddesses.

Worship

The cult of Serket is known to have existed since the 1st dynasty when she appears on a funerary stela from Saqqara, though the presence of her 'priests' seems to indicate medical magicians rather than the servants of a temple. Early Egyptian amulets of scorpions – known from Old Kingdom times – could have been apotropaic in nature and may not have represented Serket herself, though the goddess appears in anthropomorphic form as an amulet during the Late Period. As might be expected, Serket appears in many magical spells although, oddly, the majority of known spells against scorpion stings invoke Isis rather than Serket. There are, however, many spells in which Serket is said to protect and heal poisonous bites, and she appears to have been a patroness of the practicioners of magical medicine who dealt with such bites.

Ta-Bitjet

A scorpion goddess said to be the wife of Horus, Ta-Bitjet was believed to have power against poisonous bites and was invoked in many magical spells for this purpose. As is common with other minor goddesses invoked for anti-venom spells, Ta-Bitjet was sometimes conflated with the much greater deity Isis.

Gilded wooden statue of **Serket** *made to guard one side of the canopic shrine from the tomb of Tutankhamun. 18th dynasty. Egyptian Museum, Cairo.*

Inanimate Object Deities

Aten

Mythology

The mythology of the Aten – the radiant disk of the sun – is not only unique in Egyptian history but is also one of the most complex and controversial aspects of Egyptian religion. Forever associated with the heretic pharaoh Amenophis IV/Akhenaten, the Aten predates that king but rose to become a universal and almost exclusive deity during his reign – only to plunge into virtual obscurity within a generation of Akhenaten's death. The word *aten* is known to have been used from at least Middle Kingdom times to designate the solar disk and is used in this way in the Coffin Texts; and by mid-New Kingdom times a solar god named Aten appears to be well established. Tuthmosis IV issued a commemorative scarab on which the Aten functions as a god of war protecting the pharaoh, and his successor, Amenophis III, the father of Akhenaten, seems to have actively encouraged the worship of Aten. The third Amenophis stressed solar worship in many of his extensive building works; and one of the epithets of this king was Tjekhen-Aten or 'radiance of Aten', a term which was also used in several other contexts during his reign. But it was duirng the reign of Amenophis IV/Akhenaten that the ultimate elevation of the Aten occurred. Exactly what kind of god the Aten was envisaged as being at this time is not always apparent. Raymond Johnson has in the past discussed the possibility that the Aten worship promulgated by Akhenaten was one that emphasized the god as a deified form of his father, Amenophis III, but whatever the case may be in this regard, the Aten mythology propounded by Akhenaten was revolutionary and had far-reaching consequences.

Evidence such as the Great Hymn to the Aten shows not only that the god was regarded as being universal and transcendent, but also that the Aten's position relative to the king and his direct family was conceived in unique terms. Akhenaten and his queen Nefertiti served the god directly and, despite the existence of a dedicated priesthood of the Aten, Akhenaten alone was declared to have true knowledge of the god. As a result, even the most universal aspects of the theology of Atenism were short-circuited in the closed system espoused by the god's chief adherent. It could even be said

*The radiant disk of the **Aten**, depicted with a uraeus and pendent* ankh *sign, and with each ray terminating in a hand, accepts the floral offerings of Akhenaten and Nefertiti who worship the sun disk with two of their children. 18th dynasty. Limestone relief from el-Amarna. Egyptian Museum, Cairo.*

237

The **Aten** illuminates a royal
couple identified by the altered
inscription as Tutankhamun
and his wife Ankhesenamun.
Back panel of the golden
throne from the tomb of
Tutankhamun. 18th dynasty.
Egyptian Museum, Cairo.

that Atenism espoused a closed triad consisting of the Aten, Re and Akhenaten himself. Even
the high priest of the Aten was called the priest
of Akhenaten – indicating not only the elevated
position of the king in this theology but also the
effective barrier that he formed between even his
priests and the god Aten.

The Aten's relationship with other gods was also
complex. Akhenaten may have suppressed the cults
of some deities, but there remains clear evidence
that other gods were admitted in the Atenist theology.

Principal of these other deities was the sun god Re
who was equated with the Aten in certain contexts
and who was retained in the renewed titulary of
Akhenaten and incorporated in the names of two
of the king's own daughters, Nefernefrure and
Setepenre. Akhenaten also seems to have acknowledged other forms of the sun god, for example,
by making provision at his city of Akhetaten for
a tomb for the Mnevis bull which was held to be
a physical manifestation of Re. Some other deities,
such as the goddess Maat and the god Shu, were

The Royal Titulary of the Aten

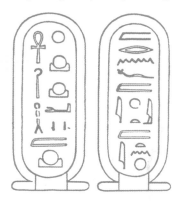

*The early form of the **Aten**'s cartouches incorporating other forms of the sun god.*

*The later, more restricted form of the **Aten**'s twin royal cartouches.*

*Detail of a limestone relief showing Nefertiti offering the early form of the **Aten**'s cartouches to the divine sun disk. 18th dynasty. Brooklyn Museum of Art.*

In his capacity as universal god and king of all, the Aten was given a titulary with two cartouche names of the same kind as those given to the Egyptian king on his coronation. It existed in two forms – an earlier version which included the names of Maat, Re-Horakhty and Shu and a later, more focused protocol of the ninth year of Akhenaten's reign which limited the identification of the Aten.

Early titulary:

Introduction:
Live, beautiful god who rejoices in Maat [the goddess is depicted rather than just the phonetic symbol for truth]
Lord of all which his disk circles
Lord of the sky, Lord of the Earth
Aten, living and great,
Illuminating the two lands
May my father live!

First cartouche:
Live Re-Horakhty who rejoices [or becomes active] in the Horizon

Second cartouche:
In his name of light [*shu*] which is in the Aten.

Conclusion:
Given life eternally forever,
Aten living and great
Who is in jubilee residing in the temple of Aten in Akhetaten.

Later titulary:

First cartouche:
Live Re, ruler of the two Horizons who rejoices [or becomes active] in the Horizon
Second cartouche:
In his name of light which comes from the Aten.

In this second version of the Aten's titulary Akhenaten replaced Re-Horakhty with Re (or possibly 'sun') and also replaced the name of the god Shu with a word for 'light' not associated with any god – thus divorcing the worship of the Aten from traditional Egyptian polytheism.

*Sandstone block showing Amenophis IV/Akhenaten and the **Aten** in his early form as a falcon-headed god wearing the disk of the sun on his head. The god's name does not yet appear in a cartouche. Egyptian Museum, Berlin.*

also accepted – as in the early cartouche names of the Aten (see inset box), though this acceptance was later restricted.

Iconography

Originally it was customary to represent Aten as a god in the form of a falcon-headed anthropomorphic deity similar to the usual depictions of Re or Re-Horakhty. However, early in the reign of Amenophis IV this iconography underwent a radical change in that the god began to be depicted in the form of the solar disk with a uraeus at its base and with streaming light rays which terminated in hands which were either left open or shown holding *ankh* signs when they fell upon the image of the king or a member of the royal family. Although the origin of this iconographic form actually predates Amenophis IV/Akhenaten and examples can be found from the reign of Amenophis II (1427–1401 BC),

under Akhenaten it became the sole manner in which the Aten was depicted.

Worship

Evidence exists of the cult of the Aten at Heliopolis during the reign of Amenophis III, but it was under Amenophis IV/Akhenaten that the cult of the god reached its peak. Upon his accession, the latter king constructed a large temple complex, which included at least three sanctuaries just outside the eastern perimeter of the temple of Amun at Karnak. Within a short time of the founding of this new temple, the worship of Amun and other gods seems to have been diminished and eventually, in the case of Amun at least, actually proscribed. Beginning in approximately his 5th year when the king changed his name to Akhenaten, a new capital – Akhetaten 'the horizon of the Aten' – was built at the virgin site of el-Amarna in Middle Egypt, and new temples

*View of el-Amarna, the site of Akhenaten's city of Akhetaten or 'the horizon of the **Aten**', looking northwest from boundary stela K.*

were built to honour the god. These included the so-called 'great temple' and 'small temple' which were constructed according to a novel architectural plan emphasizing open access to the sun rather than the traditional darkness of Egyptian shrines.

There also appears to have been temples of the Aten at Memphis, at Sesebi in Nubia and perhaps elsewhere for at least part of Akhenaten's reign, though evidence for popular acceptance of the Aten religion is decidedly lacking. Many of the rock-cut tombs cut for the nobles of el-Amarna have prayers to the Aten (often seemingly extracts from the great hymn to the god) inscribed on their doorways, and there are other formal indications of respect for Akhenaten's god among the city's ruling elite, but Atenism remained an exclusive religion – only the king and his family are depicted worshipping the god and it is only to them that the Aten holds out the gift of life. There is no real evidence for personal, individual worship of the god on the part of the ordinary Egyptian whose only access to the Aten was through the medium of the king. This situation created a religious vacuum which was unstable even from the beginning, and the presence of amulets and representations of various deities and other indications of traditional worship demonstrate that even in the new capital popular worship of the older gods – even if covert in nature – nevertheless continued.

Although the priesthoods of the various gods were powerless to stop the religious changes which came with Atenism during Akhenaten's lifetime, the religious and political realities extant at the end of the king's reign meant that a return to orthodoxy was inevitable. Akhenaten's successors returned to Thebes, and the cults of Amun and Egypt's many other gods were renewed. The Aten's temples were quickly deserted and within a few years they were torn down, often, ironically, to be used in the renewal and expansion of temples for the very gods Atenism had sought to displace.

Moon

Unlike the solar *aten*, it is uncertain that the disk of the moon was itself worshipped in Egypt as a deity during historical times, and the evidence which is extant seems to show that it was regarded rather as a symbol or manifestation of specific deities associated with the moon. Most prominent of these gods were Horus (see p. 200), Iah (see p. 111), and Thoth (see p. 215), though the lunar disk was also a symbol of Osiris according to the mythology of that god. Additionally, 14 individual deities were sometimes associated with the days of the waxing moon and 14 were associated with the waning moon.

The god Anubis attends the lunar disk which stood in contrast with the sun and which could symbolize Osiris according to Egyptian mythology. Redrawn from E. Naville, The Temple of Deir el-Bahari.

*The deities of the 14 days of the waning **moon** surround the 'lunar eye' within the moon's disk in its barque of the night. Detail of a late relief.*

241

Epilogue: A Lasting Legacy

Ritual stela of the goddess Isis shown in typical Graeco-Roman manner and with only the diminutive horns and sun disk atop her head directly betraying her Egyptian origin and identity. 1st–2nd century BC. Egyptian Museum, Cairo.

Long before the ancient Egyptian civilization reached its end, Egypt had exerted enormous influence over its neighbours, trading partners and even its enemies. Much of that influence is reflected in the presence of Egyptian deities which have been detected as far from the Nile as Persia in the east and Britain in the west. The ancient Minoans, for example, absorbed the goddess Taweret into their own culture (see p. 185), and the image of the Egyptian god Bes (see p. 102) became that of

the Greek Gorgon. Sometimes the influence was oblique, yet it was clearly present. The Achaemenid Persians, who ruled at least part of Egypt from the late 6th through to the 4th century BC, were influenced considerably by Egyptian culture and religion, and Persian rulers such as Darius the Great even commissioned Egyptian-style statues of themselves, not unlike statues of Egyptian gods. Images of the Egyptian gods intrigued and mystified outsiders for centuries and were carried to many distant lands. Statues of Egyptian deities are thus known to have stood in many ancient cities and, at the height of the Roman Empire, Roman legions carried images of the protective god Bes (see p. 102) and the great goddess Isis (see p. 146) as far afield as England. The Romans were particularly enamoured of things Egytian and the Egyptian phoenix (see p. 212) – which was compared to undying Rome – appears on the coinage of the late Roman Empire as a symbol of the Eternal City. It was also viewed as an allegory of resurrection and life after death – ideas that appealed to early Christians throughout the Empire.

Only at the very end of Egypt's ancient history when the old beliefs gave way to new monotheistic faiths, did Egypt's many deities fall into oblivion – but even then, the old ways and old gods would prove to be the seeds from which new religious ideas would continue to grow. Here, in fact, among the ancient gods and goddesses of the Nile lie the roots of many later religious traditions – and perhaps, ironically, even the concept of monotheism itself (see p. 36), as well as that of the transcendent nature of the divine, can be traced ultimately to Egyptian beginnings. While this is not to diminish fuller developments of these concepts in later religions, the influence of Egyptian deities and religion cannot be denied in the formative periods of those same religions, and particularly that of Christianity which provides an excellent case study of Egyptian influence.

Christianity took root in Egypt at an early date. By the end of the 2nd century it was already well established in the Nile Valley and soon came to replace the old religion of the gods. Doubtless the spread of the religion was aided by the fact that many aspects of Christianity were readily understandable to the Egyptians in terms of their own ancient myths and beliefs, not least the role of Jesus as the son of God. As has been pointed out, the fact that the Egyptians, since ancient times, had viewed their king as the incarnate son of a god, meant that the Christian concept of Jesus as the incarnate Son of God was far more readily embraced in Egypt than elsewhere in the Roman world.

The iconography of Christianity – precisely because it encountered the Egyptian deities at

Bronze statue of the god Horus in the dress of a Roman soldier. c. 1st century AD. Provenance unknown. British Museum.

an early and formative period in its development – was particularly affected. Often the gods are in the details. The four evangelists of the Christian tradition were frequently depicted in animal form or as animal-headed like the Egyptian gods in early Christian art, and the precursor of the St. George and the Dragon motif may possibly be first found in Hibis Temple. But even major Christian motifs may have Egyptian origins. The sacred mother and child of Christianity are certainly foreshadowed in the countless images of Isis (whom the Egyptians called the *mut-netcher* – the 'mother of god') and her infant son Horus, as is even the symbol of the cross (which is first attested in Egypt as the 'Egyptian' or *tau* cross – a form of the *ankh* sign). It has also been suggested that scenes from the Egyptian underworld books which graphically depict the fate of the damned inspired much of the later iconography of the Christian hell with its demons and punishments and it is probably impossible to know the full extent to which such pagan revenants have influenced the imagery of Christianity.

Other later religions and even secular philosphies have likewise been affected by the deities of Egypt. Greek accounts of Egyptian myths continued to influence Western cultures during the Medieval and Renaissance Periods. The philosophy of Neo-Platonism and various forms of the Hermetic mysteries all contained ideas which were essentially Egyptian, and as late as the 17th century, the German Jesuit-scholar Athanasius Kircher argued that the goddess Isis was an emanation of the queen of heaven of Roman Catholic belief.

Even today, in the 21st century, many of Egypt's gods and religious symbols continue to exist – sometimes unbeknown to their perpetuators and sometimes knowingly. Throughout the Mediterranean sailors still paint an eye on the prow of their boats for protection and to 'see' their way ahead without realizing they continue a custom begun by the ancient Egyptians with the Eye of Horus (see p. 200). In Egypt, local women desiring to have children still occasionally visit the crypts of Hathor's Temple, as that goddess retains a reputation for granting fertility almost two millennia after her cult was overthrown.

There is also a vast modern interest in ancient Egypt which often focuses on the civilization's gods and goddesses – ranging from the detached study of scholars of comparative religion to the fervent efforts of latter day pagans who desire to resurrect the ancient cults. The legacy of the gods is to be found in an amazing number of places and with ongoing reinterpretations, for the influence of Egypt's deities has far outlived the ancient civilization with a persistence which – viewed historically – may outlast our own.

Further Reading

Abbreviations

AAWLM	*Abhandlungen der Akademie der Wissenschaften und der Literatur in Mainz*
ÄAT	*Ägypten und Altes Testament*
ADAIK	*Abhandlungen des Deutschen Archäologischen Instituts Kairo*
ÄF	*Ägyptologische Forschungen*
ASAE	*Annales du Service des Antiquités de l'Égypte*
BACE	*Bulletin of the Australian Center for Egyptology*
BES	*Bulletin of the Egyptological Seminar*
BIFAO	*Bulletin de l'Institut français d'archéologie orientale*
BRL	*Bulletin of the John Rylands Library*
BSA	*Bulletin de la Société d'Anthropologie*
GM	*Göttinger Miszellen*
JAF	*Journal of American Folklore*
JANES	*Journal of the Ancient Near Eastern Society*
JARCE	*Journal of the American Research Center in Egypt*
JEA	*Journal of Egyptian Archaeology*
JNES	*Journal of Near Eastern Studies*
JSSEA	*Journal of the Society for the Study of Egyptian Antiquities*
JTS	*Journal of Theological Studies*
KMT	*KMT: A Modern Journal of Ancient Egypt*
LÄ	Helck, W., and E. Otto (eds.), *Lexikon der Ägyptologie* (Wiesbaden,1975–)
MÄS	*Münchner Ägyptologische Studien*
MDAIK	*Mitteilungen des Deutschen Archäologischen Instituts, Abteilung Kairo*
OBO	*Orbis biblicus et orientalis*
OEAE	*Oxford Encyclopedia of Ancient Egypt*
PÄ	*Probleme der Ägyptologie*
RHPR	*Revue d'Histoire et de Philosophie Religieuses*
RHR	*Revue de l'histoire de religions*
SAK	*Studien zur altägyptischen Kultur*
VA	*Varia Aegyptiaca*
ZÄS	*Zeitschrift für ägyptische Sprache und Altertumskunde*

There is a vast literature extant on ancient Egyptian religion in general and on the individual gods and goddesses themselves. The following bibliography aims to provide access to that literature through a selection of standard works and recently published articles on the major deities. For further information on the many hundreds of minor Egyptian gods and goddesses, the reader is encouraged to consult some of the excellent handbooks listed in the Introduction section below as well as the bibliographies found in the specialized studies listed under the various categories of deities.

Introduction

Assmann, J., *The Search for God in Ancient Egypt* (tr. by D. Lorton, Ithaca, 2001)

Cerny, J., *Ancient Egyptian Religion* (Westport, CT, 1979)

Frankfort, H., *Ancient Egyptian Religion: An Interpretation* (New York, 1948)

Hart, G., *A Dictionary of Egyptian Gods and Goddesses* (London, 1986)

Kemp, B.J., *Ancient Egypt: Anatomy of a Civilization* (London and New York, 1989)

Leitz, C. (ed.), Das Lexikon der ägyptischen Götter und Götterbezeichnungen I–VII (Leuven/Louvain, 2002)

Lesko, B.S., *The Great Goddesses of Egypt* (Norman, OK, 1999)

Luft, U.H., 'Religion', *OEAE*, Vol. III, pp. 139–45

Lurker, M., *The Gods and Symbols of Ancient Egypt* (tr. by B. Cumming, London, 1980)

Quirke, S., *Ancient Egyptian Religion* (London, 1992)

Shaw, I. and P. Nicholson, *The Dictionary of Ancient Egypt* (London, 1995)

Silverman, D.P., 'Deities', *OEAE*, Vol. I, pp. 369–75

Teeter, E., 'Cults: Divine Cults', *OEAE*, Vol. I, pp. 340–45

Tobin, V.A., *Theological Principles of Egyptian Religion* (New York, 1989)

Traunecker, C., *The Gods of Egypt* (tr. by D. Lorton, Ithaca, 2001)

Watterson, B., *The Gods of Ancient Egypt* (London, 1984; repr. Gloucestershire, 1996)

I Rise and Fall of the Gods

Birth of the Gods

Allen, J.P., *Genesis in Egypt: The Philosophy of Ancient Egyptian Creation Accounts* (New Haven, 1988)

Hassan, F., 'Primeval Goddess to Divine Kingship: The Mythogenesis of Power in the Early Egyptian State'. In R. Friedman and B. Adams (eds.), *The Followers of Horus: Studies dedicated to Michael Allen Hoffman 1944–1990* (Oxford, 1992) pp. 307–22

Hassan, F.A., 'The Earliest Goddesses of Egypt: Divine Mothers and Cosmic Bodies'. In L. Goodison and C. Morris (eds.), *Ancient Goddesses: The Myths and the Evidence* (Madison, WI, 1998)

Hoffman, M.A., *The Predynastic of Hierkonopolis — An Interim Report* (Oxford, 1982)

Hoffmeier, J.K., 'Some Thoughts on Genesis 1 & 2 and Egyptian Cosmology' *JANES* 15 (1983) pp. 39–49

Lesko, L.H., 'Ancient Egyptian Cosmogonies and Cosmology'. In B.E. Shafer (ed.), *Religion in Ancient Egypt: Gods, Myths, and Personal Practice* (Ithaca and London, 1991), pp. 88–122

Silverman, D.P., 'Divinity and Deities in Ancient Egypt,' In: B.E. Shafer (ed.), *Religion in Ancient Egypt: Gods, Myths, and Personal Practice* (Ithaca and London, 1991), pp. 7–87

Ucko, P.J., *Anthropomorphic Figurines of Predynastic Egypt and Neolithic Crete* (London, 1968)

Rule of the Gods

Allen, J.P., *Genesis in Egypt: The Philosophy of Ancient Egyptian Creation Accounts* (New Haven, 1988)

Bleeker, C.J., 'L'Idée de l'ordre cosmique dans l'ancienne Égypte', *RHPR* 2–3 (1962), pp. 193–200

Mysliwiec, K., 'Amon, Atum and Aton: The Evolution of Heliopolitan Influences in Thebes'. In *L'Égyptologie en 1979, 2: Axes priorities de recherches* (Paris, 1982; Cairo, 1983), pp. 285–89

Silverman, D.P., 'Divinity and Deities in Ancient Egypt'. In B.E. Shafer (ed.), *Religion in Ancient Egypt: Gods, Myths, and Personal Practice* (Ithaca and London, 1991)

Decline of the Gods

Assmann, J., *Zeit und Ewigkeit im alten Ägypten* (Heidelberg, 1975)

Bagnall, R.S., *Egypt in Late Antiquity* (Princeton, 1993)

Bell, H.I., *Cults and Creeds in Graeco-Roman Egypt* (Liverpool, 1953)

Frankfurter, D., *Religion in Roman Egypt : Assimilation and Resistance* (Princeton, 1998)

Hollis, S. T., 'Otiose Deities and the Ancient Egyptian Pantheon', *JARCE* (XXXV, 1998), pp. 61–71

Merkelbach, R., *Isis Regina, Zeus Serapis. Die griechisch-ägyptische Religion nach den Quellen dargestellt* (Stuttgart, 1995)

Witt, R.E., *Isis in the Graeco-Roman World* (Ithaca, 1971); repr. as *Isis in the Ancient World* (Baltimore, 1997)

II Nature of the Gods

Forms of the Divine

Assmann, J., *Ägypten: Theologie und Frömmigkeit einer frühen Hochkultur* (Stuttgart, 1984); trans into English as *The Search for God in Ancient Egypt* (Tr. D. Lorton, Ithaca, 2001)

Baines, J. 'On the Symbolic Context of the Principal Hieroglyph for "god"'. In U. Verhoeven and E. Graefe (eds.), *Religion und Philosophie im alten Ägypten* (Leuven, 1991), pp. 29–46

Brunner, H., 'Name, Namen, und Namenlosigkeit Gottes im Alten Ägypten'. In H. von Stietencron (ed.), *Der Name Gottes* (Düsseldorf, 1975), pp. 33–49

Cauville, S., 'Á propos des 77 génies de Pharbaithos', *BIFAO* 90 (1990), pp. 115–33

Derchain, P., 'Der ägyptische Gott als Person und Funktion'. In Wolfhart Westendorf (ed.), *Aspekte der spätägyptischen Religion* (Weisbaden, 1979), pp. 43–45.

Fischer, H. G., 'The Ancient Egyptian Attitude Towards the Monstrous'. In A.E. Farkas *et al.* (eds.), *Monsters and Demons in the Ancient and Medieval Worlds: Papers Presented in Honor of Edith Porada* (Mainz, 1987), pp. 13–26

Goedicke, H., 'God', *JSSEA* 16 (1986), pp. 57–62

Hoffmeier, J.K., *Sacred in the Vocabulary of Ancient Egypt: The term ḏsr, with special reference to Dynasties I–XX* (Göttingen, 1985)

Hornung, E., 'Tiergestaltige Götter der alten Ägypter'. In *Mensch und Tier* (Bern, 1985), pp. 11–31

Hornung, E., 'Götterwort und Götterbild im alten Ägypten'. In H.-J. Klimkeit (ed.), *Götterbild in Kunst und Schrift* (Bonn, 1984), pp. 37–60

James, E.O., *The Worship of the Sky-God* (London, 1963)

Kurth, D., 'Götter determinieren Götter', *SAK* 5 (1977), pp. 175–81

Meeks, D., 'Zoomorphie et image des dieux dans

Brady, T.A., *Sarapis and Isis: Collected Essays* (Chicago, 1978)

Brunner-Traut, E., 'Der Sehgott und der Hörgott in Literatur und Theologie'. In J. Assmann, E. Feucht and R. Grieshammer (eds.), *Fragen an die altägyptische Literatur* (Wiesbaden, 1977), pp. 125–45

Cornelius, S. *The iconography of the Canaanite gods Reshef and Baal in the Late Bronze and Iron Age I periods (c 1500–1000 BC)* (Goettingen & Fribourg, 1994)

Cruz-Uribe, E., 'Atum, Shu, and the Gods During the Amarna Period', *JSSEA* 25 (1995), pp. 15–22

Dolinska, M., 'Red and Blue Figures of Amun', *VA* 6:1–2 (April–August 1990), pp. 3–7

Eaton-Krauss, M., 'The Earliest Representation of Osiris', *VA* 3 (1987), pp. 233–36

Giveon, R., 'New Material Concerning Canaanite Gods in Egypt'. In *Proceedings of the Ninth World Congress of Jewish Studies, Jerusalem, 1985* (Jerusalem, 1986), pp. 1–4

Griffiths, J.G., 'Osiris', *OEAE*, Vol. II, pp. 615–19

Griffiths, J.G., *The Origins of Osiris and His Cult* (Leiden, 1980)

Griffiths, J.G., 'Osiris and the Moon in Iconography', *JEA* 62 (1976), pp. 153–59

Griffiths, J.G., 'Osiris', *LÄ* IV, c. 623–33

Hall, E. S., 'Harpocrates and Other Child Deities in Ancient Egyptian Sculpture', *JARCE* 14 (1977), pp. 55–58

Holmberg, S., *The God Ptah* (Lund, 1946)

Houser-Wegner, J., 'Shu', *OEAE*, Vol. III, pp. 285–86

Houser-Wegner, J., 'Nefertum', *OEAE*, Vol. II, pp. 514–16

Josephson, J.A., 'Imhotep', *OEAE*, Vol. II, pp. 151–52

Kozloff, A.P. and B.M. Bryan, with L.M. Berman, *Egypt's Dazzling Sun: Amenhotep III and His World* (Cleveland, 1992)

Lorton, D., 'Considerations on the Origin and Name of Osiris', *VA* 1 (1985), pp. 113–26

McBride, D.R., 'Nun', *OEAE*, Vol. II, pp. 557–58

Mysliwiec, K., 'Atum'. In *OEAE*, Vol. I, pp. 158–60

Mysliwiec, K., *Name. Epitheta. Ikonographie*, Vol. II, *Studien zum Gott Atum* (Hildesheim, 1979)

Ogdon, J.R., 'The Celestial Ferryman in the Pyramid Texts', *Publicaciones Ocasionales, Instituto de Egiptologia de la Argentina*, Vol. 1 (Buenos Aires, 1977)

Ogdon, J.R., 'Some Notes on the Iconography of Min', *BES* 7 (1985–86), pp. 29–41

Onstine, S., 'The Relationship Between Osiris and Re in the Book of Caverns', *JSSEA* 25 (1995), pp. 66–77; pl. 5–7

Osing, J., 'Isis und Osiris', *MDAIK* 30 (1974), pp. 91–113

Otto, E., *Ancient Egyptian Art: The Cults of Osiris and Amon* (Tr. by K. Bosse-Griffiths, New York, 1967)

Otto, E. and M. Hirmer, *Osiris und Amun, Kult und Heilige Staetten* (Munich, 1966)

Plutarch, *De Iside et Osiride* (tr. J.G. Griffiths, Cardiff, 1970)

Quaegebeur, J., *Le dieu egyptien Shai dans la religion et l'onomastique* (Leuven, 1975)

Ritner, R., 'Horus on the Crocodiles: A Juncture of Religion and Magic in Late Dynastic Egypt.' In J.P. Allen, J. Assmann, A.B. Lloyd, R.K. Ritner and D.P. Silverman (eds.), *Religion and Philosophy in Ancient Egypt* (New Haven, 1989), pp. 103–16

Romanosky, E., 'Min', *OEAE*, Vol. II, pp. 413–15

Schenkel, W., 'Amun-Re: Eine Sondierung zu Struktur und Genese altägyptischer synkretischer Götter', *SAK* 1 (1974), pp. 275–88

Schlögl, H., 'Nefertem', *LÄ* IV, c. 378–80

Schlögl, H., *Der Sonnengott auf der Blüte* (Genève, 1977)

Schlögl, H.A., *Der Gott Tatenen nach Texten und Bildern des Neuen Reiches* (Freiburg and Göttingen, 1980)

Schumacher, I., *Der Gott Sopdu, der Herr der Fremdlander* (Freiburg, 1988)

te Velde, H., 'Schu', *LÄ* V, c. 735–37

te Velde, H., 'Ptah', *LÄ* IV, c. 1177–80

Tobin, V.A., 'Amun and Amun-Re', *OEAE*, Vol. I, pp. 82–85

Van der Plas, D. (ed.), *L'Hymne à la crue du Nil*, 2 vols. (Leiden, 1986)

Van Dijk, J., 'Ptah', *OEAE*, Vol. III, pp. 74–76

Vassal, P.A., 'La Physico-Pathologie dans le Panthéon Égyptien: Les Dieux Bès et Ptah, le Nain et l'Embryon', *BSA* (1956), pp. 168–81

Vernus, P., 'Le Mythe d'une Mythe: le prétendue noyade d'Osiris', *Studi di Egittologia e di antichità Puniche* 9 (1991), pp. 19–32

Wainwright, G.A., 'Some Aspects of Amun', *JEA* 20 (1934), pp. 139–53

Wildung, D., *Imhotep und Amenhotep-Gottwerdung im alten Ägypten*, *MÄS* 36 (Munich and Berlin, 1977)

Wildung, D., 'Imhotep', *LÄ* III, c. 145–48

Wildung, D., *Egyptian Saints: Deification in Pharaonic Egypt* (New York, 1977)

Wilkinson, R.H., 'Ancient Near Eastern Raised-arm Figures and the Iconography of the Egyptian God Min', *BES* 11 (1991 92), pp. 109–18

Zandee, J., 'Der Androgyne Gott in Ägypten ein Erscheinungsbild des Wiltschöpfers'. In J. Zandee (ed.), *Religion im Erbe Ägyptens: Beitrage zur spätantiken Religiongeschichte zu Ehren von Alexander Böhlig* (Wiesbaden, 1988)

Zeidler, J., 'Zur Etymologie des Gottesnamens Osiris', *SAK* 28 (2000), pp. 309–16

Female Anthropomorphic Deities

Assmann, J., *Maat: Gerechtigkeit und Unsterblichkeit im alten Ägypten* (Munich, 1990)

Assmann, J., 'Neit spricht als Mutter und Sarg', *MDAIK* 28 (1972), p. 125

Barta, W., 'Bemerkungen zur Etymologie und Semantik der Götternamen von Isis und Osiris', *MDAIK* 34 (1978), pp. 9–13

Bergman, J., 'Isis', *LÄ* III, c. 186–203

Bianchi, R., Review of J. Eingartner, *Isis und ihre Dienerinnen in der Kunst der römnischen Kaiserzeit*, *JARCE* 30 (1993), pp. 200–01

Bleeker, C.J., 'Isis and Nephthys as Wailing Women', *Numen* 5:1 (1958), pp. 1–17

Bleeker, C.J., 'Isis as Saviour Goddess'. In S.G.F. Brandon (ed.), *The Saviour God: Comparative Studies in the Concept of Salvation Presented to Edwin Oliver James* (Manchester, 1963), pp. 1–16

Bleeker, C.J., *Hathor and Thoth: Two Key Figures of the Ancient Egyptian Religion* (Leiden, 1973)

Bleeker, C.J., 'The Egyptian Goddess Neith'. In E. Urbach, *Studies in Mysticism and Religion presented to Gershom G. Scholem on his Seventieth Birthday* (Jerusalem, 1967), pp. 41–56

Brady, T.A., *Sarapis and Isis: Collected Essays* (Chicago, 1978)

Budde, D., *Die Goettin Seschat, Wodtke und Stegbauer* (Leipzig, 2000)

Buhl, M.-L., 'The Goddesses of the Egyptian Tree Cult', *JNES* 6 (1947), pp. 80–97

Cornelius, S., 'The Egyptian iconography of the Syro-Palestinian goddesses Anat and Astarte'. In K.M. Cialowicz, J.A. Ostrowski (eds.), Les civilisations du bassin mediterraneen. Hommages a Joachim Sliwa. (Cracovie, 2000), pp. 71–77.

Daumas, F., *Le Culte d'Isis dans le Bassin oriental de la Mediterranée I: Le culte d'Isis et les Ptolemees* (Leiden, 1973)

De Meulenaere, H., 'Meskhenet à Abydos'. In U. Verhoeven and E. Grafe (eds.), *Religion und Philosophie im Alten Ägypten* (Leuven, 1991), pp. 243–51

Derchain, P., *Hathor Quadrifrons: Recherches sur la syntaxe d'un mythe égyptien* (Istanbul, 1972)

Donahue, V., 'The Goddess of the Theban Mountain', *Antiquity* 66 (1992), pp. 871–85

Dunand, F., *Le culte d'Isis dans le bassin oriental de la Méditerranée*, 3 vols. (Leiden, 1973)

Egan, R.B., 'Isis: Goddess of the Oikoumene'. In L. Hurtado, *Goddesses in Religion and Modern Debate* (Atlanta, 1990), pp. 123–42

Griffiths, J.G., 'Isis as Maat, Dikaiousune, and Iustitia'. In C. Berger, G. Clerc and N. Grimal (eds.), *Homages à Jean Leclant* (Cairo, 1994), pp. 255–64

Griffiths, J.G., 'Isis', *OEAE*, Vol. II, pp. 188–91

Hollis, S.T., 'Women of Ancient Egypt and the Sky Goddess Nut' *JAF* 100 (1987), pp. 496–503; revised and repr. in Hollis, S.J., L. Pershing, and M.J. Young (eds.), *Feminist Theory and the Study of Folklore* (Urbana, 1993), pp. 200–12

Hollis, S.T., 'Five Egyptian Goddesses in the Third Millenium B.C.', *KMT* 5:4 (1994), pp. 46–51, 82–5

Hornung, E., 'Versuch über Nephthys'. In A.B. Lloyd (ed.), *Studies in Pharaonic Religion and Society: In honor of J. Gwyn Griffiths* (London, 1992), pp. 186–88

Lesko, L.H., 'Nut', *OEAE*, Vol. II, pp. 558–59

Lichtheim, M., *Maat in Egyptian Autobiographies and Related Studies* (Freiburg, 1992)

Münster, M., *Untersuchungen zur Götin Isis vom Alten Reich bis zum Ende des Neuen Reiches* (Berlin, 1968)

Osing, J., 'Isis und Osiris', *MDAIK* 30 (1974), pp. 91–113

Parker, R., 'Lady of the Acacia', *JARCE* 4 (1965), pp. 151

Pinch, G., *Votive Offerings to Hathor* (Oxford, 1993)

Plutarch, *De Iside et Osiride* (tr. J.G. Griffiths, Cardiff, 1970)

Quaegebeur, J., 'Cleopatra VII and the Cults of the Ptolemaic Queens'. In *Cleopatra's Egypt: Age of the Ptolemies* (Brooklyn, 1989), pp. 41–54

Roberts, A., *Hathor Rising: The Power of the Goddess in Ancient Egypt* (Rochester, Vt., 1997)

Schlichting, R., 'Neit', *LÄ* IV, c. 392–94

Simon, C., 'Neith', *OEAE*, Vol. II, p. 516

te Velde, H., 'Mut', *LÄ* IV, c. 246–48

te Velde, H., 'Towards a Minimal Definition of the Goddess Mut' *Jaarbericht van het Voor-Aziatisch-Egyptisch Genootschap Ex Oriente Lux* 26 (1979–80), pp. 3–9

te Velde, H., 'Mut', *OEAE*, Vol. II, pp. 454–55

te Velde, H., 'Mut the Eye of Re'. In *Akten des Vierten Internationalen Ägyptologisches Kongresses* (Hamburg, 1989), pp. 395–401

Teeter, E., 'Maat', *OEAE*, Vol. II, pp. 319–21

Teeter, E., *The Presentation of Maat: Ritual and Legitimacy in Ancient Egypt* (Chicago, 1997)

Troy, L., *Patterns of Queenship* (Uppsala, 1986)

Troy, L., 'Mut Enthroned'. In J. van Dijk (ed.), *Essays on Ancient Egypt in honour of Herman te Velde* (Groningen, 1997), pp. 301–05

Vischak, D., 'Hathor', *OEAE*, Vol. II, pp. 82–85

Wells, R.A., 'The Mythology of Nut and the Birth of Ra', *SAK* 19 (1992), pp. 305–21

Wente, E.F., 'Hathor at the Jubilee'. In G.E. Kadish (ed.), *Studies in Honor of John A. Wilson* (Chicago, 1969), pp. 83–91

Witt, R.E., *Isis in the Graeco-Roman World* (Ithaca, 1971); repr. as *Isis in the Ancient World* (Baltimore, 1997)

Zabkar, L.V., *Hymns to Isis in Her Temple at Philae* (Hanover and London, 1988)

Mammalian Deities

Altenmüller, H., 'Bes'. In *LÄ* I, c. 720–23

Altenmüller, B., 'Anubis'. In *LÄ* I, c. 327–33

Bianchi, U., 'Seth, Osiris et l'Ethnographie', *RHR* 179 (1971), pp. 113–35

Doxey, D.M., 'Anubis', *OEAE*, Vol. I, pp. 97–98

Fischer, H.G., 'The Cult and Nome of the Goddess Bat', *JARCE* 1 (1962), pp. 7–23

Malek, J., *The Cat in Ancient Egypt* (London, 1993)

Germond, P., *Sekhmet et la protection du monde* (Geneva, 1981)

Gundlach, R., 'Thoeris', *LÄ* VI, c. 494–97

Heerma van Voss, M., *Anoebis en de Demonen* (Leiden, 1978)

Helck, W., 'Stiergotte'. In *LÄ* VI, c. 14–17

Hopfner, T., *Der Tierkult der Alten Ägypter* (Vienna, 1913)

Hornung, E., *Der Ägyptische Mythos von der Himmelskuh* (Freiberg, 1982)

Houlihan, P.F., 'Pigs', *OEAE*, Vol. III, pp. 47–48

Houser-Wegner, J., 'Taweret', *OEAE*, Vol. III, pp. 350–51

Jones, M., 'The Temple of Apis in Memphis', *JEA* 76 (1990), pp. 141–47

Kessler, D., *Die heiligen Tiere und der König.* (Wiesbaden, 1989)

Kessler, D., 'Bull Gods', *OEAE*, Vol. I, pp. 209–13

Malaise, M., 'Bès et les croyances solaires'. In S. Israelit-Groll (ed.), *Studies in Egyptology: Presented to Miriam Lichtheim* (Jerusalem, 1990), pp. 680–729

Malaise, M., 'Bès', *OEAE*, Vol. I, pp. 179–81

Malek, J., *The Cat in Ancient Egypt* (London, 1993)

Meeks, D., 'Le nom du dieu Bès et ses implications mythologiques'. In U. Luft (ed.), *The Intellectual Heritage of Egypt: Studies Presented to Lászlo Kákosy* (Budapest, 1992), pp. 423–36

Mysliwiec, K., *Die heiligen Tiere des Atum*, Vol. I, *Studien zum Gott Atum* (Hildesheim, 1978)

Ray, J.D., 'Cults: Animal Cults', *OEAE*, Vol. I, pp. 345–48

Ritner, R.K., 'Anubis and the Lunar Disc', *JEA* 71 (1985), pp. 149–55

Romano, J.F., 'The Origin of the Bes-Image', *BES* 2 (1980), pp. 39–56

Romano, J.F., 'Notes on the Historiography and History of the Bes-image in Ancient Egypt', *BACE* 9 (1998), pp. 89–105

te Velde, H., 'Some Egyptian Deities and Their Piggishness'. In U. Luft (ed.), *Intellectual Heritage of Egypt: Studies Presented to Lászlo Kákosy* (Budapest, 1992), pp. 571–78

te Velde, H., *Seth, God of Confusion, PÄ,* 2nd ed. (Leiden, 1977)

te Velde, H., 'The Cat as Sacred Animal of the Goddess Mut'. In M. Heerma Van Voss et. al. (eds.), *Studies in Egyptian Religion dedicated to Professor Jan Zandee* (Leiden, 1982), pp. 127–37

te Velde, H., 'A Few Remarks on the Religious Significance of Animals in Ancient Egypt', *Numen* 27 (1980), p. 78

te Velde, H., 'Mut, the Eye of Re', *SAKB* 3 (1988), pp. 395–403

Wilkinson, R., 'A Possible Origin for the "Shoulder Ornaments" in Egyptian Representations of Lions', *VA* 5:1 (1989), pp. 59–71

Yoyotte, J., 'Une monumentale litanie de granit: Les Sekhmet d'Amenophis III et al conjuration permanente de la déesse dangereuse', *Bulletin de la Société Française d'Égyptologie* 87–88 (1980), pp. 46–71

Zabkar, L.V., *Apedemak Lion God of Meroe: A Study in Meroitic Syncretism* (Bath, 1975)

Avian Deities

Allen, T.G., *Horus in the Pyramid Texts* (Chicago, 1915)

Assmann, J., *Egyptian Solar Religion in the New Kingdom: Re, Amun and the Crisis of Polytheism* (tr. A. Alcock, London, 1995)

Bács, T.A, 'Amun-Re-Harakhti in the Late Ramesside Royal Tombs'. In *Fs Kákosy* (1992), pp. 43–53

Blackman, A. and H.W. Fairman, 'The Myth of Horus at Edfu (II)', *JEA* 28 (1942), pp. 32–38; 29 (1943), pp. 2–36; 30 (1944), pp. 5–22

Bleeker, C.J., *Hathor and Thoth: Two Key Figures of the Ancient Egyptian Religion* (Leiden, 1973)

Brovarski, E., 'Sokar', *LÄ* V, c. 1055–74

Brunner, H., 'Chons', *LÄ* I, c. 960–63

Dodson, A., 'El Kab, City of the Vulture-Goddess', *KMT* 4 (1996–97), pp. 60–68

Doxey, D.M., 'Thoth', *OEAE*, Vol. III, pp. 398–400

Fairman, H.W., 'The Myth of Horus at Edfu (I)', *JEA* 21 (1935), pp. 26–36

Gardiner, A.H., 'The Goddess Nekhbet at the Jubilee Festival of Ramses III', *ZÄS* 48 (1910), pp. 47–51

Gardiner, A.H., 'Horus the Behdetite', *JEA* 30 (1944), pp. 23–60

Graindorge, C., 'Sokar', *OEAE*, Vol. III, pp. 305–07

Graindorge, C., *Le dieu Sokar à Thèbes au Nouvel Empire* (Wiesbaden, 1994)

Houser-Wegner, J., 'Khonsu', *OEAE*, Vol. II, p. 233

Kurth, D., 'Thoth', *LÄ* VI, c. 497–523

Meltzer, E.S., 'Horus', *OEAE*, Vol. II, pp. 119–22

Müller, M., 'Re and Re-Horakhty', *OEAE*, Vol. III, pp. 123–26

Onstine, S., 'The Relationship Between Osiris and Re in the Book of Caverns', *JSSEA* 25 (1995), pp. 66–77; pl. 5–7

Quirke, S., *The Cult of Ra* (London and New York, 2001)

Schenkel, W., 'Horus', *LÄ* III, c. 14–25

Reptile, Amphibian, Fish Deities

Borghouts, J.F., 'The Evil Eye of Apophis', *JEA* 59 (1973), pp. 114–50

Broekhuis, J., *De Godin Renenwetet* (Assen, 1971)

Brovarski, E., 'Sobek', *LÄ* V, c. 995–1031

Dolzani, C., *Il Dio Sobk* (Rome, 1961)

Doxey, D.M., 'Sobek', *OEAE*, Vol. III, pp. 300–01

Hansen, N.B., 'Snakes', *OEAE*, Vol. III, pp. 296–99

Johnson, S. B., *The Cobra Goddess of Ancient Egypt: Predynastic, Early Dynastic, and Old Kingdom Periods* (London, 1990)

Kákosy, L., 'Ouroboros on Magical Healing Statues'. In T. DuQuesne (ed.), *Hermes Aegyptiacus: Egyptological Studies for B. H. Stricker on His 85th Birthday* (Oxford, 1995), pp. 123–29

Piccione, P.A., 'Mehen, Mysteries, and Resurrection from the Coiled Serpent', *JARCE* 27 (1990), pp. 43–52

Invertebrate and Insect Deities

Bacher, I., 'Die Fliege in Kultur und Religion der alten Ägypter', M.A. Thesis (Munich, 1993)

Goyon, J.-C., 'Isis-scorpion et Isis au scorpion', *BIFAO* 78 (1978), pp. 439–57

Hansen, N.B., 'Insects', *OEAE*, Vol. 2, pp. 161–63

Keimer, L., 'Pendeloques en forme d'insectes faisant partie de colliers égyptiens', *ASAE* 32 (1932), pp. 129–50; 33 (1933), pp. 97–130, 193–200; 37 (1937), pp. 143–72

Kritsky, G., 'Beetle Gods, King Bees and Other Insects of Ancient Egypt', *KMT* 4:1 (1993), pp. 32–39

Von Känel, F., 'Scorpions', *OEAE*, Vol. 3, pp. 186–87

Inanimate Object Deities

Allen, J.P., 'Hymns: Solar Hymns', *OEAE*, Vol. II, pp. 146–48

Assmann, J., 'Aton', *LÄ* I, c. 526–40

Parker, R. and O. Neugebauer, *Egyptian Astronomical Texts: Vol. 1: The Early Decans* (Providence, 1960)

Redford, D.B., 'The Sun-disc in Akhenaten's Program: Its Worship and Its Antecedents, I', *JARCE* 13 (1976), pp. 47–61; 17 (1982), pp. 21–38

Ritner, R.K., 'Anubis and the Lunar Disc', *JEA* 71 (1985), pp. 149–55

Schlögl, H.A., 'Aten', *OEAE*, Vol. I, pp. 156–58

Wilkinson, R.H., 'The Motif of the Path of the Sun in Ramesside Royal Tombs: An Outline of Recent Research', *JSSEA* 25 (1995), pp. 78–84; pl. 8–10

Sources of Quotations

p. 15 '...it is very likely that...' F. Hassan, 'The Earliest Goddesses of Egypt: Divine Mothers and Cosmic Bodies'. In L. Goodison and C. Morris (eds.), *Ancient Goddesses: The Myths and the Evidence* (Madison, WI, 1998) p. 307

p. 16 'interesting similarities exist...' J. Hoffmeier, 'Some Thoughts on Genesis 1 & 2 and Egyptian Cosmology', *JANES* 15 (1983), p. 39

p. 21 'enables them to become young...' E. Hornung, *Conceptions of God in Ancient Egypt: The One and the Many* (Tr. by J. Baines, Ithaca, 1982; London, 1983), p. 162

p. 27 'a lion-headed goddess...' H.G. Fischer, 'The Cult and Nome of the Goddess Bat', *JARCE* 1 (1962), p. 23

p. 38 'unites the view of god...', 'monotheism with a polytheistic face' J.P. Allen, 'Monotheism: The Egyptian Roots', *Archaeology Odyssey* 7:8 (1999), p. 44

p. 55 'degree of divinity...' M.-A. Bonhéme, 'Divinity', *OEAE*, Vol. I, p. 401

Illustration Credits

Abbreviations

a = above; b = below; c = centre; l = left; r = right; t = top

Ägyptisches Museum und Papyrussammlung, Berlin 203, 240a; 12l & 64–65 Photo Jürgen Liepe, © Bildarchiv Preussischer Kulturbesitz, Berlin
University of Arizona Egyptian Expedition Archive 72bl, 74–75c, 88a, 192, 200
Ashmolean Museum, Oxford 14r
British Museum, London 18, 19a, 51l, 84–85a, 117, 137, 143, 164, 181, 191r, 194l, 243
Judi Burkhardt 27a, 86–87, 176a
Peter Clayton 16, 81a, 139, 232
Davies, N. de G., *The Rock Tombs of El-Amarna*, II, pl. v; IV, pl. xx, 239r
Egyptian Museum, Cairo 13bl, 13br, 38r, 172
Egyptian Museum, Cairo. Photo Margarete Büsing, © Bildarchiv Preussischer Kulturbesitz, Berlin 125b
Eva Engel, Göttingen 48
Photo Heidi Grassley, © Thames & Hudson Ltd, London 4–5, 22–23, 27br, 42–43a, 50, 76l, 94–95, 111a, 136, 144, 171b, 201b, 219
Harer Family Collection, San Bernardino 28bl, 156, 165l, 178
Richard Harwood 19b, 42l, 56, 56–57, 96, 107, 115al, 116r, 189r
Photo Hirmer 58l, 67, 123b, 210a
Andrea Jemolo 89b, 147, 206–07
George Johnson 15, 21a, 28a, 43ar, 74l, 75b, 79a, 81l, 81r, 89al, 90, 119, 135a, 138, 150, 153b, 157, 159a, 160r, 169a, 195
KMT: A Modern Journal of Ancient Egypt 231
K. Lange 99a
Jürgen Liepe 6a, 14l, 22l, 36, 37a, 77a, 92, 115br, 124, 131, 140, 146, 149, 170bl, 173, 174b, 177b, 185l, 186–87b, 188, 201a, 202a, 205, 212l, 213a, 217, 227b, 230, 235, 236–37, 242
Metropolitan Museum of Art, New York 79b, 126
Museum of Fine Arts, Boston 193 (Gift of the Egypt Exploration Fund); 37b (Charles Amos Cummings Bequest Fund)
Paul Nicholson 182b, 240b
Oriental Institute of the University of Chicago 186ar
Pelizaeus Museum, Hildesheim/Sh. Shalchi 78b

Photo © RMN 27bl; 151l D. Amaudet, G. Blot; 33 H. Lewandowski
John G. Ross 116l, 121l, 238
William Schenck 72a, 83a, 102–03, 113, 155b, 162l, 165r, 169bl, 190, 208b
Seminar für Ägyptologie, Cologne, photo Gisela Dettloff 216a
Albert Shoucair 105, 160l, 161r
Soprintendenza per le Antichità Egizie, Museo Egizio, Turin 64
Staatliche Sammlung Ägyptischer Kunst, Munich 155a, 220a (loaned by Bayrischen Landesbank)
Jeremy Stafford-Deitsch 30–31, 34a, 35a, 45b, 54, 73, 93, 104a, 110–11, 120, 121r, 133a, 134, 142, 145, 148, 152, 162–63, 170ar, 226
E. Strouhal 44b, 221
Frank Teichmann 24–25
Werner Forman Archive 166–67; 239l Brooklyn Museum, New York; 101 Sold at Christie's, London; 10–11 Fitzwilliam Museum, Cambridge; 128a J. Paul Getty Museum, Malibu; 20 Courtesy L'Ibis, New York; 125a, 175br E. Strouhal; 185r Museo Egizio, Turin; 186l Egyptian Museum, Cairo
Araldo De Luca/Archivio White Star 2–3, 6–7, 17a, 40–41, 48a, 68–69, 80, 158–59, 159b, 197, 214b, 222, 232–33, 234
Richard Wilkinson 12–13a, 17b, 26, 28bl, 29b, 34b, 38a, 39, 43b, 44a, 47l, 47r, 49, 51r, 55b, 58r, 59, 60, 60–61, 62, 62–63, 63, 66, 66–67, 75a, 85b, 88b, 91a, 100r, 103a, 103b, 108–09, 109bl, 112b, 114, 132l, 135b, 151r, 154, 182a, 196a, 204, 207ar, 211b, 213b, 215, 216b, 220bl, 220br
Philip Winton 1, 9, 21b, 29a, 31, 32, 35b, 42r, 45a, 55a, 76r, 77b, 78a, 78c, 81b, 83b, 89ar, 91b, 95r, 98, 99b, 100l, 104b, 106, 109br, 111br, 112a, 118, 122, 123a, 127, 128b, 129a, 129b, 132r, 133b, 141l, 153a, 161l, 168l, 168r, 169br, 171a, 174a, 175a, 175bl, 176b, 177al, 177ac, 177ar, 179l, 179r, 180, 183, 184, 189l, 191l, 194r, 196b, 198, 199, 202bl, 202br, 207al, 208a, 210b, 211a, 212r, 214al, 214ar, 218l, 218r, 223, 224, 225a, 225b, 227a, 228, 229l, 229r, 241a, 241b

Acknowledgments

The author gratefully acknowledges the help of a number of colleagues who kindly shared their research, supplied information or offered comments on sections of this book for which they had special knowledge. James P. Allen and James K. Hoffmeier deserve special mention in this regard, and thanks are also due to Stephen Quirke, Aidan Dodson and Toby Wilkinson for reading the manuscript and offering a number of helpful suggestions. Eugene Cruz-Uribe kindly supplied helpful information relating to some aspects of the later history of the Egyptian deities.

For illustrations I would particularly like to thank Richard Harwood and George Johnson, who supplied a number of photographs, as well as Ben Harer and curator Eva Kirsch for making available images of items from the Harer Family collection. Philip Winton skilfully prepared most of the line drawings used in this book and several others were kindly done by Judi Burkhardt.

A number of members of The University of Arizona Egyptian Expedition and others are to be particularly thanked for their support and assistance while this book was in the making.

Suzanne Onstine, Anne Lopez, Richard Harwood, Donald Kunz, Edith Kunz, Shang-Ying Shih, Cindy Ausec, Kaila Bussert and Jennifer Harshman were particularly helpful, as was Stephanie Denkowicz whose kind and generous support enabled much of our research which often had an impact on the present book.

Egypt's Supreme Council of Antiquities is gratefully acknowledged for allowing my continued study and archaeological research in Egypt, and special thanks go to Drs Zahi Hawass, Sabry el-Aziz, Muhammad Sughayr and Yahia el-Masry, as well as Muhammad el-Bialy, Ibrahim Suleiman and the local inspectors who have facilitated my work in Egypt over the years.

I am also very grateful to all the members of the publisher's editorial, design and production staff who brought this project to completion.

Finally, I would like to acknowledge the kind and constant help of my wife Anna and son Mark whose assistance in many ways made it possible for me to complete the present work.

Index

Page numbers in *italics* refer to illustrations
Page numbers in **bold** refer to the catalogue entry
for that deity, or group of deities